John P. Slough

JOHN P. SLOUGH

The Forgotten Civil War General

RICHARD L. MILLER

University of New Mexico Press • Albuquerque

ISBN 978-0-8263-6219-3 (cloth)
ISBN 978-0-8263-6220-9 (electronic)

Library of Congress Control Number: 2021930602

COVER ILLUSTRATION AND FRONTISPIECE
John Potts Slough. Library of Congress Prints and Photographs Division,
LC-DIG-cwpb-04625 (digital file from original neg.).
DESIGNED BY Mindy Basinger Hill
COMPOSED IN Adobe Caslon Pro and Wood Serif Regular.

＊＊＊＊＊＊

TO

Karin

＊＊＊＊＊＊

Contents

Acknowledgments

WRITING A BOOK IS A LONG JOURNEY. MINE BEGAN IN SEPTEMBER 2007 when my wife and I saw Santa Fe's plaza for the first time. After getting settled in our Southwestern-themed bed and breakfast, we strolled around the plaza's perimeter, basking in the late summer sun as we admired the shops and historic buildings. I was curious about a weathered monument in the plaza's center and even more curious when I read the monument's inscriptions, which memorialized the Union dead who fell in four Civil War battles in New Mexico Territory during early 1862. That curiosity led me to John Potts Slough, the Union commander at the battle of Glorieta Pass and the subject of this book.

Long journeys are made easier with company, and fortunately I have had many companions—friends, acquaintances, archivists, historians, and writers—who accompanied and assisted me during my journey with John Slough. Terry Seip and Bill Deverell, both professors of history at the University of Southern California, helped launch my research with recommended readings in mid-nineteenth-century American and Western American history. Many years after these initial recommendations, Professor Deverell graciously read my final manuscript and suggested publishers. Gwen Fuller, a descendant of Slough's daughter Sarah, responded to my "out of the blue" email with information about Slough and his wife, Arabella McLean Slough Probasco. Cheryl Nunn willingly tackled my many questions about the Slough family genealogy. I am especially grateful for the assistance provided by the librarians and archivists at the Public Library of Cincinnati and Hamilton County, the Cincinnati History Library and Archives, the Mahn Center for Archives and Special Collections at the Ohio University Libraries, the Kansas State Historical Society, the Chicago Historical Society, the Denver Public Library, the Colorado State Archives, the Stephen H. Hart Library and Research Center, the National Archives, the Local History Special Collections at the

Alexandria Public Library, the New Mexico State Records Center and Archives, the Fray Angélico Chávez Historical Library, and the Beinecke Rare Book and Manuscript Library, Yale University. Their suggestions facilitated my search for important primary and secondary sources.

Many friends encouraged me throughout my writing. The "Breakfast Boys," a group of eight men who have breakfasted with me every Thursday for the past seven years, have been especially supportive of this book. Two members of the group, Dick Baldwin and Jamie Snell, volunteered to read early chapters. Ed Malles, Gary Bloxham, Rebecca Morris, and my cousin, Jan Duvall—all writers—provided thoughtful comments on draft chapters. My sister-in-law, Susan Lorch, made the type of careful observations about the manuscript that only a retired English teacher can make. I am particularly appreciative of the close reading given by my friend Kelby Fletcher. Kelby brought his lawyer's analytic mind to his review of the entire manuscript and made numerous suggestions for improvement.

There are three people who deserve special mention. Carolyn Laceky has shared my excitement about writing a biography of her great-grandfather since this project began. She kindly sent me her graduate school papers on John Slough as well as a box full of primary source material she had uncovered about her great-grandfather. Throughout my research and writing, she has stayed in touch, offering family memories about Slough and giving encouragement as I finished each draft. She has made John Slough come alive for me.

It is not an exaggeration to say that without my good friend Steve Ross, I could not have written this book. An accomplished writer and historian who teaches at the University of Southern California, Steve helped me understand how serious history should be written. He spent hours reading draft after draft and offering constructive comments. Like any good teacher, he improved this book immeasurably with his thoughtful advice.

Finally, my greatest thanks are reserved for my wife, Karin. It was she who first suggested that I write a book and then lovingly supported me as I attempted something I had never done. Karin is an inveterate reader, which enabled her to let me know whenever my writing became sloppy and unclear. Her comments broadened my approach to Slough's story so that it might appeal to more than Civil War buffs and aficionados of Western history. Most importantly, she never lost confidence that I could accomplish my goal of writing a history book and she never tired of my dedication to the project. It is to her that I dedicate this work.

Introduction

JOHN SLOUGH SETTLED HIS HEAVY-SET FRAME INTO THE PARLOR'S armchair as dusk fell on Leavenworth, Kansas Territory, in late summer 1857. He had worked all day at his prospering legal and real estate practice and was grateful that friends had invited him to supper. Relaxing in the comfortable chair, he noticed that the parlor was darkening. He raised the wick of the kerosene lamp next to him, inadvertently outlining his large, balding head and broad shoulders in the shadows cast by the lamp's flame. Suddenly, shots shattered the parlor's front window. He instinctively dropped behind the armchair to await more gunfire, but his assailant had fled. Slough escaped harm this time, but the attack would not be the last attempt on his life.[1]

The American narrative has always portrayed the West as a place of terrible risk and great reward. Emigrants like John Slough crossed the continent to seek new beginnings despite the West's reputation for violence and premature death. Some came to pan gold in mountain streams or dig for precious metals in cliffs and rock outcroppings; others planned to farm or ranch, lured by rumors of fertile soil and lush grasses. Many sought their fortune in selling supplies or providing services in western boom towns. Some needed a new start, to leave behind a failed business or escape an unsatisfying marriage or avoid punishment for crimes they had committed. Others, such as adherents of the Church of Jesus Christ of Latter-day Saints, sought the frontier's haven for their religious beliefs. All believed that the West offered them opportunity, a chance to win a better life.

Those willing to move across the continent, the American narrative promised, had a greater opportunity to gain economic and social status than the less venturesome stuck in their settled lives back east. Nineteenth-century popularizers of the "go ahead system" promoted the dream of fame and fortune for any individual willing to take risks and work hard in the American land of opportunity. Those who journeyed west, said the narrative, had an even greater chance of success. "Incentive and opportunity were there," Ray Allen Billington and Martin Ridge wrote in their *Western Expansion: A History of the American Frontier*, "men and women only had to apply themselves to achieve wealth and an elevated social status." These were the pioneers whose flatboats brought them down the Ohio River, whose wagon trains dug permanent ruts in the prairie, or whose mules carried them along the Santa Fe Trail.[2]

A handful who ventured west achieved extraordinary fame and fortune. Their stories continue to enthrall our imaginations more than a century after they lived. Others failed miserably. Historians have suggested that they failed because they lacked sufficient resources to succeed in the competitive and harshly unforgiving West. They had too little capital, too little knowledge, too little preparation, or simply too little luck. They were the ones who returned east broken and beaten or, like the many fallen by illness or accident, died before they reached their destination.

In retelling the story of the American West, historians have largely overlooked a set of men whose ambition drove them to prominence in their communities yet whose shortcomings denied them the lasting fame they sought. Usually they were the sons of the "better sort" who, having gone west in search of greater opportunity, achieved success by contemporary standards but ultimately never attained their greater vision. They enjoyed the resources necessary for success; they had talent, determination, education, often a profession, and usually a circle of acquaintances who could promote their endeavors. These advantages enabled them to serve as leaders of their western communities, but, in the end, they yielded their positions to "new competitors with keener eyes and stronger frames." Denied the success they sought, they often moved to new communities to begin again. Today no monuments remember them.[3]

John Potts Slough was such a man. His early years seemed to herald later success. His father accumulated wealth and prestige during Cincinnati's antebellum boom years. That prosperity afforded Slough an education appropriate for a young man from the rising middle class, a profession as a lawyer, and marriage to the niece of a United States Supreme Court justice. His father's connections eased Slough's entry into politics in 1850 and, five years later, enabled the ambitious young man to win election to the Ohio House of Representatives. It was an auspicious beginning to a promising political career.[4]

The success Slough's father enjoyed taught the son that America's seemingly endless opportunity provided ambitious, hard-working men the prospect of fame and good fortune. Slough pursued that dream across the American continent for much of his life. From Ohio, he traveled to Kansas Territory in the late 1850s, spent the war years in Colorado Territory and Virginia, and, once the war had ended, resumed his quest in New Mexico Territory. Success did not elude Slough, at least as most Americans understood success, yet he never achieved the level of accomplishment he desired. After winning election as a young man to the Ohio House of Representatives and later establishing himself as a leader of Kansas's Democratic Party, he never gained higher elective office. He failed to earn promotion to major general during the Civil War even though contemporaries praised his victory at Glorieta Pass, his role defending Harpers Ferry in May 1862, and his military administration of Alexandria, Virginia. After the war, he longed to return to Colorado Territory as its governor, but, failing that, he accepted appointment as chief justice of New Mexico Territory. There he struggled to reform the New Mexico courts. It was as if his reach always exceeded his grasp, yet he never faltered in his search for new and better opportunity. If one career stalled, he embraced a new one; if a venture did not pan out, he embarked on another one. His life is a not a "rags to riches" tale, yet he embodied the same determination for success that the American narrative ascribes to the nineteenth-century American character.

Certainly, Slough's personality contributed to his failures. Some who knew him described Slough in highly complimentary terms. He was "straight forward" and "intelligent"; "social and agreeable"; a man who demonstrated "energy, tact, perseverance, and courage"; a "faithful and constant ally" to his Democratic colleagues. Despite this praise, Slough had an impulsive streak and a hair-trigger temper. He was overly sensitive to perceived slights, which led him to respond in ill-advised ways. His cold and aloof personality prevented him from forming close friendships and a loyal following among his contemporaries. He developed many adversaries who sought to ruin his reputation and block his advancement. All these faults undermined his efforts in the highly competitive atmosphere of mid-nineteenth-century America. Together, they thwarted his ambitions.[5]

Aside from Gary L. Roberts's study of New Mexican political violence, *Death Comes for the Chief Justice*, historians have shown little interest in

Slough even when writing about events in which he chiefly figured. As a result, they often sketch him in unidimensional terms and underestimate his impact. For example, in his well-regarded history of Kit Carson, *Blood and Thunder*, Hampton Sides characterizes Slough simply as a man with "a chip on his shoulder," while Donald Frazier dismisses him as a "short-tempered martinet" who commanded the 1st Colorado Volunteers. Curt Anders explains that Slough, "a failed Colorado lawyer," earned his brigadier general star by ignoring his principles. Darlis A. Miller blames Slough's troubles in New Mexico on his "contemptible behavior." Sides, Frazier, Anders, and Miller, as well as other historians, misread Slough because they fail to examine the complexity of his character or his achievements over a lifetime of effort. They offer a caricature rather than an historical likeness of the man. They fail to give him the recognition and importance he deserves.[6]

Slough's life merits more than brief and unreliable profiles. He enjoyed sufficient fame that newspapers widely reported on his activities between 1857 and 1867. His reputation—one could even say notoriety—among his contemporaries suggests a life worth examining; after all, he knew the period's most prominent men, among them Abraham Lincoln, Andrew Johnson, Edwin Stanton, John McLean, and Salmon Chase, as well as important Westerners such as William Gilpin, John Chivington, and William H. Larimer Jr. Because Slough's pursuit of opportunity led him across the country—Ohio, Kansas Territory, Colorado Territory, Virginia, and New Mexico Territory— and his fierce ambition frequently pushed him onto center stage, we can use his life to examine the great events of mid-century. He played a noteworthy role in them: the fight over Kansas's admission to the Union, the Colorado gold rush and Denver's beginnings, the Civil War in Virginia, and the corrosive political struggle of Reconstruction in New Mexico Territory.

Slough's importance also stems from his participation in events that have received scant attention from historians. The Wyandotte Constitutional Convention, for example, has not been examined at length since G. Raymond Gaeddert's 1940 book *The Birth of Kansas*. Most histories of Jackson's Valley Campaign have ignored the federal defense of Harpers Ferry, and occupied Alexandria, the Southern city longest under federal military control during the Civil War, has had little description until Paula Tarnapol Whitacre's recent biography of Julia Wilbur. Slough's life affords us an opening not only to events largely untouched by historians but also to the interplay between the two great themes of the mid-nineteenth century: westward expansion and the Civil War.[7]

In their examination of nineteenth-century American family life, James and Dorothy Volo note that for the aspiring, "Only death or physical incapacity relieved a man of his obligation to pursue success." John Slough certainly fulfilled that obligation to pursue success. His life evokes conflicting emotions: distaste for his hypersensitivity, impulsivity, and hotheadedness; sympathy for his enduring repeated attacks on his character; respect for his principled devotion to the rule of law; and, above all, admiration for his dogged determination to capitalize on the opportunities his era presented. Ralph Waldo Emerson famously wrote in 1862, "America is another name for opportunity." John Potts Slough well-exemplified that vision; his is a story of great opportunity and failed ambition.[8]

Part I

OHIO

1

Coming
of Age

A BOISTEROUS CROWD THRONGED THE CINCINNATI PUBLIC LANDING on a cold February day in 1829, eagerly awaiting the arrival of the president-elect of the United States. They watched as a flotilla of three paddle-boats approached the city from downriver, steamed past the crowd "amid cannon-firing and other demonstrations of applause," traveled upstream about a quarter of a mile, and then circled to sweep grandly down to the landing.[1]

On board one of the steamboats, General Andrew Jackson—Old Hickory, the Hero of New Orleans, and the newly elected seventh president of the United States—had chosen to interrupt his journey from Nashville, Tennessee, to Washington, DC, for a brief visit to Cincinnati. Perhaps wishing for some exercise after the tiring journey, Jackson disembarked, bypassed the waiting carriages, and walked to his hotel "in a simple, democratic way." Cincinnatians greeted the president-to-be warmly, cheering for him along the way even though Jackson, dressed in mourning for his wife Rachel, walked somberly through the crowd. Jackson rested at the hotel for a few hours and then boarded his steamboat to resume the inaugural trip.[2]

A young ship carpenter, Martin Slough, likely stood in the rejoicing crowd either through curiosity or support for the president-elect. He lived only a few blocks from the public landing and probably worked in one of the carpentry shops along Front Street. Martin himself had reason to rejoice. He and his wife Mary recently celebrated the birth of their first-born, a boy they named after Mary's father, John.[3]

Martin Slough was born in Pennsylvania in 1802. Two years later his family moved to Cincinnati, joining other early settlers looking to improve their circumstances in the fertile Miami Valley. By 1804, when the Slough family arrived, Cincinnati numbered about a thousand residents. The town was no longer a wilderness settlement. A frame schoolhouse had been built. Travelers lodged at the Green Tree Hotel. The town had two newspapers, the *Western Spy and Hamilton Gazette* and the *Liberty Hall and Cincinnati Mercury*. Men gathered at taverns to read newspapers, discuss politics, and conduct civic affairs. For the population's refined element, touring groups of actors regularly performed plays, starting with *The Poor Soldier* in 1801.[4]

Newcomers, like the Slough family, erected "two story hewed-log houses chinked with mortar and roofed with clapboards," replacing the earlier round-log cabins built by the first Euromerican inhabitants. Comforts had begun to appear. Houses had glass windows, oak planked flooring, and whitewashed interiors. Chairs, chests, feather beds with quilts, trundle beds, and other furnishings were common household items. Life for Cincinnati's populace, praised by contemporary Dr. Daniel Drake for their "industry, temperance, morality, and love of gain," had become considerably more comfortable since the settlement's founding in the late 1780s.[5]

Martin Slough's parents uprooted their family from Pennsylvania for the promise of a better life in the growing town on the banks of the Ohio. Little is known about Martin's father and nothing about his mother. Martin's descendants claim that the family's patriarch was Matthias Slough, a Pennsylvanian and the first colonel commissioned by General George Washington upon assuming command of the Continental Army. There was a Revolutionary War patriot named Matthias Slough, but he never left Pennsylvania. Martin's father and mother, on the other hand, crossed the Alleghenies determined to improve their circumstances and the destinies of their children. Their son Martin would show his own drive to build a comfortable, prosperous life for his family in the promising city of Cincinnati.[6]

It was the broad Ohio River, flowing from Pittsburgh at the confluence of the Allegheny and Monongahela Rivers to the Mississippi River at Cairo, Illinois, that blessed Cincinnati's early development. By the time Martin Slough's parents arrived in 1804, the river trade had been established. Flat boats, barges, and keelboats struggled against the current to upstream towns and villages or made the long haul to the Mississippi and down to New Orleans. Native and foreign-born workers poured into the city, lured by the higher wages and steadier employment than the labor-glutted eastern cities afforded. Population doubled every few years; by 1829, the year of John

Slough's birth, Cincinnati had twenty-four thousand inhabitants, making it the largest city in the West and the seventh largest in the nation. It was the focal point of emigration to the West and the region's major manufacturing center. Workers were employed in "mills and factories that produced for export great quantities of flour, spirits, textiles, castings, steam engines, farm implements, furniture, and a variety of wood and metal articles."[7]

Underpinning the city's industrial growth was steamboat construction. Although Cincinnati shipbuilders fabricated their first steamboat in 1816, the industry did not flourish until 1824, when the United States Supreme Court decided that the Constitution granted Congress the power to regulate interstate commerce. The ruling upended steamboat monopolies and opened the nation's rivers and lakes to any entrepreneur with the capital to build and operate a steamboat. Investors calculated that a steamboat, costing no more than $50,000 to build, could return as much as $25,000 profit per voyage. With solid returns and relatively little risk, Cincinnati steamboat construction entered a golden era that lasted three decades. By the end of the 1820s, more than a quarter of the steamboats plying the western rivers were constructed in Cincinnati.[8]

Martin Slough entered adulthood during the bustling 1820s and, appropriate for a boy growing up in a riverfront town, chose ship carpentry as his occupation. The earliest Cincinnati directories list no Sloughs, neither Matthias nor Martin. Martin's name, occupation, and address first appear in the 1829 directory: "Martin Slough, ship carpenter, Sycamore between 2nd and Lower Market." His father had died by 1829, leaving his mother, who worked as a milliner, to live with her son and his new family.[9]

Martin had married twenty-three-year-old Mary S. Potts in 1828. Within a year, on February 1, 1829, the couple welcomed their first child, John. Their second child, Mary, was born on April 16, 1831, in the family's new home on East Front Street. John and Mary survived cholera epidemics that ravaged Cincinnati in the summers of 1832, 1833, and 1834 and were joined by a baby brother, named after his father Martin, on June 30, 1835.[10]

During the 1830s, buoyed by Cincinnati's rising prosperity, Martin and his young family began the transition from a working-class, artisanal background to an upwardly mobile, middle-class life. Martin proved to be an ambitious and enterprising businessman willing to take advantage of the "Queen City's" vibrant economy. By 1834, he left ship carpentry to open a coffee house on

Front Street close to the Public Landing. Steamboat construction during the 1820s and early 1830s had been decentralized, with work subcontracted to craftsmen like Martin Slough. As capital flowed into Cincinnati, however, the emerging industrial capitalists centralized ownership and production and abandoned their reliance on independent artisans. Increasing competition from larger, centralized firms may have forced Martin to leave his occupation of ship carpenter, although he also recognized that owning a coffee house amid the public landing's warehouses, workshops, and stores was a good business opportunity. His decision to own a coffee house demonstrated that he had attained the economic independence desired by many early Cincinnati craftsmen.[11]

Martin operated a coffee house and boarded working men throughout the remainder of the 1830s. By the late 1830s, Cincinnati's coffee houses were under attack. Germans largely owned them, and they freely dispensed both coffee and alcohol. Public opinion, swayed by the city's increasing nativist and temperance feelings, demanded that coffee houses be suppressed. In response, the city council imposed a prohibitively expensive license on their operation.[12]

The new coffee house licensing fees forced Martin into keeping taverns. Although contemporaries described his place of business as a coffee house in 1840, the 1839–1840 city directory lists Martin and his brother-in-law, John Potts, as partners in a tavern. Hard-working and diligent, traits his son John would exhibit years later, Martin also ran a boat and provision store on the waterfront. The 1842 and 1843 city directories record that he owned a small hotel and tavern on the public landing at Walnut Street. He ran this establishment until 1845 or 1846, when he became a lumber dealer, his final occupation until his retirement in the 1870s. By 1840, the city directory also shows a residential address for the Sloughs separate from Martin's business addresses. The family lived for several years on Front Street between Vine and Race in what must have been more a commercial than residential district. The address suggests that Martin valued easy access to his businesses on the waterfront rather than the fashionable addresses on Third, Fourth, and Seventh Streets.[13]

The many craftsmen, boatmen, merchants, and businessmen who worked around the public landing gathered at Martin Slough's coffee houses and taverns, where they relaxed, enjoyed a drink with friends and fellow workers,

Antebellum Cincinnati, with its bustling steamboat trade, afforded Martin Slough ample opportunity to rise from ship carpenter to prosperous businessman. Source: Library of Congress Prints and Photographs Division, LC-DIG-ppmsca-09494.

conversed on the latest topics of interest, and read the local and eastern newspapers. Politics was always a favorite topic of conversation. Martin was a Democrat, and because the coffee houses and taverns Cincinnatians frequented often became associated with the owner's political party, his establishments served as meeting places for Democrats in the Fourth Ward, the political division that encompassed the streets closest to the Ohio River.

Martin also forged ties to Fourth Ward businessmen and politicians through his honorary membership in the Washington Fire Engine and Hose Company No. 1. By the 1840s, Cincinnati's fire companies served as the breeding ground for the city's political leadership; men often started their public careers as a fire company officer. Through his membership in the Washington Fire Engine and Hose Company No. 1, Martin met Cincinnati politicians like Othniel Looker, David Griffin, John Keown, Jonathan R. Johnston, and William Bromwell. The connections Martin made through his businesses and through the Washington Fire Engine and Hose Company facilitated his son John's entry into politics in the 1850s.[14]

One seemingly trivial piece of evidence suggests Martin's growing reputation in the Queen City. In 1842 and 1843, he was among fifty prominent Cincinnatians who recommended Guild's Patent Cooking Stove in a series of advertisements run in the *Daily Cincinnati Enquirer*. Martin's fellow endorsers included such Cincinnati notables as the well-known antislavery lawyer Salmon P. Chase; the founder of Cincinnati's first department store John Shillito; banking, railroad, and insurance magnate George Carlisle; and politician and public education reformer Nathan Guilford. These were important men in Cincinnati history. By the early 1840s, just a generation after his parents started anew in Cincinnati, Martin had joined the ranks of the Queen City's most prosperous and successful men.[15]

As his family rose in Cincinnati society, Martin had to consider an appropriate education for his eldest son. He enrolled twelve-year-old John in the preparatory department of Cincinnati College. Established in 1815, the school was housed in the "finest public building west of the [Allegheny] mountains," but by the time John entered in 1841, its building had fallen into disrepair and its president, the Reverend T. J. Biggs, struggled to pay its instructors. Martin could have sent his son to other preparatory colleges in Cincinnati. Charles Cist, in *Cincinnati in 1841*, mentions Woodward College and St. Xavier College along with Cincinnati College. But John could easily walk the six blocks from his home to Cincinnati College, while Woodward College was farther afield. And because the Sloughs were Protestant, Martin did not consider Catholic St. Xavier College as a suitable source for his son's education. John would receive his preparatory training at Cincinnati College, staying there until fire destroyed the dilapidated building in January 1845.[16]

John entered the Cincinnati Law School in 1849, the only department to survive the fire that wrecked the Cincinnati College building. The law school had been the first to open west of the Allegheny Mountains when it was founded in 1833. By the time John began his legal studies, it offered a five-month course with tuition set at $50 plus a $5 graduation fee. John had to provide his own texts: Blackstone's *Commentaries*; Walker's *Introduction to American Law*; Chitty's work on contracts, Greenleaf's on evidence, and Gould's on proceedings; Smith's *Mercantile Law*; and Holcombe's *Introduction to Equity*. John attended two "exercises" daily, either a lecture or a discussion of a text, and a weekly moot court for which the students prepared pleadings, furnished briefs, and made oral arguments. Upon passing examinations at the end of the course of study, John and his classmates would be admitted to the Cincinnati Bar.[17]

John left no diaries, journals, or personal letters during his lifetime, but another student's diary offers a glimpse of life at the Cincinnati Law School. Charles Gordon Matchette entered the law school in October 1855, six years after John matriculated. There were differences between Slough and Matchette's experiences while studying law. For example, Matchette, who came from Manchester, Ohio, stayed in boarding homes, moving several times during the term because of "bad board and usage," while John lived at home. Yet the two young men, coming from respectable Ohio families and engaged in the study of law at the same school, must have shared much in common.[18]

Succeeding at the law school required effort. Matchette considered his fellow students to be "all sharp fellows," and although he complained frequently about professors failing to appear for their lectures, he valued their tutelage and felt fondly about them individually. He considered the lessons to be "long and intricate" and had to work diligently at reading assignments, attending lectures, and preparing for moot court. By the middle of the term, he confided to his diary that he felt "somewhat worn out both in body and mind" and worried that he might fail his examinations.

Even though Matchette feared that Cincinnati's "thousands of temptations [could] make a student fall from the true mark," the young man took frequent advantage of the city's opportunities for leisure. He went to the theater for the first time shortly after arriving and became a regular theatergoer, attending a performance every few weeks and seeing *Richard III* the night before his bar examination. He also enjoyed walks in the hills surrounding Cincinnati, marveling at the vistas afforded by the city and across the river to Kentucky. He attended public lectures, worshiped at church, and called on friends, both male and female. He also delighted in less genteel pastimes, drinking with his classmates, reveling in a vaudeville "Monkey Show" at Smith and Nixon's Hall, and joining a group of men and boys who snowballed "every sleigh, Omnibus, or Milkman waggon [*sic*]" one January day.

John Slough undoubtedly availed himself of similar preoccupations, but unlike Matchette, he avoided carousing with friends. Although his father operated taverns until the mid-1840s, Slough's mother was elected an officer of the Grand Union of the Daughters of Temperance just before Slough entered law school. Nineteenth-century American mothers were responsible for the moral upbringing of their children, and Slough's behavior later in life suggests that his mother imbued him with a distaste for alcohol and its effects. Whereas Charles Gordon Matchette sported with friends in their rooms, leaving them drunk and "eating pig's feet, singing patriotic songs, and telling good stories" at four in the morning, Slough returned home after classes to spend a quiet evening studying. Achieving a solid education was more important to him than frolicking with friends.[19]

Booming Cincinnati had no shortage of lawyers when Slough entered the legal profession in 1850; roughly 180 lawyers and law firms practiced in the city. Even though his Cincinnati Law School diploma provided him with more professional standing than lawyers trained by apprenticeship, John did not open up a law office until 1853. By then, he had already launched his political career in Cincinnati's Fourth Ward, the waterfront district where his father had owned coffee houses and taverns. As early as June 1850, about the time he graduated from law school, Slough began his political apprenticeship, representing the Fourth Ward at the Hamilton County Democratic convention held in Carthage, Ohio.[20]

The Fourth Ward again sent Slough to the Hamilton County Democratic convention in August 1851. Meeting at the Mechanic's Institute in Cincinnati, the delegates addressed the process of nominating local and state candidates. The method of candidate selection was a critically important issue for Democrats, who relied on loyal delegates attending the party's convention to nominate men with appropriate Democratic credentials. But a delegated convention, in which powerful party leaders controlled the selection process, clashed with the republican belief that public interest and government by the people trumped government by the few. Charges by the Whigs that the Democratic Party threatened the country's republican foundations because its candidates had to bow to the party's leaders made Democrats sensitive about their nominating process.[21]

The Hamilton County Democratic Executive Committee decided that an ad hoc committee should examine the nomination issue. Slough, a tall, handsome, twenty-two-year-old only a year out of law school, was chosen to serve on the committee and to write its report. The committee considered the advantages of a delegated convention, but, in the end, advised the Executive Committee that, if approved by a majority of Hamilton County Democrats, a popular vote system should be adopted to select nominees.[22]

Slough's assignment to write the ad hoc committee's report marked the beginning of his ascent in politics. In September 1851, his Democratic colleagues recruited him to serve as secretary to the local committee charged with ensuring the party's success in the upcoming election. Slough campaigned diligently for Democratic candidates, addressing election rallies throughout Hamilton County, Ohio. The Fourth Ward rewarded his hard work by electing him to the Cincinnati City Council in April 1852. The following year, Cincinnati's Democratic leaders appointed him secretary to the Trustees of the Cincinnati Water Works. It is difficult to know how much Slough was involved in the utility's deliberations. Extant Cincinnati Water Works records make no mention of his duties nor his compensation. Perhaps he held the position in name only, but, at the very least, his four-year tenure as secretary contributed to his political apprenticeship.[23]

Other matters occupied Slough during this period. In addition to opening his law office in 1853, he married sixteen-year-old Arabella Sophia McLean on February 1, his twenty-fourth birthday. With his marriage to Arabella, also known as Belle, Slough became connected to the politically prominent McLean family.

Arabella was the ninth child and sixth daughter of William and Sarah McLean. Her paternal grandfather, Fergus, an Irishman and weaver by trade, embraced the American cause shortly after arriving in Wilmington, Delaware, and fought with the Continental Army at the battles of Trenton, Princeton, and Monmouth. After the Revolutionary War, he and his wife Sophia worked a small farm in Morris County, New Jersey, until 1789, when the family began moving west—like Matthias Slough's family—in search of greater opportunity. For eight years, Fergus did not put down roots, moving his family ever westward, finally settling in 1797 on a farm in Warren County, Ohio.[24]

Arabella's father, William, was born in Kentucky in 1794, a few years before the McLean family moved to Ohio. As a young man, William followed in the footsteps of his brothers John and Nathaniel. He was admitted to the bar in 1814 after being taught the rudiments of the law by his brother John. About that time, he became the editor and publisher of the *Western Star*, a weekly newspaper John and Nathaniel founded in 1807. Besides running a newspaper, all three brothers entered politics. Nathaniel served a few terms in the Ohio Legislature beginning in 1810. John represented Ohio in the United States Congress from 1813 to 1816, when he resigned to take a seat on the Ohio Supreme Court. William was elected to the United States House of Representatives from Ohio's Third Congressional District in 1822 and served until 1829. After his third term in Congress, William resumed the practice of law in Cincinnati and entered into various mercantile ventures. He died from tuberculosis in 1839, just three years after Arabella's birth. In his death notice, the *Cincinnati Gazette* described him as "urbane and social, and no man had fewer enemies."[25]

It is quite possible that Arabella's care—in part, at least—fell to her uncle John upon William's death. John had always been his brother's close friend, served as one of two executors of William's estate, and helped his brother's family with William's mercantile interests after William died. Despite John McLean's appointment to the United States Supreme Court in 1829, he was able to watch over William's family as he divided his time between Cincinnati, Washington, DC, and the old family home in Warren County, Ohio. By the early 1850s, his responsibility on the Supreme Court required him to hear cases in Cincinnati for the federal circuit court. John Slough likely met Arabella's famous uncle when McLean was in Cincinnati; perhaps McLean gave his niece to the young politician at their wedding.[26]

John Slough was an eligible bachelor when he met Arabella in 1851 or 1852. He had dark gray eyes and light brown hair and stood almost six feet tall. A contemporary described him as "decidedly a fine-looking man, tall and well built, with light hair and complexion, round face, and head approaching the Shakespearian form; in his personal relations, he is quite the gentleman, social, free, and sufficiently dignified."[27]

Whether at balls, teas, lectures, plays, or other social events, plenty of opportunities existed for Belle to notice the serious young lawyer. She claimed a place in Cincinnati society by virtue of her well-known father and uncle. The Sloughs also enjoyed a prominent position in the Queen City. John's father, Martin, was recognized as one of the city's earliest residents and an important businessman. His mother, Mary, was active in the Grand Union of the Daughters of Temperance, an organization that offered middle-class ladies the opportunity for respectable socializing while promoting alcohol reform. Martin's honorary membership in the Washington Fire Engine and Hose Company No. 1, his charter membership in the Cincinnati Pioneer Association, Mary's membership in the Daughters of Temperance, along with John's attendance at the Cincinnati Law School and sister Mary's at the Wesleyan Female College, suggest that by the 1850s the Sloughs had established themselves among Cincinnati's respectable families.[28]

More importantly, Martin Slough was well-to-do by 1850. That year's census listed the value of his real estate at $20,000, which placed him among the two hundred richest men in Cincinnati. Not quite fifty years after his father had arrived in Cincinnati, Martin could boast of wealth, status, and respectability. Son John was an appropriate match for Arabella McLean.[29]

John and Belle quickly settled into married life. The couple moved into their own house at 16 Richmond Street in the city's west end. There they had their first child, William McLean Slough, named after Arabella's father. For the next two years, Slough continued his professional pursuits. He practiced law at 256 Main Street, served as the secretary to the Trustees of the Cincinnati Water Works, and worked for the success of the Hamilton County Democracy. He was appointed as one of three secretaries for the Cincinnati Democratic Convention held on March 20, 1854, functioned as one of six secretaries at the state Democratic convention held in Columbus nine months later, and served as secretary to the Hamilton County Democratic Executive Committee in August 1855. In the five years since he first represented the Fourth Ward at the Hamilton County Democratic convention, Slough had become well-known among Cincinnati Democrats as a promising politician.[30]

John's entry into politics occurred during a tumultuous period for Cincinnati Democrats. At the state level, Ohio was experiencing an ever-shifting landscape of political coalitions—Democrats and Free Soil, Whigs and Free Soil, even Democrats and Whigs—that sought to share power and political patronage. Cincinnati suffered from the worst of this political fragmentation. The splintering began with the October 1852 elections when a coalition of Whigs and disaffected German-Protestant Democrats defeated the old-line Democratic Party. Nativist sentiment further fractured the two-party system in Cincinnati the following spring with four different parties vying for the mayor's office. The temperance movement again splintered Cincinnati party lines when seven tickets competed for the state legislative positions in the fall 1853 elections. Meanwhile, across the United States, anti-Catholic and antiforeign partisans began meeting in pursuit of a rabidly nativist agenda. They were called "Know-Nothings" because they denied participation in any anti-immigrant activity. The movement swept through the United States, North and South, winning followers and capturing state and local elections.[31]

An especially severe drought in the summer of 1854 dried up commerce on the Ohio River at the same time that increased competition from railroads undercut the steamboat trade. Unemployed workers from Cincinnati's waterfront blamed the newly arrived immigrants for their financial troubles, made worse by the recession of late 1854 and early 1855, and they flocked to the Know-Nothing cause to vent their frustrations. Anger against Cincinnati's foreigners boiled over in the 1855 Cincinnati mayoral election. To intimidate voters and prevent a Democratic victory, Know-Nothings destroyed ballot boxes and assaulted Germans in their neighborhoods on Election Day, April 2. The Germans fought back, erecting barricades on the bridges over the Miami and Erie Canal that led into the Over the Rhine district. The Know-Nothings and Germans battled for three days; two men were killed and scores wounded before the nativists gave up their efforts to breach the barricades.[32]

Ohioans who had been sympathetic to the Know-Nothings recoiled at the Cincinnati Election Day riots as antidemocratic and antirepublican. Businessmen and well-to-do farmers across the state dropped their allegiance to the movement, and Ohio's Know-Nothing party began its decline. Meanwhile, as conflict erupted in the United States Congress over the expansion of slavery into the Nebraska territory, Ohioans began to fear that the Southern slave states posed a greater threat to the republic than foreign-born citizens.[33]

By the mid-1850s, enough settlers had moved into the lands immediately west of Iowa and Missouri that Congress undertook the formal organization of the Nebraska territory. The problem posed by territorial organization was that the entire region lay above the 36-30 line established by the Missouri Compromise. If the territory sought admission to the Union as one or more states, the Missouri Compromise dictated that the new states would enter free of slavery, an eventuality that Southern congressmen and senators could not accept.

To resolve this dilemma and enable the territory's eventual admission to the Union, Democratic senator Stephen A. Douglas sought a new compromise. Douglas's solution invoked the seemingly unassailable republican principle of self-determination. His Kansas-Nebraska bill gave a territory's residents the right to decide if the territory would be admitted as a free or slave state. By repealing the Missouri Compromise and replacing it with the principle of "popular sovereignty," the Kansas-Nebraska bill empowered the people of a territory to choose slave or free. Democrats, like John Slough, cheered Senator Douglas's deft handling of the seemingly irreconcilable national problem through his espousal of popular sovereignty.

But Douglas's Kansas-Nebraska bill, passed by Congress in May 1854, infuriated antislavery Northerners because it potentially opened territories that the sacrosanct Missouri Compromise had closed forever to slavery. Moreover, they believed that the minority Southern states, which antislavery politicians and newspapers demonized as the "Slave Power," were using the Kansas-Nebraska bill for their selfish sectional interests. They feared that an oligarchy of slaveholders intended not only to extend slavery throughout the territories but also to destroy Northern rights by subordinating the nation to the slaveholders' will.[34]

The Kansas-Nebraska Act and the reopening of the slave question rallied antislavery Northerners to the antiexpansion cause and reinvigorated partisan politics. Energized by the potential threat of slavery in territories the Missouri Compromise had designated as free, conservative Whigs, antiexpansion Democrats, and Free Soilers joined together in 1854 in "fusion parties" to oppose the Kansas-Nebraska Act and to restore the Missouri Compromise. The anti-Nebraska coalitions in the Midwestern states swept the fall 1854 election. Even Hamilton County, where Slough campaigned for Democratic candidates, favored the fusionists and ousted the Democrats by a plurality of seven thousand votes.[35]

Slough's political apprenticeship occurred in a fast-changing landscape dominated by political fragmentation, violent nativism, and anti-Nebraska fusion coalitions. Throughout this period, he worked tirelessly for the Democrats. The party repaid his loyalty and hard work by nominating him to run in the 1855 general election for the Ohio House of Representatives. Although the newly formed Republican Party took the Ohio governorship and majorities in the State Senate and House of Representatives, Hamilton County voters elected Slough and seven other Democrats to the state legislature. Assuming his seat in the Ohio House on January 7, 1856, the young legislator enjoyed an enviable position in mid-nineteenth-century American life; he was the eldest son of a prosperous and respectable Cincinnati family, husband of the niece of a United States Supreme Court justice, newly elected Ohio state representative, and an emerging talent in Ohio Democratic politics. What Martin Slough had dreamed for his son, John Slough had seemingly achieved.[36]

2

"An Ardent and
Zealous Democrat"

ALTHOUGH HE WAS THE YOUNGEST AND LEAST EXPERIENCED REPRE-
sentative Hamilton County voters sent to the 52nd Ohio General Assembly,
John Slough was clearly a politician on the rise. He had enjoyed increasing responsibility among Hamilton County Democrats since his entry into politics,
yet his election to the Ohio House of Representatives in 1855 was an unusual
accomplishment. The reward most party loyalists expected in the antebellum period was election to local office, such as sheriff, coroner, or delegate
to the party's convention. Slough, however, rose quickly from party worker
to the Ohio House of Representatives in five years. His rapid promotion
was impressive, especially because the Hamilton County Democratic Party
could choose among many loyal, well-respected, and long-serving members.[1]

Family ties aided Slough's introduction to politics. His father, Martin, was
well-connected to Cincinnati politicians, especially in the Democratic Fourth
Ward, through the coffee houses and taverns that he operated in the 1830s
and 1840s. During his childhood, John Slough must have heard Democrats
discuss politics as they ate and drank in his father's establishments. He could
hardly have avoided the party's influence in Cincinnati, a Democratic stronghold throughout the antebellum period. As historian Jean Baker points out,
men like Slough were raised in communities where "the language they heard,
the activities they observed, the sentiments they inhaled were Democratic."
Listening to the patrons' constant political discourse in his father's taverns,
participating in the shared cultural traditions of Democratic Cincinnati, and
influenced by his father's Democratic affiliation, Slough naturally joined the
Democratic Party.[2]

His marriage to Arabella McLean increased the young lawyer's attractiveness as a candidate. Although Arabella's uncle, United States Supreme

Court justice John McLean, abandoned the Democratic Party in the 1830s, his prominence in national politics made the McLeans an established and well-respected Ohio political family. McLean was also related by marriage to Salmon P. Chase, another prominent Ohio politician; at one point, Chase and McLean were neighbors. Close connections existed among Cincinnati's political elite, and Slough's career likely benefited from his ties to the McLean and Chase families.[3]

Most of all, it was Slough's hard work for the Democratic Party that won the ambitious lawyer the opportunity to represent Hamilton County in the state legislature. The *Cincinnati Daily Enquirer*, a partisan Democratic newspaper, praised him as a young man of "good attainments and popular manners" and "an ardent and zealous Democrat." Slough won the nomination because, as the *Enquirer* concluded, "No man has labored harder for the success of our organization than Mr. Slough; he has been true in the darkest hour, because he is sincerely attached to our principles." Despite the attacks of Know-Nothings and anti-Nebraska fusionists on the Democratic Party in the early 1850s, Slough never faltered in his loyalty as a Democrat.[4]

Slough, along with the other Democrats elected to the 52nd General Assembly, took their seats in a legislative body overwhelmingly dominated by the Republicans. The newly established Ohio Republican Party had convened in Columbus on July 13, 1855, to nominate Salmon P. Chase for governor and to write a party platform that emphasized opposition to the Kansas-Nebraska Act and the expansion of slavery into the territories. Chase won the governorship and his party swept the Ohio House of Representatives and Senate. Twenty-nine Republicans and six Democrats sat in the Senate; in the House, seventy-nine Republicans outnumbered thirty-two Democrats. The sizable Republican majorities meant that they would control the legislative agenda, and their resistance to the Kansas-Nebraska Act and the extension of slavery would become the official policy of the State of Ohio.[5]

Slough experienced the Republican majority's strength on his first day in the legislature. Perhaps as an honor for his loyal work, the Democrats chose the freshman legislator to propose the party's candidates for House offices. Slough rose first to nominate Thomas J. S. Smith, a Dayton, Ohio, lawyer and "old line Democrat," for Speaker of the House. The House voted on party lines, 76-27, and elected the Republican candidate, Nelson Van Vorhes. Slough then proposed E. M. McCook for House clerk; McCook lost to James

S. Robinson, 75-30. Undeterred, Slough continued to nominate Democrats to House offices—first assistant clerk, second assistant clerk, sergeant-at-arms, first assistant sergeant-at-arms, second assistant sergeant-at-arms—and each of his nominations lost to the Republican candidate.[6]

Despite this humbling exposure to statehouse politics, Slough quickly settled into the work of a state legislator. Nine days into his first term on January 16, 1856, he informed the House that he intended to introduce a bill to abolish capital punishment. The next day, he proposed H.B. No. 20, "An act for providing for the punishment of crimes," which the House briefly debated and rejected.[7]

Our knowledge of Slough's performance as a freshman legislator depends on the proceedings recorded in the *Journal of the House of Representatives of the State of Ohio* and a few references in the political columns of the *Cincinnati Daily Enquirer* and the *Daily Ohio State Journal*. He faithfully attended the House sessions. He sat on two House committees, one on the militia and the other on universities, colleges, and academies, and served on a joint House-Senate committee that reconciled differences in a bill reforming the court of common pleas. He introduced a handful of resolutions and a few pieces of legislation, including bills on landlord-tenant relationships and the organization of the Ohio militia. He seldom engaged in debate and preferred that colleagues introduce bills and resolutions concerning Cincinnati and Hamilton County.[8]

The picture of Slough that emerges from contemporary records is that of a promising legislator, not yet a leader, but thoroughly engaged in the political process. His few speeches that merited newspaper coverage reflect a commitment to antebellum Democratic principles: opposition to corporate and banking "privileges," resistance to antislavery activities, fervent support of popular sovereignty, and devotion to a strict interpretation of the United States Constitution. His manner of speaking avoided the fiery partisan oratory favored by some of his Democratic associates, yet he did not hesitate to criticize bills or resolutions contrary to his Democratic beliefs. For example, in one of his rare speeches, he attacked a Republican bill that awarded special favors to the Bank of Ohio because "an article in the Democratic creed" was "to avoid the conferring of privileges that may not be equally enjoyed" by all citizens. In the end, he voted for the bill because, he admitted, his constituency approved of its provisions. Slough was partisan, but also pragmatic.[9]

Day after day, Slough and his colleagues, both Democrats and Republicans, attended to the legislation necessary to govern the state of Ohio. They passed bills that addressed the administration of courts, the oversight of the state's lunatic asylum and penitentiary, the authorization of road and bridge construction, and the regulation of railroad and insurance companies. Democrats and Republicans frequently voted together to pass legislation; Slough himself voted with the majority on almost three-quarters of the bills that reached a final reading. But on the great national concern of the day—the extension of slavery into Kansas—the Ohio House of Representatives split into opposing factions as Democrats and Republicans bitterly disagreed over the increasingly violent conflict occurring in Kansas Territory.[10]

Settlers had eagerly staked their claims in Kansas Territory once the Kansas-Nebraska Act opened the region to emigrants. Between 1854 and 1855, the territory's population increased tenfold; the March 1855 census counted more than eight thousand souls in the region. Pioneers from slaveholding states—mainly Missouri—accounted for almost 60 percent of Kansas's early population. Some of these settlers brought enslaved people into the territory, but whether they possessed slaves or not, emigrants from slaveholding states adamantly believed in their constitutional right to own slaves. Against them stood emigrants from New England, the Midwest, and the middle Atlantic states, who opposed the entry of enslaved people (and for some, even the entry of free Black people) into the territory. They did not wish to compete with slave labor and intended that the soil they tilled in Kansas would be "free soil." Little room for compromise existed between Free Soilers and slaveholders in 1855 Kansas.[11]

The dispute between the territory's proslavery and antislavery inhabitants did not stop at the Kansas border. Missouri was a slave state and many Missourians strongly believed that slavery in Kansas was essential to slavery's continued existence in Missouri. They perceived that Northern abolitionists were using the Kansas Free Soil settlers to achieve slavery's destruction, first in Kansas and then in Missouri. Northerners, who saw the Slave Power's maneuvering behind the Kansas-Nebraska Act, concluded that Southerners were manipulating Missourians to advance the Slave Power's scheme of spreading slavery throughout the republic. Both sides believed that their opponents represented a threat that had to be resisted vigorously.[12]

The tinder for the controversy—illegal voting by Missourians in Kansas elections—was lit soon after the first territorial governor, Andrew Reeder, arrived in Kansas in October 1854. Reeder called for the election of a territorial delegate to the United States Congress and more than 1,700 Missourians poured into Kansas to vote. Their presence at the polls enabled a proslavery candidate to win election as Kansas's delegate. Missourians also swayed the far more consequential election of a territorial legislature in March 1855. Although Governor Reeder took precautions to ensure a fair election, armed and determined Missourians again entered Kansas to manipulate the contest's outcome. Illegal ballots outnumbered legal ones four to one; the proslavery vote overwhelmed the antislavery vote, 5,427-791, guaranteeing a proslavery legislature.[13]

In July 1855, the new territorial legislators met in Shawnee Mission, Kansas, a stone's throw from the Missouri border, and proceeded to pass draconian laws meant to entrench slavery in the territory. When Reeder vetoed the proslavery measures, the legislature overrode his vetoes and then petitioned President Franklin Pierce to remove the governor. Pierce replaced Reeder with a former Democratic governor from Ohio, Wilson Shannon. Shannon gave the proslavery legislature in Shawnee Mission no cause for concern. On his arrival in Kansas Territory, he announced his conviction that the Shawnee Mission legislature was the territorial legislature and that its laws were the laws of the territory.

The Free Soil settlers reacted to these events by organizing their own territorial government. Between October 23 and November 11, 1855, Free Soil delegates met in Topeka and drafted a constitution that prohibited slavery in Kansas. Antislavery Kansans adopted the Topeka Constitution, 1,731-46, and selected Charles Robinson as their governor on January 15, 1856. Kansas now had two governments, one in Topeka without any legal basis and one in Shawnee Mission without any legitimacy.[14]

By fall 1855, the proslavery and antislavery camps had organized military companies and the territory experienced its first episodes of partisan violence. The confrontation known as the "Wakarusa War" began with a property dispute in Hickory Point, Kansas. On November 21, after an argument over land that dated back to the previous year, a proslavery proponent named Franklin Coleman discharged his shotgun into the chest of Free Soil settler Charles Dow, killing him instantly. Coleman and his family fled to Missouri, but the

Hickory Point Free Soil men, led by Jacob Branson, burned the cabins of two proslavery families in revenge for the murder. The local sheriff arrested Branson, who was promptly rescued by his friends and taken to Lawrence, Kansas, where a sympathetic population gave him refuge.

Angered by the Free Soil men's flouting of the law, 1,200 fully armed proslavery Missourians converged on Lawrence to bring Branson to justice and remind the Free Soilers who controlled Kansas. The citizens of Lawrence had no intention of allowing Branson to be retaken. They dug trenches and built forts while more than 600 Free Soil men encamped in the town. False reports of murder and pillage inflamed both sides, bringing each to the brink of violence. Just as the two forces were preparing for battle, Governor Shannon arrived in Lawrence on December 7 and convinced both the proslavery and Free Soil leaders to back down. Although violence had been narrowly averted in Lawrence, the drivers for armed conflict remained.[15]

The news of the near-catastrophe in Lawrence electrified the nation. It was within this atmosphere that Representative John Slough and his fellow legislators gathered on January 15, 1856, for Governor Salmon Chase's inaugural address. Recently elected as the first Republican governor of a major Northern state, Chase was already maneuvering for his party's 1856 presidential nomination. He understood that his inaugural address would be extensively covered in Northern newspapers and, if carefully constructed, would serve to promote his candidacy. He needed to deliver a speech that proclaimed unreservedly his antislavery and Republican principles.[16]

Chase projected a powerful, dignified presence as he stood before the Ohio legislators. After dispensing with his administration's goals—he called them "mundane affairs of state"—he quickly warmed to his true message. He began by describing slavery as "the creature of despotism and the deadly opposite of democracy." He argued that the founding fathers understood the evils of slavery, but the Slave Power had "wrested" the Constitution from its original purposes, converted the government into an "instrument for the maintenance and extension of slavery," and demanded the "sacrifice of freedom" through slavery's expansion into the territories. He denounced the Kansas-Nebraska Act as "nothing but evil" and popular sovereignty as "a total subversion of the fundamental principles of American institutions." At the end of his speech, he again reminded the legislators that the founding fathers had opposed slavery's extension. "No worthier object," he insisted, "can engage the united efforts of freemen" than resisting the spread of slavery. Chase had called Ohio's Republicans to battle.[17]

Not long after Chase's denunciation of the Slave Power, the Kansas-Nebraska Act, and popular sovereignty, the Republicans and Democrats in the Ohio House began to spar over the deteriorating conditions in Kansas. On the afternoon of February 5, Speaker Nelson Van Vorhes read an urgent communication from Governor Chase to both House and Senate. Chase conveyed the fears of Kansas Free State governor Charles Robinson that "an overwhelming force of citizens in Missouri" intended to invade the territory, "demolishing the towns and butchering its free State citizens." Surely thinking of the near-attack on Lawrence, Kansas, two months earlier, Chase expressed his own apprehension that great numbers of proslavery Missourians were preparing to assail the territory's Free State residents. He pressed the General Assembly to pass a resolution urging the Ohio congressional delegation to promote legislation ensuring free elections in Kansas and admitting Kansas as a free state to the Union.[18]

As soon as Van Vorhes finished reading Chase's message, Democrat William Sawyer jumped to his feet to express astonishment that Governor Chase should "thrust into our faces such inflammatory Abolition doctrines and recommendations as are contained in the Messages." His criticism led to "some skirmishing" between the Democrats and the Republicans over the printing of the governor's letter before Darius Cadwell, Republican representative from Ashtabula County, rose to offer his resolutions on Kansas.[19]

Cadwell hailed from the "Western Reserve," a region in northeastern Ohio and the political counterweight to the Democratic counties in southwestern Ohio. It was the center of antebellum Ohio radicalism, "burned over" by the religious revivals of the 1820s and 1830s that influenced Northerners to embrace abolitionism and other reform activities. Cadwell was born in Ashtabula County in 1821 and grew up during the period of the Second Great Awakening's evangelical revivals. In 1842, he undertook his legal apprenticeship at the practice of Rufus P. Ranney and Benjamin Wade. Wade had promoted the antislavery cause since the early 1830s and probably influenced his legal apprentice's opposition to slavery. Like Wade, Cadwell was an antislavery Whig in the 1840s but joined the new Ohio Republican Party. The party repaid him with election to the Ohio House of Representatives.[20]

Cadwell's prepared statement closely followed Chase's recommendations on Kansas to the Ohio General Assembly. Leaning forward slightly to make his point, Cadwell noted that Missourians had unlawfully invaded Kansas to establish slavery in the territory "by force and without authority of law." He insisted that the peace and future welfare of the United States demanded that no more slave states be admitted to the Union. Because the Topeka Constitution prohibited slavery in the territory, he recommended that Ohio's congressional delegation press for the admission of Kansas as a free state and save it from "further civil tumults, and the further effusion of blood."[21]

No aisle separated Democrats from Republicans in the 1856 Ohio House of Representatives. Cadwell sat immediately in front of John Slough, and the Cincinnati legislator reacted with distaste as Cadwell uttered his "black Republican" pronouncements practically by his side. Kansans must decide the issue of slave or free, Slough thought, not Ohio Republicans urging Congress to settle the matter. Adding to Slough's irritation was Cadwell's habit of ending his sentences with "a sort of defiant intonation." It was most annoying. Slough decided to treat the Western Reserve abolitionist with suspicion.[22]

Three days later, on February 8, Republican representative Mendall Jewitt presented a petition from the Executive Committee of the Western Anti-Slavery Society. The petition called for far more radical action than Chase's message or Cadwell's resolutions. It argued that Ohioans, by legitimizing the federal government through participation in its elections, acceded to the "holding four millions [*sic*] of human beings in the condition of chattel slaves." Because the "principles of sound morality and the requirements of justice imperatively forbid the individual to be loyal to a government thus constituted," it urged the Ohio legislators to take any steps that "may appear expedient to effect a peaceful withdrawal of Ohio from the Federal Union." The document contended that no union of free and slave states could exist and therefore challenged Ohio to form a new confederacy of states "founded upon justice and devoted to the maintenance of equal rights."[23]

Jewitt's introduction of the Western Anti-Slavery Society's petition provoked the Ohio House into heated argument over the controversial document. The *Cincinnati Daily Enquirer*'s correspondent reported that the dispute was the "first real break . . . in the uniform good feeling evinced by members toward each other," while the *Cincinnati Daily Gazette* wrote that the document "greatly excited the talking members of that body."[24]

To this point, John Slough had not addressed—at least publicly—the Republicans' various proposals for a free Kansas. The Western Anti-Slavery Society's call for Ohio's secession drove him to speak. In comments that had a "telling effect" on the House, Slough strongly condemned the document and charged the Republicans with disunion. His speech, the *Cincinnati Daily Enquirer*'s correspondent noted approvingly, caused many members of the House to wince under "its scathing influence." Despite his criticisms, the House decided, by a close vote of 52–47, to refer the document to the Republican-controlled Federal Relations Committee. In the end, the Federal Relations Committee could not endorse so extreme a measure as disunion and recommended no further consideration of the Western Anti-Slavery Society's petition.[25]

About the same time that he condemned the Western Anti-Slavery Society's petition, Slough joined the debate over Ohio's habeas corpus statute. Representative James Monroe, professor of elocution at Oberlin College and Republican from Lorain County in the Western Reserve, introduced a bill on February 14 to strengthen the rights of fugitive slaves by revising the state's habeas corpus procedures.[26]

Since the earliest days of the republic, Northern states, including Ohio, attempted to circumvent the Constitution's Fugitive Slave clause by passing personal liberty laws. Included among the laws' protections was the writ of habeas corpus, a court order used to bring an imprisoned individual before the court to determine if the person's detention was lawful. Captured fugitive slaves—or even free Black people ensnared by slave catchers—could be released if a magistrate determined that their detention was illegal. The 1850 amendments to the federal Fugitive Slave Law, however, severely restricted a fugitive slave's legal recourse. The amendments' provisions conflicted directly with the Northern states' personal liberty laws, leading to confrontations between federal and state officers attempting to enforce the laws of their respective jurisdictions.

A few weeks before Monroe introduced his habeas corpus reform bill, events in Cincinnati resulted in tragic consequences that angered and activated Ohio's antislavery community. On the bitterly cold night of January 27, 1856, a group of seventeen slaves from two plantations in Boone County, Kentucky, fled across the frozen Ohio River and sought refuge in Cincinnati as the first stop toward freedom in Canada. The large group split up once in Cincinnati to minimize any chance that they might be noticed by slave catchers. One group, consisting of eight slaves, including Margaret Garner, her husband Simon, and their four children, asked for directions to the home of their kinsman, Elijah Kite.

Disastrously, the person who gave them directions betrayed them. An arresting party of federal marshals surrounded Elijah Kite's home shortly after the Garner family's arrival and demanded the surrender of the fugitives. Certain that return to slavery was imminent, Margaret Garner used a butcher knife to slit the throat of her three-year-old daughter and would have murdered her other three children had the marshals not broken into the house and subdued her. The marshals took the terrified and distraught family to the federal courthouse to appear as fugitive slaves before the United States commissioner for Southern Ohio and then to the Hammond Street police station to spend the night in jail.

Ohio officials quickly contested the right of the federal marshals to retain the Garners. A Cincinnati attorney who volunteered to aid the runaway family argued before Judge John Burgoyne that the Garners were free because on several occasions their master had brought them into a free state. Judge Burgoyne agreed to issue a writ of habeas corpus, forcing the federal marshals to yield the family to state officers. In turn, Ohio officials agreed to produce the fugitives for their hearing before the United States commissioner. The hearing lasted several weeks as the counsels for the fugitives and the slave owner argued their case. In the end, the Garners were returned to Kentucky and sold to an owner in the Deep South.[27]

Judge Burgoyne's writ set up the type of confrontation between federal and state officials that James Monroe intended to remedy in his proposed legislation. Concerned that federal officers would simply ignore a writ of habeas corpus issued on behalf of a fugitive slave, Monroe pointed out that insufficient penalties existed in state law for any officer, federal or state, who disregarded a writ of habeas corpus. He proposed to cure this defect in Ohio law by empowering a judge to issue the writ to a second officer if the first officer ignored it. Monroe, in his argument, said that he "would be glad to see the Fugitive Slave Law . . . ignored by our Courts and our Legislature" because he regarded the law as nothing more than "waste paper." But the Fugitive Slave Law was the law of the land, so he was offering his bill as more "efficient for the protection of liberty" than Ohio's current law.[28]

John Slough reached a different conclusion about the efficiency of Monroe's bill. Specifically citing the recent events in Cincinnati, he told his colleagues that the bill would bring Ohio into conflict with the federal government because writs could be placed in the hands of two different officers, both sworn to execute them. Alluding to Monroe's opinion that the Fugitive Slave Law was "waste paper," he tartly noted that his colleague could have made his bill more "obnoxious" by declaring the supremacy of Ohio law over the acts of Congress or the Ohio courts over the federal courts. Nevertheless, he argued, Monroe's bill was incompatible with the United States Constitution and should be rejected. Surely with "calm reflection," the House members would reach the same conclusion.

No sooner had Slough finished than Darius Cadwell challenged his call for "calm reflection." Linking the Fugitive Slave Law to the Republican belief that the Slave Power threatened the very existence of liberty, Cadwell proclaimed that "the time had arrived in the demands of slavery when freemen needed fresh guards to protect personal liberty." He argued, as had James Monroe, that the bill was necessary to give "efficiency" to the writ of habeas corpus. Joseph Egley, Slough's colleague in the Hamilton County delegation, could not resist provoking the Western Reserve abolitionist. He baited Cadwell by asking him if he favored conferring equal rights on Black people. Cadwell replied that he hoped "the day is not far distant when no man in Ohio will hesitate" to say he was for equal rights. In an age when most Americans considered Black people inferior and unworthy of rights, the abolitionist's admission was astonishing.

Cadwell spoke again that afternoon as the House continued to debate Monroe's bill. He quoted United States Supreme Court justice John McLean, Arabella Slough's uncle, to strengthen his argument that the bill posed no conflict between the federal and state courts. Slough took no part in the afternoon's discussion but voted against the bill when it was presented for its third reading on March 13, 1856. Monroe's revisions to Ohio's habeas corpus law passed by a vote of 57–42.[29]

Slough left no record of his opinion of chattel slavery. Salmon Chase recorded in his journal that Slough was proslavery, which is plausible given Slough's Cincinnati origins. The Queen City's proximity to slaveholding Kentucky and its antebellum commercial ties to Southern businessmen shaped the city's pro-Southern, if not proslavery, orientation. The city manifested its hostility to Black people not only through the daily humiliations endured by its Black population but also in the terrifying racial violence that broke out in 1829, 1836, and 1841, when white mobs ransacked the city's Black neighborhoods. Free Black people did not feel welcome in the Queen City and few made it their home. In 1829, when the first major race riot occurred, 2,258 Black people lived in Cincinnati and accounted for 10.3 percent of the population. During the next thirty years, as the city's white population exploded by a factor of five, its Black population barely increased. There were only 3,172 Black people among Cincinnati's 115,438 inhabitants in 1850, an indication that free Black people preferred to live elsewhere than antebellum Cincinnati.[30]

Slough grew up on the Cincinnati riverfront, among businessmen who traded with the South and native-born white workers who felt threatened by competition from free Black labor. He might easily have adopted the proslavery feelings Chase attributed to him. Additionally, according to the *Daily Ohio State Journal*, he was a member of the "Miami Tribe," the conservative Democratic faction in Cincinnati with proslavery leanings. On the other hand, Slough's condemnation of the Western Anti-Slavery Society's call for disunion would have been shared by virtually all Northerners, and his belief that Monroe's habeas corpus bill was unconstitutional reflected his conservative interpretation of the Constitution. Neither of these positions, nor his opposition to the Republicans' antiexpansion platform, necessarily meant that Slough harbored sympathetic feelings for the South's "peculiar institution" even though he believed that no Black man was the equal of a white man.[31]

On March 18, the House finally passed, resolution by resolution, its answer to the Kansas controversy. Slough understood that he could not appear indifferent to the plight of the Kansas settlers, so he voted to approve the resolution expressing sympathy for the people of Kansas "engaged in defending themselves against lawless violence, and asserting their inherent right of self-government." It would have been insensitive and impolitic to vote against the resolution and, after all, its wording applied to both proslavery and Free State settlers. The remainder of the resolutions explicitly promoted the Republicans' antiexpansion platform. They exhorted the Ohio congressional delegation to use its best efforts to exclude slavery from the Kansas-Nebraska territory and "all territories embraced by the Missouri

Compromise." They also urged Ohio's senators and congressmen to oppose the proceedings of the proslavery legislature meeting in Shawnee Mission, Kansas, while working to admit Kansas as a free state. Slough voted against each resolution, but, as he expected, the minority Democrats could not muster sufficient votes to prevent the Republican majority from adopting antiexpansion as Ohio's policy.[32]

The Ohio House considered the 1850 Fugitive Slave Law once again on April 9, two days before the end of the session. The state Senate had sent to the House a resolution urging the Ohio congressional delegation to work for the repeal of the 1850 law, which the Senate characterized as unconstitutional, unjust, and inhumane. The House Democrats sought to counteract the resolution's certain adoption by proposing that the Ohio legislature pass its own fugitive slave law if the United States Congress repealed the national one. John Slough voted for the Democrats' amendment, and when it failed he voted against the Senate resolution. Not surprisingly, the resolution passed on a party-line vote.[33]

On April 11, 1856, the 52nd Ohio General Assembly adjourned for the remainder of the year. During the session, the House had passed scores of bills—largely on a nonpartisan basis—that addressed the economic, financial, judicial, and social issues faced by the state. The Ohio Republicans also approved a set of antiexpansion resolutions, called for the repeal of the 1850 Fugitive Slave Act, and provided judges with more latitude in issuing writs of habeas corpus to protect men and women fleeing enslavement. The House's debates over the crisis in Kansas, the legal rights of fugitive slaves, and the expansion of slavery into the territories reflected the simmering national argument that would boil over in the next four years.

It was time for Representative Slough to return to Cincinnati. His wife Arabella was seven months pregnant and would deliver their second child on June 27. Slough needed to attend to his role as father as well as his practice as an attorney. He had seemingly performed well in his first session representing Hamilton County and its Democratic constituency. He diligently attended the House's daily sessions, actively participated in its deliberations, served on several committees, and proposed a handful of bills. His political skills led a contemporary to recognize him as "the most regularly developed politician among the delegation of his county," a representative who "in the general business of legislation handles himself well." Yet rumors were circulating in the Ohio Statehouse about Slough's behavior; legislators had apparently complained about his angry outbursts. The rising Cincinnati politician needed to curb his temper, some members believed, if he expected to make his way in Ohio politics.[34]

3

〜〜〜〜〜

Disgrace and Defeat

GOVERNOR CHASE'S WARNING TO THE OHIO LEGISLATURE THAT Kansans faced "invasion, usurpation, violence, [and] bloodshed" was not mere Republican rhetoric. Political violence in the territory intensified during early 1856 as disputes between proslavery and Free State adherents degenerated into bloody confrontations. In April, militants shot proslavery sheriff Samuel Jones in the back when he attempted to arrest Free State leader S. N. Wood in Lawrence, Kansas. The attack on Jones angered the territory's chief justice and proslavery proponent, Samuel Lecompte. Judge Lecompte insisted that several Free State leaders be indicted for treason. He also directed that Lawrence's newspapers, the *Herald of Freedom* and the *Kansas Free State*, as well as the town's Free State Hotel, be "abated as nuisances." To Judge Lecompte, the two antislavery newspapers and the fortress-like Free State Hotel served as tangible proof of Free State resistance to the territory's elected government.[1]

As soon as he recovered from his wounds, Jones and federal marshal I. B. Donaldson traveled to Lawrence to execute Judge Lecompte's orders. With them rode a posse of as many as eight hundred proslavery men. On May 21, 1856, after Marshal Donaldson made his arrests, Jones and his posse positioned four six-pounder brass cannons in front of the Free State Hotel. The men shelled the hotel for an hour and then attempted to blow it up with kegs of gunpowder. Defeated in their efforts to reduce the building's stone walls, the men set the hotel on fire and turned to looting Lawrence's houses and shops. Although no Free State settlers were killed during the melee, the Northern press grossly exaggerated the results of the posse's attack. One set of headlines shrieked, "Startling News from Kansas—The War Actually Begun—Triumph of the Border Ruffians—Lawrence in Ruins—Several

Proslavery militias destroyed the Free State Hotel and sacked the town of
Lawrence, Kansas Territory, in 1856. Republicans used the outrage
to brand Democrats as supporters of violence in the defense of slavery.
Source: Wikimedia Commons/Public Domain.

Persons Slaughtered—Freedom Bloodily Subdued." For many Northerners,
the "sack of Lawrence," as the affair became known, proved the ends to which
proslavery men would go to suppress antislavery sentiment.[2]

Meanwhile, Massachusetts senator Charles Sumner delivered a particularly incendiary speech, titled "The Crime Against Kansas," before the United
States Senate. Although his ardent antislavery beliefs and florid oratory were
well-known in the Senate, this time his comments particularly enraged his
Southern colleagues. He derisively characterized Andrew P. Butler and Stephen A. Douglas as the Senate's Don Quixote and Sancho Panza for their
blind adherence to slavery and popular sovereignty. He saved his harshest
words for Butler, a courtly South Carolinian bred to regard the virtue of
white women, by calling him a "Don Quixote who had chosen a mistress
to whom he has made his vows, [a mistress] who . . . though polluted in the
sight of the world, is chaste in his sight—I mean the harlot, Slavery." That
insult was not sufficient for Charles Sumner. In his concluding remarks,
he continued to rage against South Carolina and Butler, savaging South

Carolina for its "shameful imbecility from Slavery" and mocking Butler's speeches as "loose expectorations."[3]

Butler's nephew, South Carolina congressman Preston Brooks, seethed over Sumner's venomous attack on his uncle and his state. On the afternoon of May 22, the day after the "sack of Lawrence," Brooks caught Sumner writing at his desk after the Senate had recessed for the day. Swearing that the senator had libeled both South Carolina and his uncle, Brooks wielded his gold-headed cane against Sumner's head and shoulders, beating the senator senseless. The North reacted with outrage. Brooks's attack on Sumner, in Northerners' perception, symbolized the Slave Power's determination to demolish the rights of free men. Southerners were delighted with Brooks's defense of Southern honor, sending him dozens of canes to express their approval. The House of Representatives, failing to achieve the two-thirds majority required to expel Brooks, censured the South Carolinian, while a Baltimore court fined him $300 for the egregious assault.

When he read about the "sack of Lawrence" and the Sumner caning in the *Cincinnati Daily Enquirer,* John Slough could not have foreseen the impact the two events would have on his political career. The Democratic National Convention, convened in Cincinnati on June 2, had a more immediate effect. It was an election year, and the delegates—592 men from thirty-one states—gathered in the Queen City to nominate the party's presidential and vice presidential candidates. They settled on James Buchanan as their presidential nominee. A Northerner who respected the interests of the slave states, Buchanan appealed to both moderates and conservatives. The delegates, seeking to solidify the Southern vote behind the ticket, selected John C. Breckinridge of Kentucky as Buchanan's running mate.

Slough probably missed the convention's sessions. He did not serve as a delegate and may not have had access to its proceedings. Smith & Nixon's Hall, the convention's venue, was too small for the large number of delegates, newspaper reporters, and guests. The *Cincinnati Daily Enquirer* noted that the hall was "well filled" on the convention's first day, leading the delegates to consider moving to the larger Metropolitan Hall. With the main floor reserved for delegates and the galleries packed by newspaper correspondents, little space remained for visitors like Slough to watch their party's leaders in action.[4]

Even if Slough missed the excitement within Smith & Nixon's Hall, he politicked for Stephen A. Douglas's nomination during the convention and then worked loyally for the Democratic ticket once the delegates chose Buchanan and Breckinridge. In July, Slough became secretary to the Ohio Democratic Central Committee and acting secretary to the Ohio Democratic Executive Committee. It was a key promotion for the young politician. Serving as secretary made Slough the senior official responsible for coordinating the Ohio Democratic Party's political activities. In that role, he corresponded with Democratic leaders across the state, organized election rallies in Ohio cities, and dispatched information to the state's Democratic newspapers about election results. The success of the Ohio Democratic Party in the fall elections depended in part on Slough's organizational abilities.[5]

His efforts did not go unnoticed. After Buchanan and Breckinridge won the November election, the Democratic *Columbus Statesman* showered praise on Slough for his work on behalf of Democratic candidates. The paper lauded his "energy, tact, perseverance, and courage" and claimed that "In the long course of our political life, we have never met with a more faithful and constant ally." The Democratic State Central Committee also recognized the Cincinnati politician. Meeting in Columbus on December 9, the party leaders commended him for his "very faithful and unremitting efforts" as the committee's secretary during the campaign. It was rare recognition from the state Democratic leadership. Besides Slough, the Central Committee only extended thanks to its chairman, Samuel Medary. Slough had earned the admiration of Ohio Democrats and, undoubtedly, the attention of Ohio Republicans.[6]

Slough returned to the business of legislation when the 52nd General Assembly reconvened on January 7, 1857. As part of the representatives' efforts to organize the new session, he resolved that the sergeant-at-arms obtain desks for two new members. He also proposed that the Ohio attorney general decide if members could receive mileage and per diem during the previous adjournment. The House set aside Slough's resolution about mileage and per diems—the members "laid it on the table"—so on January 14, he asked his colleagues to reconsider his request. The Republicans promptly voted to postpone his resolution indefinitely.[7]

The Republicans' peremptory rejection of his proposal to query the attorney general irritated Slough. As he listened to the roll call vote, Slough groused to his Democratic desk mate, George Robinson, "It is as I expected,

Slough sat only a few weeks in the newly opened statehouse before
his expulsion from the Ohio House of Representatives in January 1857.
Source: Courtesy of the Ohio History Connection, AL 00225.

they [the Republicans] are afraid to allow the Attorney General to give an
opinion." Darius Cadwell, who sat in front of Slough and Robinson, turned
in his chair, looked at Slough, and said, "The Attorney General would pay
no attention even if your resolution passed."

"Why not?" Slough asked.

"Because there are men in the House equally competent to determine if
we're entitled to mileage and per diems during an adjournment." Cadwell's
tone had just a hint of condescension.

Already annoyed that the Republicans had dismissed his resolution,
Slough again asked Cadwell why the attorney general would not provide
an opinion. Whether he intended to antagonize Slough or simply because
he was irritated with the Cincinnati Democrat, Cadwell shot back, "Because
the matter is too foolish to engage the Attorney General's attention."

Those were provocative words. Slough believed that Cadwell—a "black
Republican" whom he neither liked nor trusted—had deliberately called him
a fool. Knocking over his chair as he leaned over his desk, Slough angrily

spat at Cadwell, "I do not permit any man to call me a fool, either here or elsewhere."

Cadwell now lost his temper. He rose, stuck his face within five or six inches of Slough's face, and belligerently asked, "What do you propose to do about it?"

Slough answered, "This is what I propose to do about it," and struck Cadwell over the left eye. The Republican recoiled from the unexpected blow, falling back into his chair. Slough picked up his own toppled chair and, again muttering that he allowed no man to call him a fool, sat down.[8]

Slough's assault of Cadwell strangely went unnoticed among their colleagues. With the House proceeding as if nothing extraordinary had occurred, Cadwell had to interrupt Speaker Van Vorhes for permission to speak. He told the members that during the vote on Slough's resolution, he had commented to the Cincinnati Democrat that the attorney general would pay no attention to the resolution even if it passed. He acknowledged that his remark led to an argument, ending with Slough striking "a full blow" to his forehead. He then called on Slough to refute what he had said. Slough only sputtered that Cadwell's accounting had "suppressed" the "gist of the matter." Perhaps in an effort to control his anger, he declined to make any further comment, saying that he preferred that witnesses to the incident make statements to an investigating committee.[9]

The House could not ignore Slough's breach of its rules. It immediately appointed a select investigating committee of three Republicans and two Democrats. John Hunter, the committee's chairperson and one of the "most zealous" of the House Republicans, would be certain to judge the Cincinnati Democrat harshly. The committee's other two Republicans, T. M. Cook and Nelson Franklin, might offer Slough a more impartial review, although Cook tended to avoid controversy and probably would follow the opinionated John Hunter. Slough's only hope was to convince the two Democrats, Thomas J. S. Smith and Lorenzo Dow Odell, and either Cook or Franklin that Cadwell had provoked him.[10]

Two days later, Slough asked the Speaker for permission to make a statement "which should have been said earlier, but circumstances prevented." According to the *Cincinnati Daily Enquirer*'s correspondent, Darius Cadwell archly noted that he found it strange that Slough declined to speak when the altercation occurred but now had something to say. Slough must have glanced sharply at Cadwell. Instead of answering Cadwell's snide remark, he began to read a brief prepared statement.

He acknowledged "the sanctity of places set apart for legislation" yet asserted that his constituents, upon learning of Cadwell's provocation, expected him to address the insult "in the manner deemed most proper by me." He told his colleagues that Cadwell intended to insult him and therefore the insult "demanded chastisement." Slough apologized to neither Cadwell nor the House, saying only that he regretted his disregard of the legislature's rules, an admission he felt fulfilled "everything that could be properly demanded by the House." Upon Slough's finishing his statement, Cadwell rose and, with a tone "intended to be very keen and cutting," sarcastically noted that "by all means, the gentleman's apology should go on record. It was worthy to be preserved, and should be handed down to posterity as a model of parliamentary courtesy and eloquence."[11]

Slough submitted a copy of his remarks for publication in the House journal, but apparently his written words did not match his spoken ones. How the two versions differed is unknown—perhaps he omitted his assertion that Cadwell's insult "demanded chastisement"—but the Republicans concluded that he deliberately intended to manipulate the public record. They demanded that Slough furnish an exact copy of the statement he read on January 16, and when Slough stubbornly refused to acknowledge the Republicans' demand, they insisted it be stricken from the *Journal*. For the Republicans, his apparent duplicity in revising his remarks reinforced their growing belief that Slough lacked character.[12]

The select investigating committee presented its report on Thursday, January 22. The members had heard testimony from Slough and Cadwell as well as several legislators who sat close to the two men. The report varied little from the account Cadwell gave the House immediately after his altercation with Slough on the afternoon of January 14. The committee's three Republicans concluded that even though Slough believed that Cadwell insulted him, "no amount of provocation in mere words can justify a personal assault by one member on another, in a legislative assembly." Accordingly, the majority Republicans recommended that the House "take such measures for the vindication of its outraged honor and dignity, as circumstances demand." The committee's two Democrats concurred with the report's assessment of what had transpired but refused to pass judgment on their colleague. Instead, they left it "entirely to the House" to decide "how great an indignity has been offered to it."[13]

The House Republicans had no intention of ignoring Slough's misbehavior now that the select committee had delivered its report. As soon as the committee's findings were presented, Ralph Plumb, Darius Cadwell's associate from the Western Reserve, demanded that Slough make a "full and unequivocal confession . . . with an assurance that the offense shall not be repeated" for the "unjustifiable" attack he had inflicted on Cadwell. Tightening the screws, Plumb resolved that Slough be expelled from the House if he failed to apologize by the next day. The Democrats rallied to Slough's defense by arguing that he should be allowed to address the House before the representatives voted on Plumb's resolution. Plumb agreed that it was the privilege of the member "now arraigned"—as if Slough were on trial—to have an opportunity to respond.[14]

Slough refused to apologize. He again told his colleagues that he regretted his breach of the House rules. He considered his regret to be a "proper acknowledgement" of his transgression. "What more could in justice be demanded," he asked the representatives, "that would not be degrading to me?" He had violated House decorum and, in his view, his acknowledgment was sufficient. The Republicans did not agree. Slough's striking Cadwell offered them the opportunity to embarrass both the Ohio Democrats and their rising political star. They would not accept Slough's admission nor forgive his actions. After the House returned from a recess, Republican Thomas Bunker called for the immediate expulsion of Representative John P. Slough, given the "assault and battery" he had committed against Darius Cadwell.[15]

Representatives Plumb and Bunker had both offered resolutions to ban Slough from the House, but the Republicans wanted to make absolutely certain they had sufficient votes to punish him. They elected to set the resolutions aside for a week to allow undecided members to make up their minds. During that time, according to the *M'Arthur Democrat*, the affair completely absorbed the members' attention. Undoubtedly the Republican and Democratic caucuses met to ensure party discipline on the upcoming vote. The *Cincinnati Daily Enquirer* asserted that the Republicans applied the "political gag" to suppress any dissension in the decision to expel Slough, while the *Cincinnati Daily Gazette* disingenuously claimed that the Republican members agreed not to caucus, "all concurring in the opinion that it [the assault] should not be given a party bias in any manner whatsoever."[16]

Within a week, the Republicans had lined up the necessary votes to expel Slough. On January 29, the House voted on Bunker's resolution. To the Republicans' dismay, the resolution failed by one vote to gain the two-thirds majority necessary for expulsion. Dr. Franklin Flowers, a Know-Nothing who generally aligned with the Republicans, claimed confusion about the vote's purpose. Was it intended, he asked, to expel Slough or to substitute Bunker's resolution for Plumb's resolution? He proposed that the vote be reconsidered.[17]

The House was still not ready to decide the matter. Democrats argued that the Cincinnatian deserved a lesser punishment than expulsion. E. E. Hutcheson suggested that both Cadwell and Slough be disciplined because Cadwell had "the insolence to get knocked down" and Slough had "the insolence to knock his fellow member down." The Republicans had no intention of disciplining both men. They rejected Hutcheson's proposal 73-31, and then recessed for lunch and one last opportunity to convince any wavering members that Slough deserved the strongest punishment the House could wield.[18]

That afternoon at three o'clock, the legislators gathered to determine if Slough would remain a member of the Ohio House of Representatives. Word had spread quickly among Columbus's elites that Slough's fate hung in the balance. "The lobby and the galleries were thronged," the *Cincinnati Daily Gazette* reported, "and as nearly all the available space inside the bar was occupied, members were generally giving up their easy chairs to lady visitors." As Speaker Van Vorhes called the House to order and the crowd hushed their excited conversation, William Corry, John Slough's colleague in the Hamilton County delegation, advanced to the Speaker's desk to address the House.[19]

Corry was Slough's rival. Eighteen years Slough's senior, he had already made his reputation as an attorney and politician while Slough was still a boy. "Brilliant, erratic, and eccentric," he had a radical streak and, although nominally a Democrat, refused to be categorized politically. Slough, the conservative Democrat and loyal party member, and Corry, the independent thinker who disdained party labels, were political opposites. It was rumored that Corry tried to control Slough during the first legislative session and, when Slough rebelled, became a "bitter, unrelenting foe" of the freshman legislator.[20]

Standing before the massive marble Speaker's desk, Corry spoke forcefully despite his recent battle with smallpox. He explained that he would vote to expel his fellow Democrat because, he falsely claimed, the Hamilton County Democratic Party had disowned Slough after his assault on Darius Cadwell. He agreed with Cadwell that Slough had proposed a "foolish and frivolous" question when he asked for the attorney general's opinion on mileage and per diems. Moreover, the resolution demonstrated particularly "bad grace" coming from a member who wanted an additional four dollars a day when "thousands of [his] constituents . . . had not the where with to purchase the necessaries of life." As Corry attacked Slough, portraying him as an insensitive party hack, Slough angrily interrupted his rival to warn that he would hold him personally responsible "here and elsewhere." Corry coolly replied, "I am prepared to meet you here or elsewhere."[21]

After Corry finished, Democrats John Chaney, Thomas J. S. Smith, and James Holmes argued for a less extreme punishment, arguments that the *Cincinnati Daily Gazette* dismissed as "velvety dabs of disapprobation." Much to his Democratic colleagues' dismay, Slough again lost his temper when Republican Schuyler Blakeslee argued for expulsion. Slough bolted from his chair, shouting "I'll be damned if I will stand it any longer," and appeared as if he would attack Blakeslee as he had Cadwell. Only after his friends restrained him did Slough sit down.[22]

Two hours into the afternoon's session, the vote to decide Slough's fate was taken. As the clerk read the final count—71 yeas for Bunker's resolution and 32 nays—a "faint murmur" went through the galleries. The Republicans, joined by William Corry, had expelled the Cincinnati Democrat.[23]

The state's Democratic newspapers howled with outrage about the Republicans' blatantly partisan attack on Slough. Even before the final vote was taken, the *Preble County Democrat* condemned the Republicans' actions as "vindictive" and an "abuse of power." The *Cincinnati Daily Enquirer* complained that Slough "being a Democrat from this county—which is peculiarly unpopular with the Abolitionists of the Western Reserve . . . is pursued with a bitter and revengeful spite." And the *M'Arthur Democrat*, in racist language typical of antebellum Democratic newspapers, concluded that "It was spite against a Democrat and a desire to propitiate the Nigger-worshippers on the [Western] Reserve, which produced the result."[24]

The state's Republican newspapers countered that legislative bodies can never tolerate misbehavior like Slough's. The *Cincinnati Daily Gazette* editorialized that if the House failed to punish Slough for assaulting another member, then "the same right cannot be denied to others" with the result that the "halls of legislation would partake of the character of a bear garden." The Holmes County *Republican* chastised the Democratic legislators for coddling "one of its political bullies" by refusing to support Slough's expulsion. Meanwhile, newspapers across the country covered the assault and its aftermath. Not only Ohio newspapers, but newspapers in Pennsylvania, Tennessee, Virginia, Louisiana, and Washington, DC, published reports of the affair.[25]

John Slough had fallen victim to his impulsive and hotheaded nature. The Republicans used the punch he threw at Darius Cadwell to chasten the Cincinnati politician. But hot tempers and even fisticuffs were hardly rare in antebellum American politics. Slough's Democratic colleague John Chaney recalled that during his twenty-eight years serving in various legislatures, he had witnessed many incidents like Slough's assault on Cadwell, but none resulting in expulsion. Even though Chaney's recollection of legislators fighting each other described the rough-and-tumble nature of American politics, the Ohio Republicans eagerly took advantage of Slough's misconduct to rid themselves of the promising young politician and to humiliate their rivals in the Democratic Party.[26]

Slough believed that defending his honor against insult justified his physically chastising the insolent Cadwell. He told his colleagues two days after the attack that his constituents "would recognize my right, yea, would expect me to resent an insult in the manner deemed most proper by me." For many mid-nineteenth-century males, an unanswered insult threatened one's reputation because it potentially diminished others' respect. Insults—particularly ones intended to shame and provoke, as Slough interpreted Cadwell's comments—were not tolerated, even if the response meant physically attacking one's opponent. Slough's reaction was impetuous and ill-advised, but as the *Cincinnati Daily Enquirer* concluded, "Mr. Slough, in resenting Cadwell's insult, only did what most men of spirit and honor would have done."[27]

The Republicans dismissed Slough's notion of honor. Schuyler Blakeslee, in justifying his vote to expel, explained that Slough's actions offended his sense of dignity. He called on his colleagues "to manifest their correct appreciation of the true principles of honor, integrity, and manhood" by punishing the Cincinnati Democrat. Even Slough's attack on the smaller Cadwell merited Blakeslee's scorn. "Whenever I stoop to grasp the crown of Bullyism and wear it," Blakeslee contemptuously noted, "it will be by licking a man corporeally larger than myself." The *Cincinnati Daily Gazette*, in reviewing Slough's transgressions, concluded that his "unmanly and ungentlemanly conduct . . . brought upon him the vengeance of the House." Slough's behavior throughout the affair—his physical attack on Cadwell and his obstinate refusal to apologize for the assault, his seemingly deceitful effort to abridge his verbal comments for publication in the House *Journal*, and his threatening behavior toward both Corry and Blakeslee—offended his colleagues and, for the Republicans, shaped the perception of an intemperate, untrustworthy, and dishonorable politician deserving of expulsion.[28]

The Republicans also associated Slough's misbehavior with two recent atrocities: the devastation of Lawrence, Kansas, by the proslavery posse and Congressman Preston Brooks's brutal caning of Charles Sumner. They blamed the Democrats for both outrages and regarded Slough's actions as demonstrating the Democrats' propensity for violence. Schuyler Blakeslee, in arguing that the House could not tolerate Slough's attack, referenced Kansas, where men resorted to "mob violence and the shedding of blood" to usurp "the rights of the elective franchise." The Republican *Meigs County Telegraph* called Slough "an overgrown booby" who "failing to acquire notoriety intellectually . . . [is] determined to distinguish himself as an humble imitator of Bully Brooks." The *Telegraph* asserted, "Mr. Slough has acted more like a ruffian than a gentleman since the occurrence [his assault on Cadwell]," and concluded, "Ever since the attack of Brooks upon Sumner, it has been the 'mission' of Democracy to defend Ruffianism in high places." The United States Congress had failed to expel Preston Brooks; Ohio Republicans determined not to make the same mistake with John Slough.[29]

The entire affair—Cadwell's contemptuous remarks about Slough's resolution, Slough's physical response to the perceived insult, and the Republicans' determination to punish Slough with expulsion—reflected the growing antagonism between Republicans and Democrats in late antebellum politics. During the 1856 session, Republican and Democratic legislators clashed in the Ohio House over the Kansas struggles and the Fugitive Slave Law. Darius Cadwell had distinguished himself during those debates as one of the legislature's most outspoken abolitionists. John Slough, on the other hand, was a fiercely loyal Democrat. The Republican majority disdained Slough's

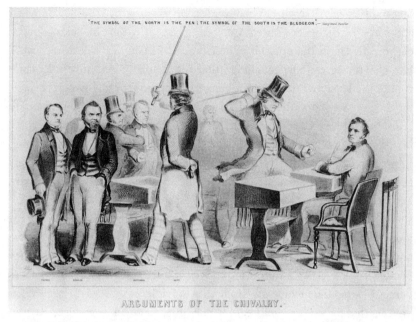

In this 1856 political cartoon, Rep. Preston Brooks viciously canes
Sen. Charles Sumner on the floor of the United States Senate. Ohio Republicans
compared Slough's attack on Darius Cadwell to Brooks's assault of Sumner.
Illustration by John L. Magee. Source: Wikimedia Commons/Public Domain.

hot-tempered, impulsive nature and used his assault on Darius Cadwell to
remove him from the House and possibly ruin his career. Their decision to
expel, rather than to censure or reprimand, was an exercise in raw political
power at the state level. In the larger national context, however, the Republicans' determination to punish the "bully" Slough mirrored the angry rift
between Republicans and Democrats as the nation neared splitting in two.

Slough fully intended to recapture his vacant seat by winning the special
election scheduled for February 16, 1857. To promote his cause, he wrote a
lengthy letter to the Hamilton County Democrats, which the *Cincinnati
Daily Enquirer* printed on February 5. He admitted that he had responded
to Cadwell's words impulsively and that his striking the Western Reserve
abolitionist violated the sanctity of the House and broke the rules of legislative propriety. Nonetheless, he asked for his constituents' forbearance. He

argued he did not deserve the harsh punishment inflicted by the Republicans, a penalty without precedent and so severe that it violated "the spirit of the constitution." Moreover, he believed that the apology he provided the House was sufficient and his expulsion had been "designed as a blow to the people of Hamilton County and the Democracy of the State generally." Slough called upon his constituents' "sense of justice and virtue of Democracy" in re-electing him to the House.[30]

His supporters responded favorably to his plea. On the evening of February 7, the Cincinnati and Hamilton County Democrats convened "an immense meeting" at the Metropolitan Hall to condemn the Republicans' "unjust, unprecedented, and bitter partisan course." Slough's desk mate in the House, George Robinson, angrily described Slough's expulsion as "an act of flagrant party tyranny and injustice . . . worthy of the scorn and execration of every manly and justice-loving mind." The crowd in Metropolitan Hall enthusiastically applauded Robinson as he spoke and concluded the meeting by resolving to restore Slough to his seat. The *Cincinnati Daily Enquirer* editorialized that every Democrat "should now go to work and use his best efforts to give Mr. Slough the vote that will, by its amount, be a rebuke to the partisans at Columbus who offered this indignity to our county."[31]

The Hamilton County Democratic Executive Committee chose Slough on February 9 to run for his vacant seat. The next day, the Republicans nominated a forty-six-year-old antislavery merchant, Robert Hosea, to oppose him. The *Cincinnati Daily Enquirer* quickly blasted Hosea in its columns. It editorialized that the citizens of Hamilton County would never support an "out and out Abolitionist," a man "indoctrinated in the [Salmon P.] Chase school of politics" who believed in "negro suffrage laws."

The *Cincinnati Daily Gazette* answered the *Enquirer* by hammering at Slough's alleged penchant for violence. "An Independent Voter—No Politician" revealed in the *Gazette's* February 13 issue that the Magnolia Lodge No. 83, Independent Order of Odd Fellows expelled Slough a few years previously for an offense similar to the one he had committed in the House. Three days later, on election day, the newspaper recounted an argument during the 1856 election that resulted in Slough knocking a Republican named Baker to the pavement and kicking him until Baker "bellowed." The *Gazette* also printed a letter from William Corry, the sole House Democrat to vote for Slough's expulsion. Corry urged the electorate to reject Slough, "an ex-member who had disgraced the City Offices by violence, Odd Fellows Hall by violence, the Ohio Legislature by violence."[32]

The race between Slough and Hosea was extraordinarily close. Both the *Gazette* and the *Enquirer* reported the day after the election that Hosea had apparently won. By February 19, however, the counting of ballots swung in Slough's favor and the newspapers reported that he had defeated Hosea by three votes. The margin was too close for the Republicans to concede the election. Even though the clerk of Hamilton County had awarded the certificate of election to Slough, the House Republicans urged Hosea to challenge the results.[33]

Now, despite his previous behavior, Slough began to act in the restrained, even-handed, gentlemanly fashion his opponents claimed he lacked. On February 20, he sent his rival a note requesting that Hosea defer contesting the election until he had a chance to examine the election results. He added that should the examination prove Hosea's victory, as Hosea's friends claimed, he would surrender his election certificate. The afternoon of Saturday, February 21, five days after the special election, Slough participated in a recount of the votes cast in the first and eleventh wards, the two wards where the election results had been disputed. The recount did not favor Slough. Robert Hosea had won the election by a mere seventeen votes.[34]

True to his word, Slough yielded his seat to Hosea. On February 23, he wrote Nelson Van Vorhes, the House Speaker, that Hosea had won the election and should be awarded the vacant seat. Slough explained his decision saying,

> In recommending this course, the undersigned [Slough] follows the
> prompting of duty. No good citizen would contend for an office awarded
> to him contrary to the manifest desire of those who exercise the elective
> franchise, and, although legal forms and technical constructions [i.e., the
> election certificate Slough possessed] might give the right to hold position,
> yet he who would take advantage of such circumstances, to hold a Represen-
> tative office, mistakes the character of this Government, and is totally unfit
> for the place he would occupy.

Upon the Speaker's reading of Slough's concession, Franklin Flowers, the representative who had called for a reconsideration of the failed first vote to expel Slough, commented that if the Cincinnati Democrat had only acted in as gentlemanly a fashion over the apology as he had in yielding the certificate, he would not have been expelled. On February 24, the Ohio House of Representatives voted unanimously to seat Hosea. Slough's Democratic adversary, William Corry, escorted the new member into the chamber to be sworn into office.[35]

Slough returned to Cincinnati to mull over his thwarted career in Ohio politics. No record exists of how his family and friends advised him or how the Hamilton County Democratic Executive Committee reacted to his loss. By late spring, he determined to start anew in Kansas Territory. Perhaps his attention to politics had stunted the growth of his law practice and he decided that Kansas Territory provided more opportunities for an attorney. More likely, he realized that his political career in Ohio was irreparably damaged and that he needed to leave the state to find new paths to political office. Humiliated by his loss to Hosea, he decided that he could no longer remain in Cincinnati. Slough's disgrace and defeat caused him to abandon the Queen City, leaving behind his law practice, his political friends, and even his family for a fresh start in Kansas.

On June 23, 1857, the *Cincinnati Daily Enquirer* reported that John Slough had departed Cincinnati for Nebraska Territory. Two weeks later, he took out a notice in the *Enquirer* to advertise his new law and real estate practice in Leavenworth, Kansas. The advertisement offered services of "claims collected, lands located, and real estate bought and sold." He also became the notary public for Leavenworth County shortly after his arrival. Slough had settled in the West, and for the next five years he sought his advancement there.[36]

Part II

KANSAS TERRITORY

4

A Righteous Fight

LONG AFTER JAMES AND MAHALA DOYLE HAD RETIRED FOR THE night, strangers pounded on the door of their cabin on Pottawatomie Creek, Kansas Territory. They pretended to be lost, but when James Doyle responded to their call for assistance, the men barged into the cabin and, at gunpoint, forced Doyle and two of his three sons outside. There they shot Doyle in the head and stabbed him in the chest. Not satisfied with murdering the father, the men laid open the skull of twenty-two-year-old William and mutilated twenty-year-old Drury, slashing his head and chest and severing his fingers from his hands and his arms from his torso.

The murderers next sought the neighboring cabin of Allen and Louise Wilkinson. Again masquerading as lost wayfarers, the men called out to Wilkinson, asking him to come to the door. Louise begged her husband to stay safely in bed, but Wilkinson welcomed the strangers. The next day, friends found his body lying in a pool of dried blood, 150 yards from his cabin. His throat had been cut.

The last victim that night of terror was William Sherman, who was staying at the cabin of James Harris. The vigilantes hoped to find William's brother, Henry, a proslavery activist, but took William prisoner instead when they discovered that they had missed Henry. Like the Doyle men and Allen Wilkinson, they brutally murdered William Sherman. They shot him in the chest, split open his skull, and nearly detached his left hand from his arm. Sherman, along with the Doyles and Allen Wilkinson, all shared proslavery sympathies.[1]

Leading the marauders was a gaunt man with spiky hair, a square jaw, and intensely piercing eyes. The band's captain—Old John Brown as the nation would know him three years later when he commanded the fateful raid on

Harpers Ferry—had arrived in Kansas in 1855 determined to save the territory from the evils of slavery. When armed Missourians threatened to overrun Lawrence, Kansas, in fall 1855, Brown and his Free State militia company, the "Liberty Guards," marched to Lawrence's defense in the short-lived Wakarusa War. He had come to fight and the Wakarusa War's peaceful conclusion only increased Brown's frustration that Free State resistance had not eradicated the proslavery movement in Kansas Territory. Brown concluded that he had to instill a "restraining fear" among the territory's proslavery men. On May 24, 1856, Brown and his antislavery followers set out for the proslavery settlement along Pottawatomie Creek. There, with guns and swords, the men murdered James, William, and Drury Doyle, Allen Wilkinson, and William Sherman, proving to Kansas and the nation that antislavery men had no qualms about using violence against the proslavery menace.[2]

The massacre along Pottawatomie Creek unleashed open warfare in Kansas Territory. Proslavery and Free State militias clashed in a series of "battles" during spring and summer 1856. Violence against individuals became commonplace. Marauders forced families from their homesteads and burned their cabins and crops. Random shots warned Free State or proslavery supporters that they were not welcome. Men were gunned down in cold blood. By late summer 1856, Kansas had become "Bleeding Kansas" in the nation's press, and acting governor Daniel H. Woodson declared the territory in open rebellion.[3]

On September 11, newly appointed governor John W. Geary arrived in Lecompton determined to end the disturbances in Kansas Territory. A "virile, energetic, strong-minded man" six feet five and a half inches tall, Geary possessed the force of character to fulfill his mission. The new governor used strong-armed persuasion to squash the territory's violence. He immediately ordered all illegal militias to disperse, issued warrants for the arrest of both Free State and proslavery agitators, and rebuked the territorial judges for their failure to uphold the law. By October, Kansans had sufficient confidence in Geary's restoration of order to begin resuming their everyday lives as farmers, merchants, and businessmen.[4]

Glowing newspaper articles, immodest promotional pamphlets, and reassuring letters written to family and friends encouraged potential emigrants to consider settling in the territory despite the episodes of terror that Kansans endured during 1856. After the harsh winter of 1856–1857, with travel to Kansas virtually impossible, the "Great Migration" began in spring 1857.

New settlers flooded the territory in search of rich bluestem prairie lands to farm or promising town lots to develop. Land speculation was rampant. Newspaperman Albert D. Richardson described the fevered land market in 1857 Leavenworth:

> Steamers were discharging freight at the levee, new buildings were springing up, all was activity. . . . Building lots, 25 x 125 feet upon the river landing, were valued at $10,000. Three or four blocks back, they sold for $2,000, and on the hills half a mile away, for $1,200. Prices were fast rising, money plentiful, and everybody speculating. . . . Hotels were crowded with strangers, eager to invest. Almost anyone could borrow gold without security or even a written promise to pay; and the faith was universal that tomorrow should be as this day and yet more abundant.

The boom in land sales became a bonanza for the territory's lawyers. Thomas Ewing Jr., a young Ohio attorney who arrived in Leavenworth in early 1856, acted as land agent for both family and acquaintances. In a letter written in June 1857, Ewing reassured Judge M. F. Moore of Sioux City, Iowa, that the "improvement here is great & prices firm or steadily advancing" and noted that he had invested Moore's cash to "first rate advantage" in Leavenworth lots. The following month, Ewing wrote his father, Thomas Ewing Sr., about several purchases, including one thousand acres of tribal lands now open for settlement. He advised his father, "I think it likely good bargains may be had in these lands." It was a heady time for risk takers.[5]

Leavenworth offered John Slough ideal refuge from the rejection he had recently experienced in Ohio. He undoubtedly had read about Kansas Territory's promise in the pages of the *Cincinnati Daily Enquirer* and recognized that its heated real estate market, with emigrants and speculators bidding up the price of land, promised an ambitious lawyer steady work and a handsome income. Additionally, Leavenworth counted many Cincinnatians among its residents, men that Slough may have known during his rise in Cincinnati politics. He understood that by cultivating their acquaintance, he could build the support necessary for his re-entry into politics, made easier by Leavenworth's solidly Democratic base. Immigrating to violence-torn Kansas Territory may have seemed foolhardy to Slough's family, but the Cincinnati politician and lawyer embraced the new start and its possibility of achieving fame and fortune.[6]

Promoters used this 1856 sheet music to encourage Free Soilers
to move to Kansas Territory. The rondel features an illustration
of the burning of the Free State Hotel. Source: Library of Congress
Prints and Photographs Division, LC-USZ62–53600.

There is no record of Slough's journey to Leavenworth, although it must have been similar to the tiresome and uncomfortable one described by John J. Ingalls, a twenty-four-year-old attorney from Middleton, Massachusetts. In September 1858, Ingalls rode by rail from Massachusetts to Cincinnati, boarded a steamboat for St. Louis, took the train from St. Louis to Herman, Missouri, and from there, booked passage on the *Duncan S. Carter* up the Missouri River to Kansas Territory. He recalled that the steamboat, capable of transporting three hundred passengers and a thousand tons of freight, was crammed with "wretched crowds of Emigrants on the lower deck." Ingalls's own accommodations were hardly better than those experienced by the horde camped out below. After supper and a stroll on the *Duncan S. Carter's* deck the first night, Ingalls retired to his stateroom, "painful with heat, and resonant with a thousand discordant sounds" from the steamboat's engines. He finally fell asleep listening to the "money clink and curses" of the gamblers playing cards all night outside his cabin door.[7]

Travel was slow and the steamboat offered few diversions to occupy its passengers. Days began at 6:30 a.m., when the crew set up breakfast tables where beds had covered the deck the night before. Ingalls recalled that while waiting for breakfast, the passengers refreshed themselves by washing in "water dirtier than I Ever saw thrown away." His shipmates then passed the day smoking, gambling, and reading, only to pause for meals of "greasy meats and chicory coffee." Even the scenery became tedious. "Vista after vista opened and receded," Ingalls wrote in a letter to his father describing the trip, "and nothing but a wall of cottonwood trees on Each side and the muddy troubled stream before and behind. . . . The time grew inexpressibly long and I could hardly remember that I had Ever been anywhere Else."

Slough undoubtedly experienced the same "inexpressibly long" steam-boat journey up the Missouri, arriving in Leavenworth, the largest city in Kansas Territory, in late June 1857. Speculators from Weston, Missouri, had established Leavenworth in 1854, shortly after President Franklin Pierce signed the Kansas-Nebraska Act and officially created Kansas Territory. They chose a spot on the western bluffs above the Missouri River less than four miles from Fort Leavenworth. Some of the first settlers expressed their Democratic politics by recommending that the new town be named "Doug-las" after Stephen A. Douglas, the author of the Kansas-Nebraska Act. In the end, the land association members agreed to "Leavenworth," reasoning that the sale of lots would be promoted by emigrants' belief that the town was near the fort.[8]

Leavenworth's location on the Missouri River, its proximity to Fort Leavenworth, and its access to branches of both the Oregon and Santa Fe Trails fostered the town's rapid growth. In early 1855, it had two hundred inhabitants. By the end of the year, the town had as many as two thousand residents and the price of lots had increased six-fold. When Slough arrived in Leavenworth two years later, the town had eight to ten thousand residents. Emigrants disembarking steamboats tied to the landing, farmers bringing their produce to market, townsmen conducting their business, and housewives shopping in the city's dry goods, clothing, grocery, and general stores thronged the streets. Within an easy walk of the steamboat landing, Slough could have patronized several hotels—the Leavenworth Hotel, Planters' House, the Fisher House, the Shawnee Hotel, the Rennick House, or the Pennsylvania House—until he found more permanent lodging. The hotels hardly met the standards of Cincinnati's finest inns—one young woman new to the territory complained that breakfast at the Planters' House consisted of "minced flies and potatoes, corn bread, and mosquito wings"—but Slough did not expect luxury in booming Leavenworth.[9]

There were five churches and four breweries. On hot evenings during the summer that Slough arrived in Leavenworth, crowds visited the Kuntz Brewery to enjoy the building's large veranda and adjoining grove, partake of refreshments, and listen to band concerts. The town's bars clamored with the sounds of "cursing democrats & the clink of billiard balls." For those citizens not inclined to drinking and gambling, the town had numerous venues that offered musical and dramatic entertainment. Despite its youth, Leavenworth provided sufficient amenities, coupled with plentiful opportunity, to afford Slough a promising escape from his losses in Ohio.[10]

Intent on establishing himself professionally before resuming his political career, Slough quickly opened a law office at the southwest corner of Second and Shawnee Streets. To gain a sense of his early months in practice, we can rely on the diary of another young lawyer. Daniel Mulford Valentine moved to Leavenworth from Iowa in July 1859, two years after John Slough arrived. With $300 as his nest egg until he engaged his first clients, Valentine leased an unfurnished house on Main Street and spent his first month in Leavenworth reading law books, writing letters, playing checkers with new friends, and visiting the district court. He rented an office and had a sign painted. He bought copies of the Kansas territorial laws and the Leavenworth city ordinances, subscribed to the *Leavenworth Times* and obtained a copy of the city directory, printed letterhead and business cards, and expanded his law library with the purchase of Chitty's *Proceedings*, Parsons's *Contracts*, and Kent's *Commentaries*. Within two months of his arrival, Valentine had gained a few clients, although most of his time in court was spent listening to other lawyers.[11]

John J. Ingalls also enjoyed attending court—his practice was in Atchison, a Kansas town twenty-five miles northwest of Leavenworth—and when not pleading a case, he watched the proceedings with other observers "like the bettors at a horse race." He wrote his father that the existence of two legal codes in Kansas Territory created novel complexities for lawyers. The territory's inferior courts typically utilized the Ohio code, while its higher courts, presided over by the territorial Supreme Court Chief Justice Samuel Lecompte, relied on the Missouri code. Despite the additional work the situation engendered, Ingalls noted that most lawyers had to practice both "law and land operations."[12]

Even in Leavenworth, with its booming land market and flourishing commercial ventures providing a steady demand for legal work, competition among lawyers was keen. Slough became the ninety-fifth lawyer admitted to the Leavenworth bar, just three years after the opening of Leavenworth's first law practice. He had left Arabella and his two sons, William and John, in Cincinnati, and, although lonely without them, he was able to devote his entire attention to his practice. One of Leavenworth's earliest and most prominent citizens remembered Slough as "a gentleman of fine appearance, courtly manners, perhaps a little austere at times, otherwise social and agreeable, a fluent speaker, a clear headed, cool, and successful practitioner. In a short time, he took rank with the foremost members of the bar of the city, doing his full share of the business in all courts." A talented lawyer, he quickly obtained a steady clientele. Only a year after his disgrace in the Ohio legislature forced him to leave Cincinnati, Slough enjoyed "an extensive and profitable [law] business" in Leavenworth.[13]

He also sought to broker land deals for clients still living in Ohio, advertising his services of "claims collected, lands located, and real estate bought and sold" several times a week in the *Cincinnati Daily Enquirer*. A November

1857 notice in his hometown newspaper recommended Slough as an attorney with a "thorough knowledge of the [Kansas] Territory and its people" who was prepared to "act advisedly in all matters entreated to his care." Slough did not rely solely on newspaper advertisements or word of mouth to build his clientele. In early December 1857, he returned to Cincinnati to discuss Kansas politics at the Young Men's Democratic Association and to promote his land brokerage business. He reunited with his family during his brief visit to the Queen City but returned to Leavenworth in mid-December without them. Nine months later, on August 4, 1858, John and Arabella's only daughter, Sarah Arabella, nicknamed Sallie, was born in Cincinnati.[14]

An attempt on Slough's life a few months before his December 1857 trip to Cincinnati must have influenced his decision that Arabella and the boys should remain in Ohio. An unknown assassin fired three shots at Slough as he sat in the parlor of a friend's house. The newspaper report offered no explanation for the attempt. Whether the assault stemmed from a business transaction turned sour, the partisan conflict still roiling Kansas, or a case of mistaken identity is unknown. Yet those three shots caused Slough to question his family's safety in Leavenworth. He did not bring Arabella and the children to Kansas until 1859.[15]

Kansas was entering a new phase in late 1857, transitioning from "Bleeding Kansas" to a period of intense debate, both territorial and national, over whether Kansas would be admitted as the nation's sixteenth slave state. Proslavery adherents in the territory insisted on their constitutional right to own slaves, a right that would be erased if Kansas joined the Union as free. Moreover, they understood that a free Kansas would weaken slavery's hold in neighboring Missouri; the vast majority of Missouri's slaves, laboring in the western counties along the Missouri River, could more readily escape bondage by crossing into a free Kansas. If slavery crumbled in Kansas and then Missouri, the North, bolstered by the admission of new free states carved out of the country's vast territories, would surely crush the "peculiar institution" within the outnumbered slave states. Slavery had to be defended in Kansas at all costs.[16]

The territory's proslavery legislature met in Lecompton on January 12, 1857, to chart Kansas's course to statehood. The legislators resolved to enshrine slavery in the draft state constitution by organizing a carefully controlled constitutional convention attended by loyal proslavery delegates.

They decided that only males residing in the territory on March 15, 1857, would participate in the election of delegates. This strategy denied the vote to Free State emigrants expected to arrive in Kansas later that spring, while enabling Missourians, who could easily enter the territory, to establish residency by March 15. Additionally, the territorial census, which determined the voting lists, so heavily favored the proslavery counties that Free State men denounced it as the "bogus census" and vowed to boycott the election of delegates. Their refusal to participate in the election and the suppression of Free State ballots meant that only 10 percent of the territory's electorate, mainly in the proslavery regions along the Missouri River, picked the convention's members. The result was as the Lecompton legislators had planned. All sixty delegates were proslavery.[17]

The Lecompton constitutional convention met in early September 1857, adjourned after five days, and reconvened on October 19. The delegates drafted a document that recognized and protected slavery in the new state. They decided to submit their proposed constitution directly to Congress for approval although the territory's electorate could choose between two options: a constitution with slavery or one that merely prohibited the future importation of slaves. Because the latter option left untouched the status of Kansas's currently enslaved Black people as well as that of any child born of slaves in the future, the choice between a constitution "with slavery" and a constitution "without slavery" still ensured that Kansas entered the United States as a slave state. It was an unacceptable choice for Kansas's growing number of Free State residents.

It was also a gambit that threatened to unravel the national Democratic Party. Stephen A. Douglas and the Northern Democrats condemned the Lecompton Constitution as antithetical to popular sovereignty, the principle contained in the Kansas-Nebraska Act that empowered territorial residents themselves to accept or reject slavery. They argued that the constitution's slavery clause did not reflect the will of most Kansans and the constitution's direct submission to Congress did not allow Kansans to reject it at the polls. Southern Democrats, regarding Kansas as their only hope for a slave state among those to be carved out of the Great Plains, insisted that the Lecompton constitutional convention had the prerogative to submit its proposed constitution directly to Congress. President James Buchanan decided to support the Southern Democrats. Believing that party discipline would ultimately hold the Northern Democrats in line, yet at the same time fearing the Southern Democrats' threat of secession, Buchanan declared the election of delegates to the Lecompton constitutional convention as "fair and just" and accepted their decision to forgo a territorial referendum on the draft constitution.[18]

Except for the most resolute proponents of slavery, Kansas Democrats realized that supporting the Lecompton Constitution might well destroy the party's chance for electoral success in the new state. They understood that the latest influx of settlers irrevocably transformed Kansas into a Free State territory. Drawn from Ohio, Indiana, Illinois, and the other states of the old Northwest, many of the new settlers shared the Democratic Party's antipathy toward African Americans. They had no desire to compete for land or employment with a race they considered to be inferior. The Kansas Democratic Party believed it could win the votes of white Kansans if it embraced a policy of no Black people—slave or free—in the territory.[19]

Kansas Democrats opposed to the Lecompton Constitution convened in Leavenworth on December 24, 1857, to repudiate the proslavery document. John Slough, seeking to resume the political career he had abandoned in Ohio, attended the meeting. While the *Daily Ohio State Journal* claimed that Kansas Democrats' "ultra-pro-slavery" position forced the Cincinnati expatriate to become a "free statesman," Slough's rejection of the Lecompton Constitution stemmed more from his support of Stephen A. Douglas, dating back to the 1856 Democratic National Convention in Cincinnati, and his deeply held belief that territorial residents should decide for themselves whether Kansas would be slave or free. Slough embraced the principle of popular sovereignty without reservation. He would not support a constitution that ran counter to the people's will and exhorted his fellow Democrats to oppose the Lecompton Constitution. The fight, he said, was "a righteous one."[20]

The participants at the Leavenworth meeting asked Slough and six other men to draft resolutions "expressive of the sense of the Convention." The committee presented its resolutions the day after Christmas. Their draft condemned the Lecompton convention's actions as "an infraction of the Constitution of the United States" and "destructive to the right . . . of the people for self-government." It proclaimed the Democrats' opposition to "Sectionalism and Fanaticism," especially the attempts by Missourians to control Kansas elections through "innumerable and gross frauds." It endorsed the administration of the current territorial governor, Robert J. Walker, as "corresponding with the true intent and meaning of popular sovereignty." Above all, the draft showered praise on Stephen A. Douglas, calling him "a champion, intelligent of facts, bold of action, strong of logic, grand of oratory, and possessed of all the elements of greatness, willing to bring to bear all the powers of his great intellect and heart, in defence [sic] of the doctrine of popular sovereignty."[21]

Having read their committee's handiwork, Slough and George W. Perkins, a Leavenworth probate court judge, urged the meeting to accept the draft resolutions. It did, unanimously, and then approved a petition to the United State Congress calling upon the House and Senate to reject the Lecompton Constitution and to pass a bill for a new constitutional convention whose work would be submitted to Kansans for ratification or rejection.

Three days before Slough and the Democrats met in Leavenworth, Kansans voted on the "with slavery" and "without slavery" provisions of the Lecompton Constitution. Once again, Free State proponents boycotted the election. Their refusal to participate meant that voters heavily favored the "with slavery" clause, 6,226 votes to 569 votes for the watered-down "without slavery" option. Writing in the *Ohio Statesman*, Slough reported that the polling had been a "farce" with Kansas "again invaded by large numbers of Missourians, and many voted many times." He predicted that Congress would refuse to admit Kansas under the Lecompton Constitution once the facts about the fraudulent returns became known. In a second letter to the *Ohio Statesman* a few days later, Slough noted that Kansans had "firmly determined on resistance" to the Lecompton Constitution and warned that any action by Congress to admit Kansas under it would be "a signal of civil war."[22]

By now, Free State leaders realized that the strategy of shunning territorial elections had failed to overturn the proslavery legislature or its efforts. They called on Kansans to reject the Lecompton Constitution in a special referendum held on January 4, 1858. Their supporters responded by casting more than ten thousand votes against the proslavery document. Kansans had clearly spoken against it. Although the nation's representatives and senators continued to spar, sometimes viciously, over ratifying the Lecompton Constitution, the fight over Lecompton was finished in Kansas Territory. Kansans would not accept a state constitution that protected slavery even if their action delayed the territory's march to statehood. A new constitutional convention had to be called.

5

〇〇〇〇〇〇

Fruitless
Labor

JOHN J. INGALLS REMEMBERED WYANDOTTE, KANSAS TERRITORY, AS a "pleasant village" perched above the juncture of the Kansas and Missouri Rivers. There, during the dog days of July 1859, fifty-two delegates, John J. Ingalls and John Slough among them, drafted the territory's fourth attempt at a state constitution. They met in Lipman Myer's Hall, a four-story building just off the Wyandotte levee and one of the territory's largest structures. Each day for twenty-one days, Slough and his fellow delegates climbed a wooden stairway to the third-floor meeting room—the lower two floors served as a warehouse—where they deliberated over the very shape and essence that Kansas would assume as a state. And while three previous constitutional conventions failed to draft a document acceptable to both Kansans and the United States Congress, these fifty-two delegates crafted a constitution that won Kansas's admission as the nation's thirty-fourth state.[1]

The territory's first constitution, written by Free State adherents in Topeka in 1855, prohibited slavery in Kansas. Southern congressmen convinced their colleagues to reject the constitution because, they argued, the Topeka convention was an extra-legal assembly. Two years later, when the Kansas territorial legislature rigged a proslavery constitutional convention, the Free State faction bitterly opposed the convention's handiwork, the Lecompton Constitution. Despite the efforts of Southern Democrats and the Buchanan administration to strong-arm acceptance of the Lecompton Constitution, a coalition of Northern Democrats, Republicans, and Know-Nothings blocked its ratification in the Senate.[2]

The stalemate in the United States Congress over the Lecompton Constitution encouraged Free State proponents to attempt a third constitution for Kansas. Assembling in Leavenworth in February 1858, the delegates drafted a constitution that prohibited slavery in the new state, while granting equal rights of citizenship, including the vote, to Black males. Free State Kansans approved the radical document in May 1858, but the constitution found little favor in the United States Congress. Like its two predecessors, the Leavenworth Constitution failed to gain the necessary congressional approval for ratification.[3]

A year later, Kansans elected delegates to the territory's fourth constitutional convention to convene in Wyandotte on July 5, 1859. The Kansas Republican Party had been organized only a few weeks previously in Osawatomie, yet the voters chose to send thirty-five Republicans to the convention. Only seventeen delegates were Democrats. The Topeka, Lecompton, and Leavenworth conventions had been dominated by one faction, Free State or proslavery, to the exclusion of the other. Wyandotte was the first convention in which two sides, Republican and Democrat, freely participated. Both parties clearly recognized the political leverage that the new constitution would confer once Kansas became a state. Both Democrats and Republicans fought determinedly throughout the convention to gain as much power as possible. They clashed frequently, heatedly, and at times very personally as they labored over the draft document. Outnumbered two to one, the convention's Democrats invariably lost their battles with the Republicans.

John Slough led the delegation from Leavenworth County, ten members and the largest Democratic contingent at the Wyandotte constitutional convention. Two years earlier, he had fled Cincinnati as a political outcast only to regain political and professional prominence in Kansas Territory. His Leavenworth law practice thrived during 1858 and 1859. He and his law partner, Alexander Paddock, established an "extensive and profitable" business in land transactions. By early 1859, Slough stood at "the head of the bar of [Leavenworth] county" and was counted among the many prosperous Cincinnatians in Leavenworth. His friends had begun to address him as "Colonel Slough." Mid-nineteenth-century American frontier communities often bestowed honorary titles on their leaders and Slough, once demonized as a "bully" and an "overgrown booby," enjoyed the prestige that the title conferred.[4]

He joined the Kansas Democratic Party's leadership in 1859. By summer, he assumed the same party office—secretary to the territory's Democratic Executive Committee—that had propelled his political career in Ohio. His friendship with Kansas's new territorial governor, Samuel Medary, benefited his political rise. The two men had worked together on the Ohio Democratic Executive Committee in 1856, and Medary sought Slough's support when he became Kansas's sixth and final territorial governor. Medary and other key political connections, plus the Kansas Democratic Party's need for leadership unsullied by proslavery associations, enabled Slough to move rapidly up the territorial party's ranks.[5]

Medary intended to convene the Wyandotte constitutional convention and request that Slough serve as its president prior to the meeting's organization. Illness, however, forced him to relinquish the honor of opening the assembly to Samuel A. Stinson. On July 5, the convention's first day, Stinson dutifully passed along Medary's recommendation that Slough initially manage the proceedings. The Republicans refused to have a Democrat in the president's chair, even temporarily. They selected Samuel A. Kingman to serve until the delegates elected the convention's permanent president, James Winchell.[6]

The territory's Republican newspapers seized on Slough's defeat to belittle the Democrats. The highly partisan *Leavenworth Times* lampooned their efforts to nominate Slough. Describing the convention's opening moments, the *Times*'s correspondent wrote, "Assuming the look of a martyred saint, he [Stinson] proceeded to inform the Convention that the Democratic Governor was suffering from a gripe of the bowels (brought on probably by the great Republican majority) and was unable to perform the melancholy duty of inaugurating the Constitutional Convention." When Stinson nominated Slough as the convention's president pro tempore, "There was quite a commotion as the immense bulk of the Legislative prize-fighter made a break for the coveted 'chair.'" The Republicans voted against the Leavenworth Democrat "of knock-down fame" and chose Kingman. Kansas politics denied Slough the president's chair, although, as the *Times*'s sarcasm suggests, he had not escaped the ignominy of his disgrace in Ohio.[7]

Neither the Republican delegates' rejection of his nomination nor the Leavenworth *Times*'s mockery of his previous legislative experience caused Slough to withdraw from leading the Democratic delegates. His was not the most prominent Democratic voice; fellow Leavenworth delegates William McDowell, the most rabid of the Democratic contingent, and Samuel Stinson, tall, handsome, and magnetic, spoke more frequently and fervently than did Slough. But a close reading of the convention's *Proceedings* reveals Slough's constant presence, raising questions of procedure, calling for votes on motions, signing minority reports, suggesting amendments, and offering his own resolutions. Despite the long meetings, the stifling atmosphere caused by unusually hot summer weather, and the tensions between Republicans and Democrats, he unfailingly spoke politely, thoughtfully, and with determination. The hot-tempered, impulsive young legislator from the Ohio House of Representatives now led the Democratic effort to shape the Kansas state constitution.[8]

Still pugnacious in defense of his party and its principles, Slough fought to weaken the Republican control of the convention's proceedings. Shortly after it opened, he battled with the Republicans over the right of certain delegates to be seated. On July 7, he argued at length that delegates from Wyandotte, Morris, and Chase Counties should be recognized as duly elected members of the convention. The three counties had not existed when the territorial legislature decided upon the apportionment of delegates to the convention; therefore, the Republicans claimed, no legal basis existed for admitting delegates from any of the three counties. Slough countered that denying the delegates seats disenfranchised the counties' residents. He reminded the members that only a few days earlier, the nation had commemorated the Declaration of Independence and their forefathers' resistance to taxation without representation. He marveled that so soon after the July 4 celebration, the Republican-led Committee on Credentials intended to deny Kansans their representation at the convention. "Shall we ask these people," Slough inquired, "to sustain a government in which they have no voice in framing? Certainly not."[9]

Republican James Blunt was the first to reply to Slough's question. Pointing to the Democratic side of the aisle, Blunt said, "That same hydra-headed monster that has been so long treading us down to dust, appears here today for the purpose of annoying us, and tempting us to put our foot on it in such a manner as to make this Constitution null and void." As the legislation enabling the selection of the convention's delegates made no mention of Wyandotte, Chase, and Morris Counties, admitting delegates from the three counties would destroy the legitimacy of the convention's work. Blunt believed that the Democrats' efforts to seat these delegates was no less than a strategy to sabotage Kansas statehood.[10]

Slough and Blunt had laid out their parties' positions on credentialing the three counties' delegates. Slough's steadfast adherence to the principle of popular sovereignty meant that all Kansans deserved the right of representation. He believed that refusing to seat the elected delegates from Wyandotte, Chase, and Morris Counties undermined that most basic of democratic rights. For Blunt, a strict interpretation of the law apportioning representation to the convention meant that adding delegates from unrepresented counties could not be justified. Underneath the two men's positions lay partisan politics; Slough and the Democrats believed that the additional delegates would bolster their numbers, while Blunt and the Republicans feared that the delegates would diminish their power. In the end, the Republicans refused to recognize the delegates, offering them honorary, nonvoting seats instead.[11]

J. Edmond Bennett from Wyandotte County angrily denounced the Republican decision to deny representation to his constituents. Standing before President James Winchell and the assembly, he refused the honorary seat, remarking, "Sir, the action of the Republican members in this convention clearly demonstrates to my mind that you are unwilling to permit Kansas to become a State at present if there should be a probability of her becoming at once Democratic." When Solon Thacher moved that Bennett's comments be expunged from the *Proceedings* as "scurrilous and false," Slough defended Bennett's right to dissent without censure. Most Democrats and a handful of Republicans voted against Thacher's motion, but it prevailed 33-16, and Bennett's remarks were expunged. "The whole contest looked to us *meanly partisan*," the Kansas *Herald of Freedom* editorialized, "and unworthy [of] the delegates of a great State, who had assembled to frame their functional law."[12]

Democrats and Republicans fought throughout the convention, especially about the future of African Americans in the new state. The controversy over a free or slave state had been resolved prior to the delegates' arrival in Wyandotte. The ascendency of Free State settlers in the territory, the failure of the Lecompton Constitution, and the solid Republican majority at the Wyandotte convention ended any possibility that Kansas would be a slave state. On July 18, Slough joined the majority in prohibiting slavery within Kansas. Only one delegate, a member of the 1855 proslavery territorial legislature, voted against the resolution. Kansas would be slave-free the moment it entered the Union.[13]

The rights of Black Kansans, however, remained a point of contention between the two parties. One day after the members voted for a free Kansas, Leavenworth Democrat William McDowell resolved that "No negro or mulatto shall come into or settle in this State after the adoption of this Constitution." McDowell wished to prevent free Black people from residing in Kansas. Slough and the Democrats wanted to debate McDowell's resolution, but the Republicans voted to table it. Slough was troubled by the Republicans' unwillingness to discuss a proposal favored by many Kansans, that Black people should not be allowed in the new state. He believed that the territory's voters, and not the convention's delegates, should decide the issue of exclusion, and he considered the Republicans' action short-sighted and antidemocratic.[14]

Time and again, the convention's Republicans and Democrats clashed over the status of Black people in a free Kansas. The constitution's draft Bill of Rights, and its implications for the federal Fugitive Slave Law, resulted in impassioned debate among the delegates. Republican Samuel Houston proposed wording that declared all men to be created "free and independent" and endowed with inalienable rights, including the "right to their own persons." Democrat Benjamin Wrigley countered that under the Fugitive Slave Act, any escaped slave entering Kansas would not be "free and independent" and would have no personal rights. William McDowell took up Wrigley's argument by reminding the delegates that their first duty was to support the nation's Constitution. He asked rhetorically "whether or not the Supreme Court of the United States has construed the Constitution . . . that it is the right of the owner of a slave escaped from his service, to demand the return of that slave" even if the slave had entered a free state. McDowell clearly thought that Houston's amendment abridged the Fugitive Slave Law by granting all men, including escaped slaves, the "right to their own persons."[15]

Neither side of the aisle hesitated to use invective in describing their opponents' positions. Samuel Stinson, for example, attacked the Republicans' opposition to the Fugitive Slave Law as a "fanatical" doctrine. James Blunt, on the other hand, acidly pointed out that only the Democrats, eager to "obey the commands of their *Southern masters*," regarded the wording of the Kansas Bill of Rights as an evasion of the Fugitive Slave Law. In the end, the delegates accepted compromise language that echoed the Declaration of Independence: "All men are possessed of equal and inalienable natural rights, among which are those of life, liberty, and the pursuit of happiness."[16]

Throughout the convention, the Democrats sought to limit the rights of Black Kansans while the more radical Republicans attempted to expand them. Slough spoke little during these debates; he said at one point that he was opposed to making long speeches, although his votes always reflected the conservative position on race favored by Democrats. He opposed Black suffrage and supported efforts to limit African Americans' rights by the use of "white" to modify "persons" or "males." Surprisingly, he believed that male Indians who were United States citizens by treaty should be allowed to vote, a position based more on his interpretation of the law than his acceptance of the country's Indigenous people. He agreed with the majority of the delegates that women should not vote but should attend to the "greater and more complicated responsibilities" of wife and mother. While he believed that Kansas voters should decide whether the new state should exclude Black settlers, he was not willing to place the issue of women's suffrage before them.[17]

Slough overcame his reservations about long speeches to comment on schooling for Black children and his belief in racial segregation. In one of his rare speeches, he proposed that Kansas prohibit white and Black children from attending the same common schools and universities. He denied that he opposed the education of Black children and claimed that he wished to promote Black people "as far as they are capable of elevation." But he could never consent, by vote or action, that "those upon whom Nature's God has stamped inferiority, shall ever associate with my children in our common schools." He supported segregated schools as long as Black Kansans funded their own institutions, but he was personally not willing to contribute to the education of Black children.[18]

Slough avoided employing the racial slurs so commonly used in mid-nineteenth-century America, but his arguments against mingling white and Black children in public schools would have resonated in white households throughout the territory. Samuel Houston, whose amendment to the Kansas Bill of Rights recognized all men as "free and independent," argued for separate schools because he understood that white Kansans did not want their children educated with Black children. Republican Samuel Kingman admitted in the debate over segregated schools that his constituents were not "a negro-loving race of people." The *White Cloud Kansas Chief* concluded that the Republican delegates had little regard for Black Kansans because they worked for "the interests of the FREE WHITE MAN." Slough's racial prejudices were common among both his Democratic and Republican colleagues.[19]

Not all the delegates dismissed Black people as an inferior and undeserving race. The radical Republicans—James Blunt, Solon Thacher, William Hutchison, and John Ritchie—denounced the Democrats' insistent opposition to Black rights. Thacher asserted that Slough's proposal for segregated schools proved that "the Democracy is the same now as in the bloody days of '55 and '56." Recalling the depredations of proslavery militias, Ritchie vowed that he would not be frightened by the Democrats' "howls" about Black rights after he had fought for four years "in defence [sic] of my own liberty and that of my wife and children." These words, evoking the hatreds and hardships of "Bleeding Kansas," were bitter words, and for John Slough, who had never embraced the proslavery faction in Kansas, they were unfair and insulting accusations. The radical Republicans' tirades against the Democrats alienated Slough and his colleagues and led to significant repercussions later in the convention.[20]

By the meeting's midpoint—a time when the summer's oppressive heat and the demands of drafting a state constitution had begun to wear on the delegates—the assembly embarked on its most famous and contentious debate. On the afternoon of July 15, Slough introduced two southern Nebraskans, Mills S. Reeves and William H. Taylor, to the assembly. Reeves and Taylor advocated eloquently for the annexation to Kansas of the Nebraska territory south of the Platte River. The issue of the new state's boundaries occupied the delegates for several days, and their arguments for a "big Kansas" or a "little Kansas" assumed the same partisan character that typified much of the convention's proceedings, fueling its increasingly hostile atmosphere.

Reeves and Taylor offered compelling reasons for annexing the "Platte District" to Kansas. They pointed to the natural boundary created by the Platte River, argued that the annexation would strengthen Kansas's candidacy for the Pacific railroad route, and extolled the region's hard-working population and its agricultural and commercial advantages. Despite these reasons, the Republican delegates opposed annexation because they feared it would diminish their power and benefit the Democrats politically. Solon Thacher warned that annexation would "once more subject us to the unbearable oppression of the Democratic party," while James Blood argued that the "pro-slavery party of this nation" wanted annexation to undermine the admission of a free Kansas to the Union. The Democrats angrily responded to the Republicans' refusal to enlarge Kansas's boundaries. Samuel Stinson, shouting in his clear, high-pitched voice over President Winchell's objections, threatened that if the Republicans defeated annexation, "the Democratic party will go before the people of the Territory and throw it into the teeth of the Republican party." Despite his threat, the Republicans blocked annexation.[21]

Undoubtedly the convention's long hours and challenging work took their toll on the delegates' cordiality. Partisan bitterness also rubbed raw any good feelings that the delegates had for the opposition. The members had worked together for several weeks to draft a constitution. They had agreed on much: the framework for the executive, legislative, and judicial branches; the rights to be accorded Kansas's citizens; the nature of banking and corporations; the rules surrounding elections; the organization of counties and townships; and the methods for finance and taxation. Slough played an active part in many of these discussions, proposing, for example, annual sessions and a smaller legislature, suggesting that the governor have veto power, and recommending that a majority of all legislators (and not just those present) be required to pass bills. Laboring to draft a constitution worthy of statehood, Slough grew increasingly irritated with the Republicans and their perceived refusal to compromise. Other delegates shared his anger toward the opposition. As the convention moved toward its conclusion, the tension between Republicans and Democrats threatened to erupt into violence.[22]

On Friday, July 22, William McDowell attempted to revive the annexation issue by proposing that the convention petition Congress to attach the Platte District to Kansas. The delegates rejected McDowell's resolution, ending the Democrats' campaign to annex southern Nebraska. In the course of their debate, John Ritchie raised the possibility that real estate—"corner lots"—had been proffered in exchange for a vote to locate the new capital in Lawrence. The possibility that bribes had been offered for votes troubled the assembly's members, especially when Democrat Elijah M. Hubbard confirmed that Republican William Hutchison had offered him "a good lot" in Lawrence if Hubbard voted for Lawrence as the state capital. After a special committee delivered its report into the alleged corruption, it fell to John Slough, the only delegate at the Wyandotte convention to have been expelled from a legislative body, to propose that the members eject Hutchison for attempting to bribe Hubbard.[23]

Slough refused to give up the issue even after President Winchell ruled the Democratic leader out of order. After all, it was the Democrats' best opportunity to embarrass the Republicans. The next morning, Slough recommended that a committee investigate the possibility that Hutchison had committed perjury in testifying to the special committee about the alleged bribe offered to Hubbard. This time his resolution prevailed. Slough and his Democratic colleague from Leavenworth, Adam McCune, joined Republicans Robert Graham, James Blood, and George Lillie on the special committee examining whether Hutchison had perjured himself.[24]

The committee's findings split along party lines. Slough and McCune's report called for Hutchison's expulsion. Lillie and Blood submitted their own report in which they absolved Hutchison of perjury. Robert Graham refused to sign either report because he believed that both Hutchison and Hubbard should be expelled. James Blunt, who unfailingly attacked the Democrats whenever the opportunity arose, complained that the Democrats, responsible for "the most glaring election frauds on record," demonstrated "very bad grace" in charging Hutchison with corruption. He moved to table the committee's reports. Indeed, the Republicans decided to suppress the entire matter by refusing to print any testimony about the alleged bribe in the *Proceedings*.[25]

Angered by the Republicans' apparent determination to protect Hutchison's reputation at all costs, the Democrats did not consider the matter settled. On July 28, the penultimate day of the convention, William McDowell argued that the members should reconsider their decision to table the investigating committee's testimony. Solon Thacher wearily replied that he hoped the matter would be "allowed to sleep quietly," but if the Democrats wished to pursue the charge of corruption, he felt it his duty to pursue Elijah Hubbard and others "with the same strict even-handed justice."[26]

With Thacher's threat, the room went still. The Leavenworth *Times* described the atmosphere as the "calm ... which portends a hurricane." Samuel Stinson rose to challenge Thacher, asking him to name those men Thacher considered guilty of corruption. The Republican answered without hesitation, "Samuel A. Stinson."[27]

Stinson had had enough. Speaking over President Winchell's demands for order and his fellow Democrats' cries of "Go on, Stinson, go on," the Leavenworth Democrat denounced Thacher's allegation as "infamously and willfully false" and a charge intended "to shield corruption, to gild infamy" by incriminating innocent members. He demanded that the issue of Hutchison's attempted bribery be reopened and a vote taken. With Winchell frantically hammering the president's desk for order, Stinson denied Thacher's charge of corruption as "maliciously and damnably false" and sat down. William McDowell stood to defend his friend Stinson. President Winchell attempted to regain control of the proceedings by asking McDowell if he would abide by the "strict rule" of debate. "Pale and tremulous with excitement," McDowell replied that he intended to call "a liar, a liar, and a coward, a coward."[28]

The exchange between Winchell and McDowell drove the delegates out of their chairs. Winchell demanded that the sergeant-at-arms restore order, but the stout McDowell, shaking his cane in rage, blustered "Let the Sergeant-At-Arms come on!" "Nearly all the gentlemen in the Hall were upon their feet," reported the *White Cloud Kansas Chief*, "and some were ready to produce their weapons."[29]

Democrats and Republicans surged at each other, "a large number prepared for hot work." Leading the Democrats was John Slough, his temper boiling over. Slough was a large man, almost six feet tall and two hundred pounds, but looming in front of him was Republican William McCulloch, a massive Scotsman "six feet three by two feet six." McCulloch faced Slough, raised his fists into the air, and thundered, "Order shall be maintained. If you want a fight, come on!" Slough, the blood draining from his face so that he looked as if "something had crawled in him and died," thought better of a brawl and returned to his seat. Winchell called for order again and the other delegates sat down. The "hurricane" had passed.[30]

The Democrats met in caucus that evening. Slough and his colleagues were indignant that the Republicans refused to compromise on several issues the Democrats considered essential for the constitution's ratification. They especially resented its provisions on apportionment that awarded the Republicans control of the statehouse through gerrymandered legislative districts. The Democrats had argued that every county, regardless of size, should receive at least one seat, but their opponents pushed through a plan that diluted Democratic votes by attaching smaller Democratic counties to larger Republican ones. Some of the convention's more moderate Democrats had approached their Republican counterparts about "some face-saving change to the apportionment provisions so that they might justify signing the Constitution." The Republicans, fully in charge of the draft constitution, turned down their request.[31]

During the evening's long and stormy meeting, the Democrats discussed whether they would approve a constitution they considered seriously flawed. Territorial Governor Samuel Medary attended the meeting to advocate for its approval. John Slough disagreed with his old ally from Ohio. He argued against the constitution; refusing to sign it, he believed, would send a powerful message about its shortcomings to the people of Kansas and the United States Congress. In the end, Slough's position prevailed by a narrow margin; the Democratic delegation would not sign the Wyandotte Constitution.[32]

The next day, after William Hutchison proposed adopting the constitution, Slough slowly rose to address his fellow delegates. He spoke not as the arrogant and angry young Democrat from the Ohio House of Representatives, but as the statesmanlike leader of the Democratic delegation at Wyandotte. Although he complained that a severe headache hampered his efforts, he carefully offered, without resorting to partisan attacks, the reasons why he would not sign the constitution. He began by complimenting the work of the delegates, saying that the document they had framed was "a good one—perhaps, I might say, a model instrument." Then he enumerated, one by one, the document's failures. He criticized the decision to exclude the south Platte region from the state's northern boundary and the Pikes Peak region from its western one. He described the proposed size of the legislature as extravagant and argued that denying the vote to Native tribes granted citizenship by treaty placed Kansas "in a position of antagonism to the treaty making power of the country." He condemned the requirement that residents had to be registered in the territory in order to vote for or against the constitution. Above all, he believed that two failures—the failure to allow Kansans to vote on the issue of Black exclusion and the failure of the constitution to base legislative representation on population—had resulted in a "colored and distorted" document that he could not sign.

"I sincerely regret this, sir," Slough said to President Winchell, "because I have labored since the moment I came here to the present hour, arduously and earnestly from morning till night, to endeavor to make this Constitution an instrument calculated to promote the well-being of the people of Kansas, and such as one as would secure their endorsement and our admission into the Union. . . . I regret, therefore, Mr. President, the circumstances which compel me thus to act."[33]

Slough wearily sat down, and, after Solon Thacher attacked the Democrats one final time, the delegates voted to adopt the constitution, thirty-four yeas to thirteen nays. With evening falling, President Winchell called the county delegations to sign the constitution. The first one he called was Leavenworth County. No one came forward. When Winchell asked the Leavenworth delegates if any desired to sign the constitution, Slough and his colleagues all replied no. They would not lend their names to a document they had just spent twenty-one days drafting.[34]

Slough's strategy of signaling a flawed constitution by refusing to sign it failed to persuade Kansans. On October 4, 1859, voters overwhelmingly approved the Wyandotte Constitution; nearly sixteen thousand votes were cast, with two-thirds favoring adoption. Because Southerners in the United States Senate refused to ratify the Wyandotte Constitution and admit Kansas as a free state, another sixteen months passed before the territory gained statehood. Finally, after senators from six seceded Southern states had resigned from Congress, the remaining United States senators voted on January 29, 1861, to admit Kansas to the Union. Despite Slough's misgivings about the Wyandotte Constitution, the work that he and his fifty-one colleagues performed at Lipman Myer's Hall in July 1859 accomplished the goal of transforming Kansas Territory into a state.

6

Two
Elections

JOHN SLOUGH WAS A FIGHTER. ALTHOUGH NOT A BRAWLER, AS REPUB-
lican newspapers portrayed him, he was a man willing to experience defeat
in the pursuit of his dreams. He had struggled throughout the Wyandotte
convention to gain some advantage for the outnumbered Democrats. In the
end, suffering from a headache likely produced by stress, he watched the Republicans single-handedly adopt a constitution that he and his Democratic
colleagues had repudiated as inadequate. In October, Kansans ignored the
Democrats' call for rejection, approved the Wyandotte Constitution, and
solidified the Republican hold over Kansas politics. While other politicians
would have quietly returned to private life once they realized that voters
favored the opposing party, Slough continued to battle for political office.

On October 25, 1859, he called the Kansas Democratic convention to order
in Leavenworth. The delegates selected eleven candidates to run for state
office in the December 6 election. They nominated the current territorial
governor, Samuel Medary, for state governor and enthusiastically chose John
Slough for the office of lieutenant governor. Of the eleven men nominated
that day, only Slough was chosen by acclamation. The promising political
career he had thrown away in Ohio seemed again to be within his reach.[1]

Kansas's Democratic newspapers applauded the nomination of Medary
and Slough. The *Topeka Tribune* praised Medary's performance as territorial
governor and described Slough as a "worthy candidate" who would make "a
good and efficient" lieutenant governor. The *Herald of Freedom* concluded
that Medary "wins the respect of all" while Slough "no doubt will make a
credible presiding officer in the Senate." The newspaper bragged that the
Democratic slate offered voters "a very good ticket," one in which the new
state government would be in "safe hands."[2]

Samuel Medary and John Slough ran together on the 1859 Democratic ticket for Kansas state office. Prior to Kansas, the men served together on the Ohio Democratic State Committee. Source: Courtesy of the Ohio History Connection, AL 02903.

The Democratic newspapers' praise of Medary and Slough seems restrained compared to the attacks by Republican editors. The *Emporia Weekly News*, reporting on a drunken banquet given in Medary's honor, sarcastically noted that "he [Medary] is making the most of his time" during his last days as territorial governor. The *White Cloud Kansas Chief* informed its readers that Medary had been "the chief liar and blackguard" of Ohio Democratic politics. Predictably, the two newspapers also served up Slough's troubles in the Ohio House of Representatives. The *Weekly News* reminded its subscribers that the Ohio legislature had expelled him for conduct unbecoming a gentleman, while the *Kansas Chief* derided him as the legislature's "shoulder-hitter."[3]

Slough and Medary kicked off their campaigns at Leavenworth's Stockton Hall on October 29, 1859, and then spent much of November speaking to voters across Kansas's counties. Upon completing the month-long campaign, the fifty-eight-year-old Medary complained to an acquaintance about the gubernatorial canvass's "long and arduous" politicking. Electioneering in 1850s Kansas was hard. Antebellum politicians often maintained a grueling schedule of appearances, sometimes speaking in several towns in one day, then traveling on barely passible roads to the next county. In a letter written to his father in January 1859, John J. Ingalls described the state of overland travel in northeastern Kansas. Riding in a coach "having no regard whatever to the comfort of passengers," he spent six hours traveling on "extremely bad" roads, "ice alternating with mud," from Sumner to Leavenworth. He needed more than ten hours the next day to cover the thirty-five miles between Leavenworth and Lawrence. At the end of a day, the larger Kansas cities afforded campaigning politicians comfortable lodging, but the smaller territorial towns offered only crowded, dirty, and unpleasant inns. In addition to the challenges presented by 1850s travel, candidates often had to speak before rowdy and hostile audiences. Ingalls recalled facing "a crowd of yelling miscreants, who would have been glad to have pitched me in the Missouri" when he ran for election as a delegate to the Wyandotte convention. Slough left no record of his days campaigning for the office of lieutenant governor, although he surely experienced the same stresses and strains described by Ingalls.[4]

While the two men sought votes to become Kansas's first elected governor and lieutenant governor, John Brown's campaign to root out slavery, so bloodily commenced in Kansas Territory, entered its final phase back east. On the night of October 16, 1859, Brown and eighteen followers stole into Harpers Ferry, Virginia, captured the federal arsenal and armory, and seized several local residents as hostages. Brown believed that this daring act would spark rebellion among the surrounding countryside's enslaved Black people. He planned to arm them once they joined the insurrection, withdraw to the mountains, and wage guerrilla war against slaveholders. Virginia's slaves failed to rally to his side, but the citizens of Harpers Ferry fought back, trapping Brown and his men in the arsenal. United States Marines under Col. Robert E. Lee ended the raid by battering down the arsenal's door. Brown was wounded, captured, and imprisoned. The old abolitionist's scheme to free the slaves lasted less than thirty-six hours.

Brown and his conspirators were quickly tried and found guilty of murder, inciting slaves to rebellion, and treason against the state of Virginia. His conviction provided editorial ammunition for Kansas's Democratic newspapers, especially in the midst of the gubernatorial campaign. The *Topeka Tribune*, judging that Brown "will only receive his just deserts in being hanged," criticized the Republican candidates for state office as John Brown apologists. The *Herald of Freedom* demanded that the territory's Republicans denounce Brown's treasonous raid. Even the Republican *White Cloud Kansas Chief* lamented "poor, old, crazy John Brown" and his "dozen white fools and three or four black allies."[5]

Two days before Brown's execution on December 2, 1859, and six days before the Kansas gubernatorial election, Abraham Lincoln began a week-long speaking tour in Kansas Territory. Ever mindful of his political career, Lincoln decided to test in Kansas the themes he might use if he decided to run for the presidency. A Kansas speaking tour would also provide the opportunity to woo the territory's Republicans. He could lend support, at least indirectly, to the Republican candidates seeking election on December 6 and perhaps earn the backing of the territory's six delegates at the 1860 Republican presidential nominating convention.[6]

Lincoln arrived in Elwood, Kansas Territory, on November 30, 1859. He delivered an impromptu address that evening in the dining room of the Great Western Hotel. He gave speeches in Troy, Doniphan, and Atchison the next two days and arrived in Leavenworth on December 3. A welcoming party greeted him as his coach entered the city. Accompanied by a brass band playing marches and military airs, they escorted Lincoln to a reception at the Mansion House, where Leavenworth's citizens could shake hands with the Illinois politician.

Lincoln spoke that evening before a packed house in Stockton's Hall, the venue where Medary and Slough had launched their campaign for state office five weeks earlier. The *Leavenworth Weekly Herald* reported that the hall was "filled to overflowing at an early hour" and that many Democrats—perhaps John Slough among them—attended the event. Lincoln talked for two hours, arguing against slavery and Douglas's principle of popular sovereignty. He was clearly a man of great energy. He had given five speeches in four days, yet after talking at length that evening, Lincoln retired to the rooms of the *Leavenworth Conservative*'s editor to swap tales until the early hours of the morning. He gave his final address in Leavenworth on December 5 and left two days later for his home in Springfield, Illinois.[7]

While Lincoln rested in Leavenworth on December 6, Kansans went to the polls to choose a governor, lieutenant governor, and other state officials. Samuel Medary did not feel optimistic about the election's outcome. He confided to another Democrat, John Halderman, that the Democratic ticket would likely be defeated by a thousand votes. He was mortified that Kansas would enter the Union as a "black Old John Brown state" rather than as a Democratic one, but admitted that "it is our own faults [*sic*]" that the slate of candidates failed to energize Democratic voters in northern Kansas. The final tabulation of votes confirmed Medary's fears. He lost to Charles Robinson by more than 2,500 votes. Slough lost by a similar margin to J. P. Root in the lieutenant governor's race, although he carried his home town of Leavenworth.[8]

The Republican *Emporia Weekly News* mocked the Democrats' defeat in a satirical poem titled "Sammedary, O" after Samuel Medary. Two verses ridiculed Medary and Slough's failure at the polls:

> He [Medary] did his work so faithfully,
> That straightway he was sent
> To regulate the Kansas boys,
> By Buck [Buchanan], the President.
> But here, alas! he failed, and up
> Salt River he must go—
> The fittest place, on top of earth,
> For Sammedary, O.
> And Bully Slough, the fighting-cock—
> More stomach he than brains—
> He sought for office, and has got—
> His trouble for his pains.
> Tis not to fancy pugilists
> The people honor show;
> So Johnny has to emigrate
> With Sammedary, O.

After lampooning several Democrats who also lost their races in Kansas, the poem finished by slamming President James Buchanan:

> Old Buck, the Presidential Stag—
> God help his poor old soul!
> Of this Republic's destinies
> He soon must yield control;

And o'er his name, that mighty tide,
Oblivion will flow,
And he will aye forgotten be,
Like Sammedary, O.

The *Weekly News's* prediction that "oblivion" would follow Medary and Buchanan was prescient. Both men retired from public life after leaving office in 1861. Slough, on the other hand, shrugged off his defeat and ran for public office again within a year.[9]

His loss in the lieutenant governor's race did not tarnish his reputation within the Kansas Democratic Party. On March 27, 1860, the party selected him and eleven other delegates to attend the Democrats' presidential nominating convention in Charleston, South Carolina. The twelve men evidently did not attend the convention. No Kansas newspaper recorded their departure for South Carolina, and the convention's *Proceedings* did not list the Kansas delegation, nor any other territorial delegation, among the convention's members. Slough must have been disappointed when he read the newspapers' accounts of the Charleston meeting. By missing it, he was not able to watch his hero, Stephen A. Douglas, battle for the very existence of the Democratic Party.[10]

Southern Democrats determined before the 1860 presidential nominating convention that the Democratic Party's platform had to include a clear-cut statement of the federal government's obligation to protect slavery in all the states and territories; otherwise, the Southern Democrats would abandon the party. The threat arose from more than their determination to defend the ownership of slaves; the Southern planter class and their political spokesmen believed that slavery's destruction would ruin the Southern economy and devastate the Southern way of life. Northern Democrats, led by Stephen A. Douglas, steadfastly opposed the outright endorsement of slavery wherever it was found. They argued that popular sovereignty, and not a blind adherence to the institution of slavery, must form the bedrock of Democratic principles.

With the Northern and Southern Democrats deadlocked over the party's position on slavery, Alabama's William Yancey warned the Charleston delegates that either they accept the Lower South's platform protecting the institution or witness the Lower South delegates' exit from the convention. Douglas and his followers, who constituted the majority of delegates at

Charleston, refused to accept any platform inconsistent with their support of popular sovereignty. With the Northern delegates' rejection of the Lower South's platform, the convention's members watched Yancey and fifty Southern delegates walk out of the assembly hall. Despite numerous ballots, the remaining delegates could not reach the necessary two-thirds majority to nominate a presidential candidate. Frustrated, they adjourned the Charlestown convention to reconvene in Baltimore in June.

The delay did not change the outcome. When Douglas's supporters refused to seat delegates espousing secession, one-third of the Baltimore convention's members withdrew, splitting the party into two irreconcilable factions. The Southern delegates convened their own convention and nominated John Breckinridge of Kentucky as their presidential candidate. Northern Democrats responded by nominating Stephen A. Douglas. The Democratic Party had dominated the presidency for John Slough's entire life. Now, divided into competing southern and northern parties, the Democrats could not block Republican Abraham Lincoln's path to the White House.[11]

Three months after the Democratic Party's catastrophe at Baltimore, Slough ran for mayor of Leavenworth. The *Topeka Tribune* had no doubt that he would become the next mayor of the Democratic stronghold. "We are convinced," the newspaper wrote, "that no one is better qualified or more worthy to assume the official responsibilities . . . than this gentleman." Atchison's *Weekly Champion and Press* lauded Slough as "one of the best of the Democracy in Kansas, and personally one of the best fellows," but feared he would be overwhelmed by "the gallant Republicans of Leavenworth." The *Weekly Champion* had the better gauge of Leavenworth voters. The Republican candidate, James L. McDowell, beat Slough by 221 votes. Indeed, the Republicans captured virtually all the city's offices—mayor, city attorney, recorder, auditor, treasurer, and marshal—and a majority of the city council and school trustee positions.[12]

In part, the fractured Democratic Party cost Slough the election. An anonymous letter sent to the *Cincinnati Daily Enquirer* claimed that the acrimony between Leavenworth's "Breckinridge men" and "Douglas men" had become so extreme that the former refused to vote for the Democratic ticket. Slough in particular had become "the special object of the malice and opposition of the Breckinridge party" because of his long-term support of Stephen A. Douglas. With Leavenworth's citizens increasingly Republican, the *Enquirer*'s correspondent concluded that a divided Democratic Party had no chance at the polls. In truth, the Democrats' hold on Leavenworth had slipped even before the party split into "Breckinridge men" and "Douglas men." The previous year, the Democratic candidate for mayor had barely eked out a victory, winning election by a mere thirty-two votes. The close 1859 mayoral election foreshadowed the 1860 results. Slough's defeat stemmed more from the rising Republican ascendency in Kansas Territory—indeed across the Northern states—than from a Democratic Party in disarray.[13]

In 1859, Slough led the Democratic delegation at the Wyandotte constitutional convention and ran for the second highest elective office in Kansas. A year later, with the Republican sweep of the Leavenworth city election, his political career was finished. His lucrative law practice in land transactions was also struggling, slowed by the severe drought that devastated Kansas and ended its land boom.

For a year and a half, beginning in June 1859, Kansas farmers saw little rain. They tried crop after crop—first wheat, then corn, then buckwheat, and finally turnips—but each planting died in the ground from lack of moisture. By autumn 1860, the drought affected every corner of Kansas except the northeastern counties along the Missouri River. Nearly a third of Kansans were destitute. As winter closed in, Slough, William McDowell, John Ewing, and other prominent men solicited "coats, pants, vests, shawls, blankets, &c" for Leavenworth's "numerous poor and needy." Slough's own financial well-being had suffered. Despite contemporary reports that he had prospered as a Leavenworth lawyer, the 1860 census valued his personal property at a mere $400.[14]

Slough verified the drought's catastrophic effect in a letter to the *Cincinnati Daily Enquirer* dated February 13, 1861. During the 1860 growing season, he wrote, "scarce enough rain fell in Kansas to constitute an ordinary rainstorm." This "unparalleled" weather caused total crop failures in large sections of the territory. Compounding the drought's severity, many farmers, men of "little or no means," had borrowed money for improvements or additional land purchases after the bountiful harvests of the late 1850s. With their cash tied up in mortgages and loans, they were forced off their land when their crops dried up and they could not cover their debts. "There is little money, and but scanty stocks of clothing and provisions to be found within our borders," Slough informed the *Enquirer*'s readers. "There has been, is, and must continue to be for some time to come, considerable want and perhaps suffering among our people."[15]

Slough's motivation in writing his letter to the *Enquirer* was to request aid for his penniless neighbors. Yet even in his appeal, he invoked territorial politics. A New Yorker, Thaddeus Hyatt, and two Kansans, William F. M. Arny and Samuel Pomeroy, had organized a national relief effort for Kansas in August 1860. The three men decided that Hyatt would raise money in the East and authorize the payment of freighting and other costs to send provisions to Kansas. Arny would solicit money and provisions in the West, and Pomeroy would distribute the donations to the county and township relief committees.[16]

Hyatt, Arny, and Pomeroy were all Republicans, and Pomeroy was actively campaigning to become one of the United States senators from Kansas. Slough implied in his letter to the *Enquirer* that Pomeroy was involved in the relief effort not from genuine concern for his fellow Kansans but from a desire for "*weighty arguments*" to support his campaign for the Senate. Moreover, he implied that Hyatt and Arny—men with "other than proper motives"—had issued appeals for relief possibly to siphon off donations for their own use. Slough advised donors to send money directly to people they knew in Kansas, otherwise "you will have no guarantee that your contributions will not be misapplied, and your generous sympathy wasted." His desire to see relief contributions reach needy and deserving Kansans more likely resulted in his making enemies among the three men he accused.[17]

With his political career stalled and his law practice languishing from the drought's impact on land transactions, Slough once again looked west for a new start. He had seen gold seekers on their way to the Rocky Mountains after the ore had been discovered in the streams flowing into the South Platte River. They had flocked to Leavenworth and other Missouri River towns in 1859 and 1860 to outfit their grub stakes and begin the long trek to the Rocky Mountains. The prospects for financial gain posed by the Pikes Peak gold rush, Slough decided, outweighed the potential risks of leaving Leavenworth. Several of his acquaintances, including William Larimer, George Perkins, and Edward Berthoud, had already left Kansas Territory to seek their fortune in Denver and the surrounding mining towns. Slough had worked with these men, knew them to be shrewd businessmen, and valued their judgment. He had also probably read in the newspapers that recently ceded land claims by the Cheyenne and Arapaho tribes opened settlement in the Rocky Mountain region to white farmers and ranchers. He concluded that the region's rapidly growing population promised opportunity for a lawyer experienced in land transactions.[18]

Slough's decision to leave Leavenworth was not an easy one to make. He had reunited with his family in 1859 but now, considering resettlement in Denver, he concluded that a frontier gold rush town was not a suitable place for mothers and their children. Another separation from his family would be difficult, yet Slough decided that Arabella and their four children—six-year-old William, four-year-old John, two-year-old Sallie, and six-month-old Martin—had to return to Cincinnati. A few weeks after he wrote his letter to the *Enquirer* about the Kansas drought, he closed his law practice and, alone, boarded an overland stage for Denver.

Part III

COLORADO TERRITORY

7

***

Gilpin's Pet Lambs

DENVER SPRANG FROM THE 1858 DISCOVERY OF GOLD ON THE SOUTH Platte River. Although early diggings yielded little ore, gold seekers rushed to the Rocky Mountain region, enticed by land promoters and guide books promising easy riches. These emigrants, nicknamed "Argonauts" after the mythological Greeks who pursued the Golden Fleece, were familiar with California Gold Rush tales and believed they could replicate the same miracle in the Rocky Mountains. Among them were farmers and small businessmen, hard hit by the Depression of 1857, who sought the solution to their financial problems in the gold-laden streams and canyon walls of the Rockies.[1]

Midway between the country's eastern cities and the Rocky Mountains lay Kansas; gold seekers had to travel through the territory to reach the South Platte. The residents of Leavenworth, Lawrence, and other Kansas towns quickly recognized that outfitting emigrants before their long trek across the plains might be a promising source of income. On September 13, 1858, John Slough joined William H. Larimer Jr., Judge George Perkins, and other Leavenworth business leaders to discuss the promotion of their city in supplying the anticipated rush to the Rocky Mountain gold fields. Within a few weeks of their meeting, Larimer himself headed west in search of riches. He led a band of men to the mining settlement on Cherry Creek, where they occupied the St. Charles Land Company's claim; named the questionably obtained one square mile of land after Kansas's territorial governor, James W. Denver; and officially established the Denver City Town Company.[2]

It may have been Larimer who convinced Slough to invest in Denver City property. While attending the Wyandotte Constitutional Convention in July 1859, Slough authorized the purchase of a corner lot at McGaa and

D streets. It seems doubtful that he intended this property to be anything but an investment, yet by 1861 he realized that Denver offered more than speculative real estate. The town could furnish an escape from his reputation as the "legislative prize-fighter" and the chance for a new financial and professional start. Opportunity beckoned from Denver, and Slough responded.[3]

He left Leavenworth in late March or early April 1861, traveling seven days on a Central Overland California and Pikes Peak stagecoach to Denver. If the COC & PP (as contemporaries shortened the stage company's lengthy name) had booked a full complement of nine passengers, Slough would have had to squeeze his large bulk into the small space allotted him and endure long hours sitting in one position. Sometimes he and the other passengers walked alongside the coach for a mile or two, but after a while, they would climb on board to resume the seemingly unending journey. Even the novelty of traveling across the Great American Plains faded quickly and, as Jerome C. Smiley recalled in his 1901 history of Denver, the landscape's "apparently endless stretches became most tiresome to the sight." But the four mules that pulled the heavy Concord stagecoach plodded steadily hour after hour, and eventually Slough and his fellow pilgrims reached their destination at the confluence of Cherry Creek and the South Platte River.[4]

Slough may well have questioned his decision to leave Kansas when, stepping down from the coach, he glanced at the ramshackle storefronts lining Denver's muddy main street. He had left his family and the comforts of Leavenworth only to arrive during one of the frontier town's "bust" periods. Six months earlier, Denver's population quickly shrank when thousands of gold seekers, either failing to discover gold or realizing that extracting it required an enormous amount of labor, decided to retrace their steps east before winter set in. With their departure, business slowed and real estate prices dropped precipitously; Denver's promise had tarnished. Yet Slough decided to stay and enter the town's civic life. By May 1861, he was appointed judge of its appellate court.[5]

Denver was a raw frontier town when Slough arrived. Although it claimed two theaters, a few clubs and fraternal organizations, a handful of churches, and two small private schools, it was little more than the mining camps it supplied. One pioneer family described Denver as "an exceedingly primitive town, consisting of numerous tents and numbers of crude and ill constructed cabins, with nearly as many rum shops and low saloons as cabins." As Slough

Denver boomed in the early 1860s supplying goods and
services to prospectors working the Rocky Mountain gold fields.
Source: Courtesy of History Colorado, ID 89.451.554.

explored the fledgling town, he found that two streets, lined mainly with
one-story businesses, made up its commercial district; the other streets were
sprinkled with shanties, tents, or empty lots. Wooden sidewalks, constructed
of "uneven boards that would spring up and down in the most unexpected
way," afforded the newly arrived lawyer scant protection from the mud that
seemed to be everywhere.[6]

Supplies were prohibitively expensive. With finished lumber, glass, nails,
and other building materials virtually unavailable during Denver's first years,
frame houses and shops with false fronts did not appear until the mid-1860s.
Many homes lacked basic furnishings and relied on crudely constructed
wooden benches and chairs. Outside the hastily built homes and shops,
mules, hogs, and dogs wandered Denver's streets in great numbers and provided sport for drunken sharpshooters. Even Denver's efforts to provide more
refined pastimes than taking pot shots at stray animals fell woefully short
of the diversions Slough had enjoyed in Cincinnati and Leavenworth. The
Apollo Hall, for example, offered a second-story theater with rude benches
for patrons, candles to light the stage, and performances interrupted by
the boisterous shouts of men in the saloon downstairs. Less genteel forms

of entertainment were exceedingly popular. In August 1861, two thousand people gathered around a corral outside of Denver to watch a prize fight between Con Orem and Enoch Davis. Stakes were $500 per side, an amount that led both boxers to endure terrible punishment at each other's hands. After 109 rounds, Con Orem had beaten Enoch Davis into delirium and was declared the winner.[7]

Not many of Denver's early inhabitants cared about the town's appearance or its few amenities. Most were transients who had no stake in its development. The 1860 census counted 4,749 residents in Denver, including many men solely interested in striking it rich in the gold fields. As historian Lyle Dorsett described the gold seekers' lack of civic involvement,

> Without them and the mining hinterland there would have been no town at all; yet, their presence obstructed the building of a stable, attractive community. . . . They seldom did anything voluntarily to help the town because they had no vested interest there and never planned to have any. Aside from spending money on outfitting themselves for the mountains, their earnings were spent on gambling, liquor, and prostitutes. Whatever was left over went for room and board. Consequently, Denver's streets were overrun with drunken and disorderly vagrants, as well as bands of toughs who robbed, assaulted, and even murdered innocent victims at will.

The town relied on vigilante justice to achieve some semblance of law and order. Even though Slough served as judge of the "Appellate Court of the People's Government of Denver," for many of the town's early residents, no police, no formal court system, indeed no government was better than one that cost money.[8]

It was the threat of civil war that brought territorial government to Denver and the Rocky Mountain mining communities. Kansas Territory had extended to the Rockies, but the territorial government never exercised control over its far western lands. When Kansas joined the Union on January 29, 1861, its newly established western border was more than 175 miles east of the Colorado gold fields. Kansas's admission briefly left the Rocky Mountain region without a recognized government. To fill the void, lame-duck president James Buchanan signed the document creating Colorado Territory just four days before Lincoln's inauguration on March 4, 1861.

Lincoln's appointment of a governor for Colorado Territory assumed

William Gilpin, Colorado's
first territorial governor,
enlisted Slough's help in raising
a regiment of volunteers in
July and August 1861. Source:
Courtesy of History Colorado,
ID 89.451.893.

critical importance with war looming over the nation. Several candidates, including Slough's associate, William H. Larimer Jr., lobbied for the appointment, but Lincoln chose a well-qualified Westerner, William Gilpin, to become the territory's chief executive. Six feet tall with broad shoulders and an energetic personality, Gilpin first saw the Rocky Mountain country in 1843 as a member of John C. Frémont's expedition to discover a route over the continental divide. During the next fifteen years, Gilpin gained an intimate knowledge of the West. He briefly lived in the Willamette Valley in what was to become Oregon Territory, fought in the US-Mexican War, and commanded a mounted infantry battalion charged with protecting travelers on the Santa Fe Trail. By 1860, with the publication of his book *The Central Gold Region*, Gilpin was nationally known for his advocacy of western settlement. He was also a well-connected Republican whose friends urged Lincoln to appoint him governor of Colorado Territory.[9]

Having traveled to Washington, DC, to promote his candidacy, Gilpin remained in the Capital after the Senate confirmed his appointment on March 22, 1861. He was anxious to meet with the president, secretary of war Simon Cameron, and secretary of the treasury Salmon P. Chase to obtain their instructions for governing the new territory. But on April 12, South Carolina troops fired on Fort Sumter and the Lincoln administration became enmeshed in the promise of war. The most Gilpin could accomplish was a hasty, late-evening conversation with Lincoln and Cameron outside the White House. Lincoln directed him to leave immediately for Denver so that he could organize the territory's resistance to any efforts to wrest it from the Union. Gilpin departed Washington, DC, shortly thereafter.[10]

Colorado's citizens enthusiastically received their new executive when Gilpin arrived in Denver the afternoon of May 27. That evening, he spoke to a gathering of residents in front of the brightly illuminated Tremont House. The crowd heartily cheered his "well-worded and appropriate" remarks, which were followed by a cannon salvo. On May 30, the Denver town fathers suspended business to devote the day to welcoming Governor Gilpin. Despite his recent arrival in Denver, Judge John Slough joined the territory's leaders in the round of speeches saluting the new governor. Delegations from Golden, Central City, and other Rocky Mountain towns listened to the welcoming remarks throughout the afternoon and evening before honoring Gilpin at a dinner and ball at the Golden City Hall.[11]

Gilpin neither basked in the limelight of his reception nor tarried in getting to know his constituents, but quickly set to work. His administration faced many challenges in the spring of 1861, not the least of which was the threat of insurrection. Many Southerners, presumably secessionists, populated the territory. Men from Georgia had settled the original camps along Cherry Creek, followed by emigrants from other slaveholding states. By 1861, the territory held large numbers of residents "with outspoken loyalty to the course and purpose of the seceding States." Confederate sympathizers soon began organizing for possible military action. Wishing to keep their efforts secret, they posted unassuming notices throughout the territory with offers to buy serviceable rifles, pistols, and ammunition.[12]

Rumors of insurrection in the territory alarmed Gilpin and his colleagues. Territorial chief justice Benjamin F. Hall warned President Lincoln that six thousand men with strong Southern proclivities lived in the territory and their leaders were plotting with Confederate officers in Missouri, Arkansas, and Texas. Intensifying the threat to the territory, Hall believed that the Arapaho and other tribes had entered into the pay of the Confederate government. Fearing that the rebellion would reach the territory, Governor Gilpin moved quickly to forestall any possible insurgency. In June, he appointed a military staff, complete with adjutant general, quartermaster, and paymaster (although he had no funds to pay any troops) and directed his purchasing agent to buy all available arms and ammunition, regardless of condition. Despite these efforts, Denver and the mining towns remained woefully unprotected. Lacking soldiers to resist a rebel invasion or insurrection, Gilpin ordered the raising of two companies of volunteers in July 1861.[13]

War provides ambitious men, like John Slough, with opportunity. The territory needed officers for its fledgling military force and Gilpin called upon the judge to serve as the territory's recruiting officer and captain of Company A. Slough's tenure as captain was brief. He had applied to the War Department to raise a regiment of cavalry, but before the War Department answered his application, Governor Gilpin appointed Slough colonel of the territory's first regiment, the 1st Colorado Volunteer Infantry.[14]

Gilpin left no record why he chose Slough to lead the 1st Colorado Volunteers. Mid-nineteenth-century politics was fueled by political patronage, and Gilpin would have been expected to offer the colonelcy to a friend or acquaintance with Republican credentials. Slough may have overcome this objection by shrewdly embracing a nonpartisan stance. Along with 425 other Colorado residents, he had signed a petition in July 1861 urging the territory's citizens to send a delegate to the United States Congress who will "present himself independently, as the representative of the whole people, untrammeled by any party allegiances, pledges, or preferences." He and other Coloradans set aside their party prejudices during the territory's early months, which enabled Gilpin to appoint the Democrat Slough and a Republican Slough knew from Kansas, Samuel F. Tappan, as the 1st Colorado's colonel and lieutenant colonel. Even the *Colorado Republican and Rocky Mountain Herald* praised Slough's promotion to command, calling him "a deserving and patriotic officer," although the rival *Rocky Mountain News* snidely commented that Slough and Tappan were "scarcely warm in their new uniforms before—presto change—the former is dubbed Colonel, and the latter Lieut. Colonel."[15]

Slough, who had used his honorary title of "colonel" since his arrival in Denver, may have misled Gilpin about his military background, but he did not have to misrepresent his leadership experience. He could point to Kansas, where he served as delegate to the Wyandotte constitutional convention and ran on the state's first gubernatorial ticket. Locally, he presided as judge of Denver's appellate court and had established himself among the city's prominent citizens. Moreover, Slough knew how to cultivate men who could advance his ambitions. He was among the first territorial leaders that Gilpin met and quickly became friends with the new governor. He understood that Gilpin needed his assistance and, as the territory's recruiting officer, worked hard to enlist the volunteers who would save Colorado from the secessionist threat. In turn, he earned the new governor's respect and trust.[16]

Slough detested the rebellion and readily embraced the opportunity to defend the Union. He also recognized that, more than frontier law or politics, a colonel's commission, especially in wartime, offered him the chance for the advancement his ambition craved. He resigned his position as Denver's appellate court judge in August and decided not to run for city office when the first territorial elections occurred in fall 1861. No longer an attorney or a politician, Slough exchanged his waistcoat and cravat for a Union officer's uniform.[17]

At the time Slough began recruiting volunteers, digging for gold in the Rocky Mountains had become unproductive. Life was hard in the gold fields and the men labored long hours for little return. Regardless of the weather, hot or cold, fair or stormy, the men working the gold fields lived outdoors. They cooked their meals of bacon, corn cakes, pancakes, and coffee over outdoor fires and ate their monotonous and unappetizing fare seated on a log. They slept in tents or rude shanties, if they had any protection from the elements, and covered the ground with a blanket or two for their bedding. After a short time working their claims, they "became utterly indifferent to their appearances," unwashed, unshaven, bedraggled, wearing filthy, torn clothing. As a result of these hardships, volunteering to fight appealed to the miners, not only as a patriotic and exciting adventure, but also as an attractive alternative to flailing away with a pick. Colorado's men eagerly answered the call to arms. As Byron Sanford, who eventually served as a lieutenant in the Colorado Volunteers, wrote his wife Molly, "They do not have to drum up the recruits, they come in from all quarters, from the mines, the shops and stores, all ready to fight for their country."[18]

The territory quartered the first recruits in houses and tents along Ferry Street, then moved the troops to Denver's "old Buffalo House." Because the regiment could not be permanently housed or trained in makeshift quarters, Slough and his officers searched the area surrounding Denver for a location suitable for barracks and a parade ground. They chose a thirty-acre site two miles south of town on a bluff overlooking the South Platte River. The troops were put to work in late summer 1861 constructing the officers' headquarters, enlisted men's quarters, mess rooms, guardhouse, hospital, and other buildings. By the time they completed construction, the new encampment, named Camp Weld after territorial secretary Lewis Lanyard Weld, cost $40,000, not including the soldier's labor, an amount considered exorbitant by some of the territory's citizens.[19]

Slough ordered his third in command, Maj. John M. Chivington, to assume overall responsibility for drilling the men. Chivington was born in 1821 in Warren County, Ohio, northeast of Slough's hometown of Cincinnati. Unlike Slough, who benefited from his father's contacts during his early career, Chivington lost his father early in life and had to support himself as an apprentice carpenter. He experienced a religious conversion in 1842 while attending a revival, decided to enter the ministry, and was ordained in the Methodist Episcopal Church. He served as an itinerant Methodist minister assigned to parishes in Ohio, Illinois, and Missouri before being appointed presiding elder in Nebraska Territory. In 1860, he became presiding elder in the Rocky Mountain District.[20]

Chivington was ambitious, charismatic, a formidable six feet four inches tall, and more than 250 pounds. A contemporary described him as a man "of herculean frame and gigantic stature" while the *Nebraska City News* extolled his "great energy and force of character." He became a vocal opponent of slavery with the passage of the Kansas-Nebraska Act and subsequently joined the Republican Party. When Governor Gilpin formed the 1st Colorado, Chivington based his request for an officer's commission on his antislavery beliefs. He wrote Gilpin, "I feel compelled to strike a blow in person for the destruction of human slavery and to help in some measure to make this a truly free country. I must respectfully decline an appointment as a non-combatant officer [Gilpin had offered him the regiment's chaplaincy], and at the same time urgently request a fighting commission instead." Chivington joined Slough and Tappan as the 1st Colorado's senior officers. They were an odd trio: Slough, the conservative Democrat who held little regard for Black people, and his two subordinate officers, Tappan and Chivington, both Republicans and ardent abolitionists.[21]

Without any military experience, Slough, Tappan, and Chivington had to rely on manuals, such as Hardee's *Rifle & Light Infantry Tactics* and General

Maj. John Chivington conspired against Slough to replace him as colonel of the 1st Colorado Volunteer Infantry. Source: Courtesy of the William A. Keleher Pictorial Collection, University of New Mexico, ID 000–742–0041.tif.

of the Army Winfield Scott's *Infantry Tactics or Rules for the Exercise and Maneuvers of the United States Infantry*, to learn their trade. Drill was the first order of business as the 1st Colorado's officers struggled to teach the most basic requirements of soldiering. Mornings and afternoons, they drilled the new recruits, followed by a dress parade each evening. Sightseers from Denver visited Camp Weld even before it was completed to watch the troops practice their newly acquired skills. On September 14, Slough received the Denver City Council "in his usual gentlemanly manner" and led the visitors on a tour of Camp Weld's recent improvements. Afterwards the council members enjoyed a demonstration of the soldiers' drilling. In an effort to rationalize the difficulty of training new recruits, Slough apologized for the men's "awkwardness" and ungraciously joked that "when a child was most particularly required to do its best, it was most sure to cut up and do its darndest." His disdainful comment may have charmed his important visitors but it also demonstrated an arrogance and superiority that soon drove a wedge between him and his men.[22]

Slough and Tappan squabbled about training their volunteers. On September 19, just five days after the Denver City Council's outing to Camp Weld, Tappan complained about Slough's manner in correcting his errors when drilling the troops. "We are all liable to give incorrect orders," he wrote his commanding officer, "and the men under my command have strict orders not to change position in any particular, when I fail to give orders correctly. . . . I make no claim to a correct knowledge of military matters . . . but you must remember you yourself while drilling the battalion not long since gave [illegible word] orders that were not correct and which would not have been executed if I had not taken the liberty to give the order you intended to give." Tappan assured Slough that he would obey him as his superior officer but warned Slough that he could not treat him as a gentleman if Slough continued to berate him.[23]

Both officers struggled with Chivington. Slough described the 1st Colorado's major as that "crazy preacher who thinks he is Napoleon Bonaparte," while Tappan feared that Chivington was actively undermining his relationship with the troops. "From the earliest organization of our regiment" Tappan wrote Chivington, "you have done your utmost by outspoken remarks and secret intimations to destroy my influence as an officer in the regiment." Tappan's perception that Chivington wanted to undercut his superior officers' authority was accurate, although Chivington's target was not Tappan, but the regiment's colonel.[24]

Slough desperately needed his officers' support because a lack of discipline plagued "Gilpin's Pet Lambs," as Denver's residents derisively nicknamed the 1st Colorado. From the beginning, Slough confronted serious breaches of the peace between his troops and the local civilians. Drunkenness often underlay the disturbances. On August 16, 1861, for example, men from Slough's Company A argued with a German saloon keeper, Moses Adler, over a bar bill. The next evening, Pvt. Thomas Rogers returned to the saloon to continue the dispute. Standing in the street and loudly complaining that Adler had insulted him, Rogers challenged the bartender to a fight. Adler stormed out of his saloon armed with a knife. Within seconds, he struck the soldier several times, plunging the blade into his lung just above the heart. Rogers died in the street in a pool of blood. He was probably Company A's first casualty.[25]

A few days later, soldiers from Company B tangled with a crowd of intoxicated civilians. That morning, Company A and Company B had stood at attention on Larimer Street as two ladies presented Gilpin and Slough with a "most beautiful piece of workmanship in rich silk with gilt stars" to serve as Company A's banner. Slough grandly promised the crowd that the flag would never be lost in battle so long as "one of the company should live to bear it." After the ceremony, as Company B was returning to quarters, a group of prosecessionist men insulted the soldiers and then, according to the *Colorado Republican and Rocky Mountain Herald*, fired on them. The ensuing brawl upset Denver's respectable citizenry, compelling the *Herald* to allay their fears by reporting that the town had been "peaceable" since the altercation.[26]

The soldiers easily slipped away from their quarters to patronize one of Denver's thirty-five saloons. Even after the 1st Colorado moved to Camp Weld, they smuggled past the sentries to walk the two miles into town to procure liquor. Drunkenness among the ranks became such an impediment to military discipline that the territorial legislature passed a bill in late September prohibiting the sale of alcohol to soldiers. Slough announced his intention to enforce the regulation vigorously through a notice in the *Colorado Republican and Rocky Mountain Herald*, but his efforts had little effect in reducing drunkenness among the troops. Three months later, in early January 1862, the *Herald* complained that the prohibition against the sale of liquor was "wholly without force as ever" and called on Denver's saloon keepers to stop supplying spirits to the soldiers.[27]

More than alcohol-fueled brawls, the 1st Colorado's practice of commandeering food and clothing turned Denver's citizens against the volunteer soldiers. Slough understood his responsibility to supply his troops. Just one week after he began recruitment, he placed the first of several advertisements in the *Rocky Mountain News* requesting bids for "clothing, subsistence, and transportation." But the territory's lack of revenue and Denver's distance from eastern markets severely hampered his efforts to obtain adequate food, uniforms, arms, and accoutrements. By late October, with the weather turning cold, Slough was reduced to begging Denver's citizens to donate blankets, quilts, and buffalo robes for "the comfort of those who have volunteered for your defense, and who are now suffering."[28]

Denver in 1861 imported virtually everything required by its residents. Most goods had to be transported by wagon from the Missouri River across almost seven hundred miles of prairie. Each wagon hauled four or five tons of freight; thirty-five to forty wagons traveling in a mile-long wagon train averaged only ten to fifteen miles a day along the Platte River route. In fair weather, the trip might require two months to complete, but when the weather turned foul, moving freight stopped altogether. The vast distance between the Missouri River docks and the town of Denver, the threat of Indian and bandit attacks en route, and rate collusion among the shipping agencies meant that every supply delivered to Denver commanded a high price. Even staples like flour, sugar, cornmeal, potatoes, lard, bacon, and beef had to be imported and cost dearly.[29]

To make matters worse, the new territorial treasury had no money to purchase supplies or pay its soldiers. During their brief meeting outside the White House, Lincoln had instructed Gilpin to issue personal drafts to pay for the territory's defense and assured the newly appointed governor that the War Department would honor them. Gilpin followed the president's instructions and paid Denver's businessmen with vouchers he promised the War Department would repay in gold. Denver's merchants accepted them at first, although as early as August 1861, just a few weeks after Slough began recruitment, the *Rocky Mountain News* lamented that merchants were reluctant to extend credit to "Uncle Sam," a predicament that the newspaper described as "extremely embarrassing to Captain Slough." When rumors reached Denver in November that the War Department would not honor the vouchers, many of Denver's shopkeepers shut off credit to Gilpin and supplies to the 1st Colorado.[30]

The soldiers responded by taking what they needed. Maj. John Chivington recalled twenty years later that the officers and men considered trading vouchers for supplies as a "fair deal." Merchants had only two choices: they could accept the vouchers as proof of the government's indebtedness or they could refuse to accept them. Regardless, the troops appropriated their goods. The standoff over credit led to ugly confrontations between soldiers and shopkeepers. One night, when E. L. Gallatin was working late in John Landis's saddle and harness shop, several soldiers entered the store, pointed their cocked pistols at the saddler, and demanded belts. After searching the premises, the soldiers took what they wanted, gave Gallatin a voucher for $35, and left in search of clothing. Only the intervention of Slough and territorial secretary Lewis Weld prevented the men from requisitioning coats at a clothing store. Weld promised that he would do everything possible to secure coats for them. Satisfied with his pledge, the soldiers returned to Camp Weld.[31]

Slough and Weld were not always successful in protecting Denver's businessmen from the appropriation of their merchandise. Ovando James Hollister, in his first-hand history of the 1st Colorado, relates how a Denver shopkeeper complained to Slough that soldiers had robbed his store, explaining that "they were in pressing need of some clothing, and [the] government having failed to furnish them, they were compelled to take it." In an effort to identify the thieves, Slough ordered several men to appear before him and the merchant, but the merchant's memory failed when one soldier drew a pair of steel knuckles from his pocket. Slough then decided to search the barracks for the stolen items. True to his belief that purloining needed supplies was a necessary evil, Chivington warned the men to hide what they had taken. Nothing was found, the shopkeeper left Camp Weld unsatisfied, and Chivington endeared himself to his men by subverting Slough's attempt to maintain discipline.[32]

Not only did the troops steal from Denver's storekeepers, they also raided civilian pantries and hen houses. On Christmas Eve 1861, the men treated themselves to a dinner of "eggs, hams, oysters, champaigne [sic], cheese, and vegetables" that they had foraged from their neighbors' larders. Some of the men were drunk by Christmas morning and, becoming "more scurrilous than ever," forced the sheriff, city marshal, and a posse of police to quell their rowdy behavior. Hollister admitted that the 1st Colorado's actions had become "rough" on the town but rationalized their misconduct by explaining that "we had been dogs now four months without pay." For Gilpin's Pet Lambs, Denver was "lawful 'loot.'"[33]

The soldiers' lives were not all daytime drill and nighttime forays to procure liquor and other supplies. On Sundays, which the men had at leisure, a considerable portion of the camp attended Divine Services, led by the regiment's chaplain, the Reverend J. H. Kehler. Others spent the day reading books and newspapers. Those soldiers wishing more active pursuits played baseball, an "excellent exercise of the muscle, besides being good amusement" according to the *Colorado Republican and Rocky Mountain Herald*. Capt. Ned Wynkoop organized a drama group to entertain the regiment with performances in Camp Weld's theater. The officers and men also enjoyed plays in Denver. According to the *Herald*, companies paraded along Larimer Street accompanied by fife and drum before breaking ranks to attend the theater. Slough himself attended the occasional theatrical performance. On Saturday evening, November 30, 1861, he joined members of Denver's elite, including territorial secretary Lewis Weld, newly elected mayor C. A. Cook, and city marshal W. M. Keith, to celebrate the opening of the new People's Theater. A sold-out audience, which the *Rocky Mountain News* boasted could not be "easily eclipsed" for its "size, style, intelligence, and respectability," delighted in performances of the "Mistletoe Bough" and "My Neighbor's Wife."[34]

Slough and his officers often hosted dinners in the officers' mess or invited civilian friends to full dress balls with music provided by the regiment's band. Slough, Chivington, and several other officers attended a dinner on December 22, 1861, in honor of the regiment's Company H, soon to depart Camp Weld for Fort Wise, two hundred miles southeast of Denver. After dinner, Slough spoke to the gathered officers and men and awkwardly told them that he was "happy to meet, and unite, feelingly, with his men under such circumstances as the present." He acknowledged that he was unpopular among the men, that many considered him "arbitrary and severe" because they "failed to perceive the necessity of a strict system of discipline and drill as a foundation for all success in warfare." Nonetheless, the day was "approaching when all would thank him for the course he had pursued." "He was proud of his regiment," Slough told the men, and he assured them that "when we meet the enemy together in the shock of battle, you will have cause to be justly proud of your Colonel, as I am ever proud of you."[35]

It was a poignant and heartfelt speech, given on the eve of a new year in which the 1st Colorado would likely be tested in battle. The men warmly applauded their colonel as he sat down. But the reserved John Slough could not stir the men's blood like John Milton Chivington could. When his superior officer finished speaking, the major stood and, with fire in his eyes, thundered, "I wish to say that I desire to be with you in the storm of battle— aye, in your very van, to lead you to victory, or to fall and mingle my bones with yours, skeleton to skeleton, on the same ensanguined field." The dinner erupted into "immense cheering." Chivington had promised what the men wanted to hear: he would be no coward when they faced the enemy together. Unfortunately for Slough, the 1st Colorado Volunteers preferred their feisty, personable major to a stiff, remote, and autocratic colonel.[36]

8

"The Great Mogul
of the Colorado First"

DRUNKENNESS, BRAWLING, PILFERING: ALL SERIOUS INFRACTIONS
that Colonel Slough struggled to suppress among the Colorado volunteers.
His efforts to instill discipline through confinement and other punishments
only soured the men's opinion of their commander. To make matters worse,
Slough had been ordered to protect Denver. His refusal to acknowledge his
men's clamoring to join the war back east caused some of the 1st Colorado to
question his loyalty and doubt his courage. From the moment they enlisted,
Gilpin's Pet Lambs longed to experience the thrill of battle and resented any
delay in fighting rebels. Only a few days after newly commissioned Captain
Slough began recruiting volunteers for Company A, the *Rocky Mountain News*
corrected the misperception that the local men were joining the United States
Army. The newspaper reminded the recruits that they had enrolled in the
1st Colorado Volunteer Infantry; their responsibility lay with guarding the
territory and not marching elsewhere to battle rebels.[1]

In November, a serious misunderstanding about a soldier's duty to obey
resulted in insubordination in the ranks. Recruited as mounted infantry, men
from Company K refused to muster for roll call when they learned that they
would be organized as a regular infantry unit. Fueling Company K's anger
about their reassignment was the regiment's lack of activity; the men had
grown weary of camp life and were anxious to confront the rebels. Slough
arrested Company's K's captain, Charles P. Marion, in an effort to restore
discipline. When the men of Company K vowed that they would release their
captain from the city jail and leave Colorado Territory to crush the rebellion
elsewhere, Slough disarmed the men and disbanded the company. The new
colonel had dealt appropriately with Company K's insubordination, but his
actions only increased the dissatisfaction among the men.[2]

It is not surprising that the Colorado Volunteers itched to prove themselves in battle. During the summer and fall of 1861, they read newspaper
accounts of one Union disaster after another. Catastrophes at Manassas,
Wilson's Creek, and Ball's Bluff led to a "general feeling of gloom and depression" among Denver's loyal population, and they frustrated the troops
drilling incessantly at Camp Weld. Confederate forces had also humiliated
the U.S. Army in New Mexico Territory. In July 1861, Confederate lieutenant
colonel John R. Baylor and troopers from the Second Texas Mounted Infantry invaded the town of Mesilla, just across the Texas border in New
Mexico. Opposing the Texans were twice as many federal soldiers at Fort
Fillmore under the command of veteran officer Maj. Isaac Lynde. Lynde
decided to leave the fort's protection and attack the Confederates, but when
the Texans stoutly resisted the federal advance, Lynde ordered his men to
fall back, abandon Fort Fillmore, and retreat to Fort Stanton, 150 miles away.
Baylor pursued the federals and, when the Texans overtook the strung-out
Union column at San Augustin Pass on July 28, Lynde's entire command
was captured.[3]

The potential impact of the fiasco in southern New Mexico Territory was
not lost on the *Rocky Mountain News*. In an article titled "Threatening," the
newspaper reported the rebels' capture of Fort Fillmore and noted that the
result gave "cause for some alarm for our own safety." The paper reasoned that
the Texans may decide to move north through New Mexico's Rio Grande
Valley, "a country easy of conquest, and rich in supplies and arms," to arrive
at Colorado's borders. If that occurred, the newspaper warned, "the extensive
military preparations made by Governor Gilpin were not commenced a whit
too soon." Fortunately for Colorado, Baylor kept his troops in southern New
Mexico to protect the recently created Confederate Territory of Arizona.[4]

Pressure on Slough to lead the 1st Colorado against the rebels increased
in early 1862 when a brigade of Texans massed on the Texas–New Mexico
border. Henry Hopkins Sibley, an 1838 West Point graduate, US-Mexican
War veteran, and cavalryman experienced in frontier duty, convinced Confederate president Jefferson Davis in summer 1861 that an army of Texas
volunteers could easily capture New Mexico's Fort Craig and Fort Union.
Davis authorized him to raise at least two regiments of cavalry and a battery
of howitzers to drive the federals from New Mexico Territory. Whether
Davis approved a grander plan is unknown, but Sibley apparently conceived

of a campaign in which his army would plunder the federal supply depots and forts in New Mexico Territory, win control of the Colorado gold fields, and march to the Pacific Ocean to seize California ports for the blockaded South.[5]

By late October 1861, Sibley and his newly recruited Confederate Army of New Mexico began the seven-hundred-mile march from San Antonio to Fort Bliss, Texas, on the New Mexico border. The Texans needed almost two months to reach Fort Bliss and another six weeks to recover from the fatigue, hunger, thirst, and disease they had suffered during their march. It was not until January 10, 1862, that Sibley's 2,500-man brigade crossed the Rio Grande into New Mexico Territory. The Texans' initial target was Fort Craig, where Col. Edward R. S. Canby and a garrison of 1,200 US Army regulars and 2,600 untrained New Mexico volunteers and militiamen awaited the rebels.[6]

Canby had been aware of the Texans' arrival at Fort Bliss and requested reinforcements before the Confederate Army marched into New Mexico. On New Year's Day 1862, he dispatched an urgent request to Governor Gilpin to send Colorado volunteers to Fort Wise to relieve its garrison for reassignment to New Mexico. Gilpin had already ordered the 1st Colorado's Companies B, F, and H, under the command of Lt. Col. Samuel Tappan, to march to Fort Wise, but Canby's anxious message unsettled Denver's residents. The citizens feared that if the Texans swept aside the loyal forces in New Mexico, Denver would surely be the rebels' next objective.[7]

Tension among the troops remaining at Camp Weld became unbearable with the news from New Mexico Territory. The officers and men desperately wanted to join the federal forces at Fort Craig in their stand against the rebel threat, yet Colonel Slough had no orders to reinforce Colonel Canby. Confusing Slough's inaction with indecision, the officers determined to take matters into their own hands. On February 5, Capt. Ned Wynkoop drafted a petition demanding that Slough order the 1st Colorado to New Mexico. Noting that their colonel seemed hesitant to move without orders, the petition pledged to relieve Slough of "a portion of that responsibility." Maj. John Chivington, Adj. J. A. Davidson, six captains, and thirteen first and second lieutenants all signed the letter. Of the officers at Camp Weld, only one captain, Samuel Robbins, refused to sign the petition. Robbins had replaced the cashiered Captain Marion after Company K's uprising in

November, and chose not to add his name to what he probably considered an insubordinate act.[8]

Chivington's campaign to undermine Slough's authority did not stop with his signing Wynkoop's ill-advised petition. He also ignored the command structure by writing Maj. Gen. David Hunter about the regiment's unsettled state. Hunter, the Western Department's commanding officer, rebuked Chivington for his presumption, to which the major replied that he "would be very much pleased to be dismissed from the service for trying to get my regiment to the front." Hunter ignored the major's posturing.[9]

Two days after the officers at Camp Weld signed Wynkoop's petition, the controversy over the regiment's inaction erupted into public view. On February 7, the *Rocky Mountain News* published an anonymous letter that provocatively questioned why the regiment remained in Colorado Territory when rebel victory seemed imminent in New Mexico. Signed by "Union," the letter noted that a Confederate force "with strength and determination, is now threatening the Federal forts, boasting that in sixty days New Mexico will have been subjugated . . . and the Rebel army will be at, or near the city of Denver." Both Colonel Canby and New Mexico territorial governor Henry Connelly had requested that the Colorado troops help stem the Texans' advance, yet "silence prevails with the powers that control our political destinies." "Union" charged that in Gilpin's absence (the governor had returned to Washington to lobby for repayment of the territory's vouchers), acting territorial governor Lewis Lanyard Weld feared ordering the 1st Colorado to New Mexico. Instead, he preferred to sit idly by until the rebels' approach forced him to "flee into some cañon in the mountains to secretly fortify himself, or to make hasty passage down the Platte."

Could the regiment's cowardice be the cause of its inaction? No, "Union" claimed, the Colorado troops were "impatient for a fight." The real reason for the regiment's inertia was Colonel Slough's faintheartedness. The volunteers had not left Camp Weld because "the God of War, the Great Mogul of this Colorado First, would rather be a living *coward* than a *dead* hero." "Union" urged the men to demand to be led into battle when "you can so soon and so gallantly prove yourself to be all the people say you are—the *bravest* of the *brave*." In the letter's last sentence, "Union" revealed his motivation for calling Slough a coward. "Let the Major lead you on," he declared, "and success is certain." "Union" wanted Chivington to replace Slough.[10]

Slough always had difficulty controlling his anger, and "Union's" insinuations of cowardice infuriated him. Because the anonymous author had defamed him as well as promoted insurrection within the 1st Colorado, he was determined to uncover his attacker's identity. The same evening the letter appeared in the *Rocky Mountain News*, the colonel sent a messenger requesting that the *News*'s editor, William Byers, reveal "Union's" identity. Byers's answer must not have satisfied Slough, for the next morning he stormed into the *News*'s office angrily demanding "Union's" name. Byers showed "Union's" letter to the colonel, although the pseudonymous letter gave no hint of "Union's" identity. Frustrated, Slough left the newspaper's office threatening that he would hold Byers personally responsible for any unflattering comment the newspaper published about him.[11]

Byers resolved to teach the upstart colonel a lesson about threats. In an editorial in which he recounted his exchange with Slough, Byers reminded his readers—as if anyone would question the feisty editor's position in the matter—that "*we control our columns and that he* [Slough] *shall not*." Byers then attacked Slough's character. The newspaperman lectured the colonel, warning him that if he appealed "to *might*, or ruffianism to gratify his revenge [against the *Rocky Mountain News* or possibly 'Union'], *he* becomes the violator of the law." "Ruffianism"—the term that Republican newspapers leveled against both Slough and the Democratic Party—had again been used to describe the Cincinnati Democrat's behavior. In back-to-back editions of the *Rocky Mountain News*, Slough was insulted twice. "Union" had called him a coward; Byers had called him a ruffian.[12]

In the same February 8 edition of the *News*, one of Slough's subordinates, Company D's Capt. Jacob Downing, published a letter that sought to refute "Union's" implication that the Colorado volunteers feared the Texans. Downing included in his rebuttal the text of Wynkoop's petition to move the 1st Colorado to New Mexico. He reasoned that as the regiment's officers had signed Wynkoop's petition, there was no doubt that the officers wanted to attack the rebels. Furthermore, he assured the *News*'s readers that "there is not a half dozen men in all the companies of said regiment, from Company A to Company K, who would not fight a secessionist with the fierceness and determination of a Bengal tiger."[13]

Slough's embarrassment was complete. Not only had "Union" challenged his bravery and Byers his character, now one of his junior officers publicly

Capt. Jacob Downing joined
Chivington's efforts to defame Slough
by publishing letters attacking his
character in the *Rocky Mountain
News*. Source: Courtesy of History
Colorado, PH.PROP.5186.

revealed the dissension among the 1st Colorado's officers. Slough could not
tolerate what he saw as unjustified attacks, and Captain Downing became
the target of his wrath. The same day as the *News* published Downing's letter,
Slough placed him and his lieutenant, Eli Dickerson, under house arrest.[14]

No one knows why Slough arrested Dickerson, although he probably
released the lieutenant quickly. Captain Downing was another matter. The
Colorado Republican and Rocky Mountain Herald claimed that Downing's
February 8 letter to the *Rocky Mountain News*, and especially his decision
to make public Wynkoop's petition, prompted his confinement to quarters.
"Union" himself claimed that Slough arrested Downing because of a critical
letter about Slough that Downing published in the *Rocky Mountain News*.
But Slough had Downing arrested before Downing's letter appeared on
Denver's streets in the *News*'s February 8 edition. It was more likely that
Slough suspected that his captain had used the "Union" pseudonym to con-
ceal his identity as the author of the February 7 attack on Slough and Weld.
Perhaps Byers revealed Downing as "Union" when Slough visited the *Rocky
Mountain News* early on February 8 and Slough reacted by arresting his
captain that afternoon.[15]

Downing's likely responsibility for "Union's" letter is perplexing. Nothing in his history suggests a personal, deeply rooted animosity against either Slough or Weld. After studying law in Chicago, he moved to Denver in 1859 or 1860 where he opened a law office. He briefly served as judge of the Denver Court of Common Pleas before resuming his law practice. Upon the 1st Colorado's organization in August 1861, Governor Gilpin commissioned him as Company D's captain. No record exists of a conflict between Slough and Downing, either as Denver attorneys or as officers striving to train the unruly Colorado volunteers. And although Downing was likely a Republican, there is no evidence of partisan animosity between Downing and Slough or a political feud between Downing and Weld.[16]

Then what—or who—prompted him to write a scurrilous attack against Slough? Captain Downing wanted a major's cluster and there was one man— John Chivington—whose own advancement would facilitate Downing's promotion. The ambitious and aggressive major was determined to lead the 1st Colorado. He had already begun to undercut Slough by turning a blind eye to the troops' theft of supplies, signing Wynkoop's petition demanding that Slough move the 1st Colorado without orders, and complaining to Major General Hunter about the regiment's inactivity. Anonymously slandering Slough as a coward would further destroy the colonel's reputation and perhaps lead to his removal as commander of the 1st Colorado. Chivington and his supporter Downing would then be promoted to colonel and major. Chivington's plot to discredit Slough involved "Union," and although Downing probably wrote the letter, Chivington had a hand in it.[17]

"Union's" February 7 letter provided fodder for the circulation battle between Byers's *Rocky Mountain News* and its cross-town rival, the *Colorado Republican and Rocky Mountain Herald*, edited by Thomas Gibson. Byers and Gibson originally founded the *Rocky Mountain News*, Denver's first newspaper, but in summer 1859, Gibson left the boom town for Mountain City to establish the *Rocky Mountain Gold Reporter and Mountain City Herald*. He returned to Denver in fall 1859 to publish a string of newspapers. By the time he printed the first *Colorado Republican and Rocky Mountain Herald*, he and Byers had long forgotten their initial partnership and had become ferocious competitors.[18]

The fight for the territory's governmental printing contract further fueled the conflict between the two newspapermen. Much to Byers's surprise and dismay, Governor Gilpin awarded the territory's lucrative printing contract to Thomas Gibson shortly after Gilpin arrived in Denver. Byers could forgive neither the governor nor the *Herald*'s editor for denying him "the income derived from the right to print the official post office letter list, government patents and land sales, the minutes of the town council meetings and territorial legislatures, and other government documents." Moreover, while serving as acting governor in Gilpin's absence, Lewis Lanyard Weld refused secretary of state William Seward's request to share the printing contract between the two Denver newspapers, explaining that he considered the *Rocky Mountain News* to be "venal, irresponsible, and touched with secessionism." Byers responded to these attacks on his business by using the *News*'s columns to criticize Gibson, Gilpin, and Weld.[19]

Little wonder that Gibson attacked when the *Rocky Mountain News* printed "Union's" denunciation of Slough and Weld. In an article titled "The *News* a Traitor," dated February 10, 1862, Gibson savaged Byers's decision to publish "Union's" letter. His editorial argued that the letter "not only stigmatized, abused, misrepresented and maligned the actions past, present, and prospective of Governor Gilpin, Col. Slough, and the other civil and military leaders of the Territory, but by exaggerated appeals to the volunteers of Colorado, it attempted to excite insubordination and mutiny among them." Gibson's piece minced no words. It condemned "Union's" letter as "Rebellious in its intention, traitorous in its authorship, and treason was marked in every effort to place it before the people." Nor did Gibson ignore the *News*'s responsibility for printing "Union's" letter, criticizing the *News* for its "express design of spreading abroad insurrectionary and seditious sentiments to excite Rebellion." These were strong words, especially when published in a city infected with war fever.[20]

One can imagine Byers smoldering at Gibson's editorial when he replied, "Our contemporary [the *Herald*] was jubilant yesterday over what it calls the treason of the *News*; and why does it so rejoice? Simply because its editor, Thomas Gibson, has sworn to crush us; to devote his time, his energy, his money, his credit, his very life to break us down." Byers denied any hint of disloyalty by labeling the charge of sedition as "bosh" and ended his rebuttal with the patriotic claim that "we have always said to the soldiers, *'Boys stand by your Country's flag: Let what may come, never*—NEVER DESERT THAT POST OF HONOR.'" Byer's melodramatic words ignored the contradiction in calling the 1st Colorado to serve their country faithfully while publishing "Union's" letter encouraging them to disobey their commanding officer.[21]

Slough himself may have been drawn into Byers and Gibson's print war. In the same issue that the *Herald* accused the *News* of spreading "insurrectionary and seditious sentiments," a correspondent named "Cincinnati"—a *nom de plume* appropriate for Slough—denied "Union's" charge of cowardice against the 1st Colorado's commander. "As a townsman of the Colonel, so totally wronged," "Cincinnati" declared "the utter falsity of all the charges against him where personal bravery is concerned." "Cincinnati" blamed Byers and his close friend, territorial representative Hiram Bennet, for instigating "Union's" letter in order to tarnish Slough, Weld, and, by association, William Gilpin. Having avoided politics upon his arrival in Colorado Territory, Slough was now entangled in Byers's vendetta against Gilpin and Weld.[22]

The 1st Colorado's colonel soon had more pressing matters than defending his reputation in the Denver newspapers. On February 14, Acting Governor Weld received the orders that the 1st Colorado anxiously awaited. Maj. Gen. David Hunter wrote Weld requesting that he "act promptly" and send "all available forces you can possibly spare" to reinforce Canby in New Mexico. Much had to be accomplished before the 1st Colorado could leave Camp Weld. Although Denver's merchants continued to refuse the regiment's vouchers, the men had to obtain all the necessities of war—food, ammunition, tents, extra boots and clothing, bandages and medical equipment—and load them into "miserable little rickety concerns" for the long haul to New Mexico.[23]

The volunteers continued their habit of getting drunk and disturbing the peace during their last days before departing Denver. The *Herald* reported that on the evening of February 14, intoxicated soldiers threw rocks at the newspaper's office, seemingly angered by the *Herald*'s criticism of "Union" and the *Rocky Mountain News*. The drunken soldiers also vented their ire against the town's drinking establishments by breaking the windows of several saloons.[24]

Despite this horseplay, preparations for the campaign were complete by February 22 and the order to march was given. One by one, the companies formed their columns, except for Captain Downing's Company D. Downing had remained confined since his arrest two weeks previously and his men refused to march without him. Knowing that the campaign ahead would require every soldier, Slough quickly resolved the impasse by sending word to bring Downing before him. When the junior officer appeared, Slough bluntly asked him if he was "Union." Downing denied writing the letter (although he did not deny authoring it) and Slough released him to the cheers of the regiment. Around three o'clock in the afternoon, Company D assumed its place in the line of march, and, under a wintry sky that promised snow, Gilpin's Pet Lambs departed Camp Weld "in high glee" and finally bound for the war.[25]

9

ooooooo

"We Have Saved this Territory"

MUTINY DURING THE CIVIL WAR WAS DEFINED AS "RESISTANCE TO lawful military authority" and encompassed "extreme insubordination, as individually resisting by force, or collectively rising against or opposing military authority." Moreover, the Articles of War emphasized that an officer or enlisted man "who so much as lifted a weapon or offered violence against an officer while in the execution of his duty" could be sentenced to death. Execution by firing squad was the punishment for mutiny.[1]

Barely a week had passed since the jubilant 1st Colorado left Camp Weld when Slough faced mutiny within his ranks. The campaign's first days had been arduous. Traveling through countryside with rutted and broken roads, burdened with wagons "unfit for hard service" and animals "too badly used up to stand the journey," the volunteers made little progress. The first day the men glumly tramped through snow and bitterly cold wind. They struggled the second day as well, but with each succeeding day the soldiers covered more miles. By the time they stopped for the night at a site they named Camp Colorado, the 1st Colorado had managed to march seventy miles in six days.[2]

The next morning, Company I refused to break camp as the remainder of the regiment prepared to resume its march. Mostly German immigrants, Company I's men chafed at the allotment of only two wagons for personal baggage when the other, largely native-born companies had been provided with three. They resolved not to walk another step until the shortcoming was rectified.

Slough rode over to Company I's camp to resolve the delay and get the column moving. Despite his direct command to fall in, the men of Company I did not obey; they would not continue the march without a third wagon. His back stiffening, Slough ordered Company A to disarm the recalcitrant

Germans. Lt. Charles Kerber, Company I's commander and a German himself, directed his men to load their muskets. Glaring up at the mounted Slough, he told his superior officer that "no company could disarm them and make them take their place in the line of march." Slough coldly looked down at the obstinate Kerber, pulled his revolver, and ordered Company E to assist Company A in disarming the Germans.[3]

Kerber and his men now moved from insubordination to mutiny. Company I pointed their loaded muskets at their colonel while one of its members menacingly threatened, "You shoot Kerber and we'll put sixty holes through you." Slough lost his nerve. He turned to Major Chivington, gave orders for the day's march, and rode away. In his retelling of the incident almost thirty years later, Chivington cast himself as the peacemaker. Rather than enforcing military discipline by arresting Kerber or any of the mutineers, he chose to ignore Company I's disobedience. He patiently explained to the angry soldiers that their lack of a third wagon had nothing to do with their nationality and that a wagon would be given to them as soon as one was procured. Trusting Chivington's word—a confidence Slough did not share—the men of Company I fell into ranks.[4]

Civil War volunteers commonly disdained their superior officers, especially "shoulder-strap gentry" who had done little to earn their rank. Coming from a society that valued individualism and egalitarianism, enlisted men often reacted negatively when they believed that an officer had ignored their rights or acted in a superior fashion. If they considered the officer's actions especially egregious, they reacted by obstinately refusing orders and even threatening violence. Although the men of the 1st Colorado demonstrated an especially unruly and independent streak, their dislike of their stiff-necked colonel, their refusal to accept military discipline, and their determination to defend their individual rights were characteristics not unlike other Civil War units.[5]

The Colorado volunteers disliked Slough for many reasons. Some blamed him for failing to obtain the supplies they needed and the back pay they had earned. Others questioned his loyalty to the Union, given his perceived lack of concern about the Confederate invasion of New Mexico. Many resented his efforts to instill an "arbitrary and severe" discipline. Above all, the men loathed his haughty and reserved manner. As Pvt. Ovando Hollister observed shortly after Company I's mutiny, "How little some men understand human nature. He had been our Colonel six months; had never spoken to us; and

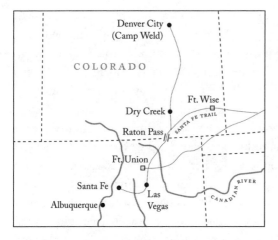

The route of the Coloradans to Glorieta Pass from Thomas Edrington and John Taylor, *The Battle of Glorieta Pass: A Gettysburg in the West, March 26–28, 1862,* University of New Mexico Press, 1998.

on the eve of an important expedition . . . could not see that a few words were indispensable, to a good understanding. . . . [T]he men seem to lack confidence in him. Why I cannot say—nor can they, I think. His aristocratic style savors more of an eastern society than of the free-and-easy border to which he should have been acclimated."[6]

Hollister's perceptive label of Slough as an elitist has the ring of truth. Raised in one of Cincinnati's *nouveau riche* families, Slough mixed easily with gentlemen from his own class, but either struggled with, or did not see the point of, establishing a relationship with the 1st Colorado's rank and file. As Hollister recalled, Slough was an officer whose "personal contact with his men was never of a kind to make him beloved." His remote and austere personality, his determination to forge his volunteers into a disciplined regiment, and his Eastern "aristocratic style" served to poison the feelings of Gilpin's Pet Lambs about their commanding officer.[7]

On March 5, as the 1st Colorado marched along the Rockies toward New Mexico, Slough received disquieting news from Lieutenant Colonel Tappan. Tappan and three companies of the 1st Colorado had garrisoned Fort Wise since the beginning of the year, but on March 1 were ordered to rejoin the regiment. While marching to rendezvous with Slough's troops, Tappan received an anxious dispatch from Col. Gabriel Paul, commander of Fort Union in northern New Mexico. Paul informed him that Sibley's brigade had routed Canby's regulars and volunteers at a Rio Grande ford named

Valverde and were headed north toward Albuquerque and Santa Fe. Paul anticipated that the rebels would attack Fort Union as soon as they arrived in northern New Mexico and urged Tappan to hurry to the fort's defense. In turn, Tappan forwarded Paul's request to Slough.[8]

Slough wasted no time reacting to Tappan's dispatch. He gathered his men, relayed the news from New Mexico, and asked if they would endure a forced march to Fort Union for the "honor and prosperity of the Republic." Personal belongings—the very items that had caused Company I to mutiny a few days earlier—were discarded as the regiment pushed forward. On March 7, Tappan's and Slough's commands reunited. The combined force now followed the Santa Fe Trail, the nine-hundred-mile trade route that connected Santa Fe with the Missouri River. The well-traveled track did not make the Colorado volunteers' progress easier. Before reaching Fort Union, the men had to struggle over Raton Pass, 7,834 feet high, on the eastern side of the Sangre de Cristo Mountains. As they descended the pass during the late afternoon of March 9, a messenger, sent by an increasingly frantic Colonel Paul, informed Slough that the Texans had captured Albuquerque and Santa Fe. Paul pressed the Coloradans to hasten their march as he expected the Texans to appear before Fort Union any day.[9]

Years after the war's end, Chivington recalled that upon reading Paul's urgent plea for help, Slough boarded a conveniently available mail coach en route to Fort Union, leaving his major to rally the troops for more days of hard marching. Chivington assembled the ranks after a quick evening meal, informed them about the fort's dire circumstances, and asked all men willing to march through the night to step two paces forward. Every soldier volunteered. Leaving behind everything except four days' rations, their arms, and their blankets, the regiment rapidly departed for Fort Union.[10]

Whether quelling Company I's mutiny or mobilizing the men for another forced march, Chivington gave himself a central and heroic role in his postwar reminiscences. Contemporary accounts by Pvts. Ovando Hollister and Charles Gardiner failed to mention the major's dramatic appeal to save Fort Union. Neither man recalled Chivington asking for volunteers to step "two paces forward." Gardiner, in a letter he wrote to his mother in May 1862, grumbled that the troops "were ordered to report in *one* hour, for a *force march*, with four days 'grub' and one Blanket." Hollister simply stated that the men "proceeded with all possible and impossible speed" toward Fort

Union after Slough received "some jumbled intelligence" about the Texans' advance. He described his comrades' willingness to march through the night as other than voluntary, saying that they cursed and complained that "there was no call for it but the Colonel's caprice." Regardless, the men tramped eighty miles in forty-eight hours to reach their destination.[11]

No doubt the 1st Colorado's march from Camp Weld to Fort Union had an epic quality. The volunteers walked three hundred miles in two and a half weeks; they covered almost half of the distance in the forced marches of the final few days. Lacking adequate provisions and transportation when they left Denver, the men had to appropriate food, horses, and mules from the ranchers and farmers along their route. Twice the men discarded superfluous clothing and equipment in order to hasten their pace; by the last two days, with their exhausted horses and mules dying in their harnesses, the men had to abandon many of their wagons. They endured snow and bitter cold early in the expedition, the precipitous climb over Raton Pass, and a "furious windstorm, a mountain hurricane" during the last thirty miles of hard marching. Yet the men, many of whom blamed their colonel for these hardships, met every challenge in their race against Sibley's Texans. Their determination to reach Fort Union before the rebels turned the tables on the confident Sibley, forcing him to react to the 1st Colorado instead of capturing the undermanned Fort Union on his own schedule.[12]

The Coloradans' objective, located 110 miles northeast of Santa Fe, was a "simple field-work of moderate size" with dirt walls and projecting artillery bastions at each corner. Company F, the regiment's only mounted unit, arrived at Fort Union around dusk on March 11; the remainder of the regiment straggled in well after dark. Colonel Paul and his eight-hundred-man garrison must have been relieved to see the Coloradans, yet apparently no preparations had been made to feed or accommodate them. Some of the men broke into the sutler's store, owned by a German named Spiegelberg, and carried off champagne, cheese, and crackers. Others had no food, but were given "rot gut" whisky to fend off the cold.[13]

Fort Union's ample stores were eventually distributed to the hungry, shoddily clad, and poorly armed Coloradans, but Gilpin's Pet Lambs saw no reason to forgo stealing, drinking, and brawling while they remained at the fort. The men's drunkenness sometimes led to violence. When Lt. Issa Gray attempted to disperse several intoxicated enlisted men and noncommissioned officers from Company K, Sgt. Darius Philbrook challenged Gray's authority and shot the lieutenant several times as Gray attempted to arrest him. Although the wounded officer survived, Philbrook was arrested, court-martialed, and executed, a sentence that Chivington lamented as "a very hard fate" for a "fine soldier."[14]

Despite the regiment's drunkenness and thievery, the regular army officers and men stationed at Fort Union welcomed the Colorado volunteers and their colonel. A correspondent to the *Rocky Mountain News* reported that Slough "stands well" with the fort's officers. He did not fare well with the fort's commander, Colonel Paul. Slough quickly rankled Paul, insisting that he outranked the veteran soldier because his commission as colonel preceded Paul's commission by four months. Paul was chagrined by Slough's audacity. An 1834 graduate of West Point, a veteran of the Seminole and US-Mexican Wars, and an experienced army officer, he now had to yield command to an untested Denver lawyer on the eve of battle. Paul promptly dashed off a protest to the army's adjutant general in Washington, DC. "I had the mortification," he wrote on March 11, the day Slough arrived at Fort Union, "to discover that his commission was senior to mine and thus I am deprived of a command which I had taken so much pains to organize and with which I expected to reap laurels. An officer of only six months' service, and without experience, takes precedence over one of many years' service, and who has been frequently in battle." Paul's complaint went nowhere. Slough and his troops left Fort Union in search of rebels before the War Department had an opportunity to respond.[15]

Although Canby clearly instructed Paul to remain at Fort Union until further orders, the commander of the Department of New Mexico sent Slough more ambiguous instructions. Canby wrote the 1st Colorado's colonel, "If you have been joined by a sufficient force to act independently against the enemy, advise me of your plans and movements, that I may cooperate. In this you must be guided by your own judgment and discretion, but nothing must be left to chance." Canby also advised Slough to "harass the enemy by partisan operations. . . . Obstruct his movements and cut off his supplies." Slough chose to interpret Canby's orders liberally. Guided by his own "judgment and discretion," he concluded that he had latitude to move against the Texans.[16]

On March 22 and March 23, Slough and 1,342 men left Fort Union. The force included the 1st Colorado plus a sizable proportion of the infantry and cavalry already at Fort Union when Slough and his men arrived. Most damaging to the fort's defenses, Slough ordered the outpost's two batteries, totaling eight guns, to accompany the expedition. It was more than enough force to "harass the enemy by partisan operations."[17]

Several explanations can be offered for Slough's bold move. It may have been his arrogance and ambition that caused him to ignore Canby's admonition to leave nothing to chance. Perhaps he left Fort Union's safety to disprove "Union's" charge of cowardice. He may have reasoned that the topographical advantages of northern New Mexico's mountains, valleys, and passes provided opportunities to harry the rebels and obstruct their advance, thereby offering better protection for Fort Union than allowing the Texans to approach its questionable defenses. Whatever his rationale, he decided to leave a minimum garrison at the fort and take almost all the federal forces forty-five miles south to Bernal Springs. There, as he explained in a note to Paul on March 22, the federal troops could block any Confederate advance on Fort Union while "harassing the enemy and protecting Santa Fe from depredation."[18]

In Paul's eyes, Slough had willfully disobeyed Canby's orders, especially the commanding officer's direction to leave a "reliable garrison" at Fort Union. On March 24, Paul again wrote the War Department to protest Slough's decision to strip Fort Union of both infantry and artillery and to ignore Canby's March 16 order to Paul to remain at the fort until further instructions. He enclosed five pieces of correspondence, including Canby's March 16 order as well as his own pleas to Slough to leave a sufficient force at Fort Union. Paul justified his action by writing, "My object in this communication is to throw responsibility of any disaster which may occur on the right shoulders." Fort Union's commander was not going to let any upstart volunteer colonel ruin his reputation in the event of a military reversal.[19]

With Slough and the Coloradans in northern New Mexico, Sibley realized that his brigade could no longer tarry in Albuquerque; the Confederates had to attack before Slough and Canby united their commands. Sibley decided to divide the Confederate Army of New Mexico into three parts, each leaving Albuquerque by a different route for northern New Mexico. The three contingents would eventually rendezvous just below Las Vegas, New Mexico, where the Santa Fe Trail turned north toward Fort Union. Col. Tom Green's detachment took the southernmost road toward Anton

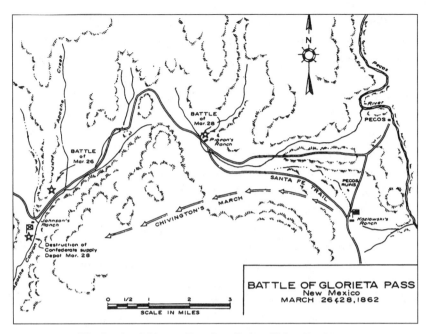

The Battle of Glorieta Pass from Robert Utley, *Fort Union National Monument, New Mexico*, National Park Service Historical Handbook Series No. 35, 1962.

Chico; Green may have had the assignment of falling back to Albuquerque should Colonel Canby bring the Fort Craig garrison up the Rio Grande valley. The largest contingent, under Lt. Col. William "Dirty Shirt" Scurry, followed the military road north from Albuquerque to Galisteo. The third unit, under Maj. Charles Pyron, swung northeast to Santa Fe and then east along the Santa Fe Trail.[20]

The evening of March 25, Pyron and his Confederates stopped at Johnson's Ranch on the western edge of Glorieta Pass. Pyron did not know that an advance force under Maj. John Chivington, sent by Slough to reconnoiter the Santa Fe Trail, was camped at Kozlowski's Ranch, only eleven miles away. Seven miles northwest of Kozlowski's Ranch and two miles from a major stagecoach stop known as Pigeon's Ranch, the Santa Fe Trail reached the summit of Glorieta Pass. The road then dropped south and southwestward through Apache Canyon, "a small valley of cultivated fields" before reaching Johnson's Ranch, where Pyron's Texans shivered around their fires.[21]

In the early hours of March 26, Pyron sent four mounted scouts east to search for Union troops before he and his command continued their advance. The scouts, members of a unit colorfully named "The Brigands," passed through Pigeon's Ranch well before sunrise. Chivington also sent scouts westward from his encampment at Kozlowski's Ranch. Somehow in the dark along the Santa Fe Trail, the twenty federal troopers missed the four rebel scouts. When Chivington's men reached Pigeon's Ranch, its proprietor, Alexander Valle, told them that rebel scouts had already passed through the stagecoach stop. The twenty troopers turned around, retraced their steps, and quickly took the unaware rebels prisoner. Chivington now knew what Pyron did not; the enemy was only a few miles away.[22]

Around 10:00 a.m., Chivington and his troops set out from Kozlowski's Ranch determined to engage the Texans. Meanwhile, Pyron, concerned that his four scouts had not returned to camp, ordered a party of thirty troopers with two artillery pieces to ride in search of either the missing scouts or the enemy. It was these thirty Confederate troopers who ran headlong into Chivington's column at the northeastern end of Apache Canyon. The rest of Pyron's command was not far behind and quickly engaged the Yankees.

The two forces numbered about four hundred men each. Pyron had the advantage of two six-pounder guns; he also had "veterans" who had fought the month previously at Valverde. Most of the federal troops were untested in battle. Nonetheless, Chivington assumed the offensive. He followed the same plan throughout the day's fight at Apache Canyon, sending infantry up the sides of the canyon in an attempt to flank the Texans while using his cavalry to charge the rebel center.[23]

The federals' first attempt to break the Confederate line was unsuccessful, in great part because the officer commanding the cavalry failed to order the charge. But the Colorado volunteers assigned to pressure the Confederate left and right flanks succeeded in forcing Pyron to withdraw his forces deeper into Apache Canyon. Chivington now turned to the 1st Colorado's Company F, the only mounted infantry in the regiment, to strike the Confederate center a second time. In a fierce fight at extremely close range, Company F overran the rebels, "trampling them under the horses' feet," and drove them backwards to a narrow defile at the southwestern edge of Apache Canyon. Nightfall rescued the rebels from another Yankee attack. Worried that Confederate reinforcements might be nearby, Chivington ordered his men to gather up the Union dead and wounded and fall back to Pigeon's Ranch. With the Yankees' withdrawal, Pyron ordered his men to return to Johnson's Ranch.[24]

The opposing sides spent March 27 awaiting reinforcements. Lieutenant Colonel Scurry's Texans arrived first. Having learned the evening of March 26 that Pyron's detachment was engaged, Scurry rallied his men for an exhausting night march from Galisteo. They stumbled into Johnson's Ranch around 3:00 a.m. the next morning. Scurry ordered his men to form a defensive line to repel the Union attack he expected later that day.[25]

Chivington also sent couriers to alert his commanding officer about the fight at Apache Canyon. Slough and the remainder of the federal force left Bernal Springs mid-morning on March 27 and reunited with Chivington's force at Kozlowski's Ranch between 2:00 and 3:00 a.m. on March 28. Although the federals had marched thirty-four miles in eighteen hours, Slough gathered his key officers in the predawn hours. They were cold and exhausted but nonetheless had to plan the battle they anticipated later that day. They decided that Slough would lead the main column through Glorieta Pass to attack the Confederates head-on at Johnson's Ranch. At the same time, Chivington would take a strong detachment across Glorieta Mesa, which bordered Glorieta Pass, to fall on the enemy's flank or rear, squeezing the rebels between the two federal forces.[26]

It was a foolhardy plan, extremely difficult to execute for untried officers in unknown territory and with no means of communication. With the Union forces split between Slough and Chivington, Scurry could use his superior numbers to overwhelm one force, then the other. In that event, Colonel Paul's worst fears would come to pass. Slough's inexperience would sacrifice the Union army in northern New Mexico and lead to the fall of Fort Union.

Around 8:30 a.m. on March 28, Slough and his command departed Kozlowski's Ranch for Glorieta Pass. Just two miles beyond the ranch, Chivington's 488-man detachment turned southwest on the Galisteo Road to cross Glorieta Mesa. The rest of the Union column quickly covered the five miles to Pigeon's Ranch. There, orders were given to fall out, stack arms, and fill canteens as the men would have no access to water along the Santa Fe Trail.

Scurry did not intend to wait any longer at Johnson's Ranch for a Yankee attack. Leaving his supply train guarded mostly by teamsters and wounded men, he led more than 1,200 Texans eastward on the Santa Fe Trail around the same time that the federals set forth from Kozlowski's Ranch. Sometime after 10:30 a.m., they pulled up in thickets to the west of Pigeon's Ranch and watched the Yankees lounging and chatting among themselves less than a mile away.[27]

Unaware of the rebels' presence, the federal column would have stumbled upon the Confederate line with disastrous consequences once they resumed their march. Fortunately, as his troops rested and refilled their canteens, Slough sent a detachment of cavalry under Captains Walker and Chapin to reconnoiter the terrain west of Pigeon's Ranch. Looking down the Santa Fe Trail, the two officers caught a glimpse of Scurry's artillery. Walker ordered his troopers to dismount and deploy as skirmishers while Chapin rode back to Pigeon's Ranch to warn Slough. Soon, the 1st Colorado's Company C along with a four-gun battery arrived in support of Walker's cavalrymen. Shots were briefly exchanged and then both sides disengaged to allow their commanders to assess the situation.[28]

Slough did not know how many Confederates his eight hundred men faced, but he guessed that his troops were outnumbered. As a result, he decided to fight defensively, taking advantage of the terrain afforded by the narrow valley that sheltered Pigeon's Ranch. Canyon wall to canyon wall was less than a mile and at times only a few hundred yards. Pines, piñon, and juniper thickly covered the ground that rose to a prominent rocky ridge on the north side of the valley. To the south, land climbed precipitously to the flat top of Glorieta Mesa. Slough chose his positions well. Throughout the day's fight, he used elevations on either side of the valley to help secure his flanks. In the center of his line, he placed one, and sometimes both of his four-gun batteries.[29]

Scurry chose to concentrate on the Union left during the first phase of the battle. While his three guns engaged the Union artillery in a counterbattery duel, Scurry reinforced his right, extending his line in an effort to outflank the federal left. The Yankees responded by slowly falling back as the weight of the Confederate numbers pressed on their line. Finally, on Slough's orders, the federal soldiers retired into the wooded slopes behind them, retreating up and over the prominence known today as Windmill Hill to take a new position in front of Pigeon's Ranch.[30]

On the Union right, a bold move led by Lt. Charles Kerber—the same lieutenant who had stared down Slough's revolver in the dispute over Company I's baggage wagons—threatened the Confederate left. Kerber noticed that a deep arroyo running perpendicular to the rebel line might afford his men cover to sneak behind the Texans. He directed his company to move stealthily along the gully toward the enemy line, but before they accomplished their objective, Confederate soldiers spotted them. Scurry responded by throwing two companies from the Fourth Texas against the single Yankee company. The Confederate numbers, along with the disadvantage of being trapped in the arroyo, meant that the men of Company I had to fight desperately to extricate themselves. Kerber's attempt to turn the rebel flank cost his company fifteen men killed, nineteen wounded, and five captured in only a half hour of vicious hand-to-hand fighting.[31]

Slough knew by early afternoon that his men were battling a larger force, although he expected Chivington's detachment to fall on the Confederate southern flank or rear at any moment. Around 2:00 p.m., he established a new defensive position just to the west of Pigeon's Ranch. The Union line took the shape of a fishhook, its eye anchored on a rough ledge of rocks to the north of Pigeon's Ranch, its shank deployed in front of the ranch, and its hook bending around the wooded and rocky Artillery Hill to the south. It was a strong position, especially because Slough could shelter artillery and supporting infantry behind an adobe wall in the Union center.[32]

Scurry decided to concentrate his attack against the federal battery behind the adobe wall. It was the tactic that won the day at Valverde and Scurry expected it to succeed again. About 3:00 p.m., the rebel center rose and, screaming from the tension and excitement of battle, rushed across the four hundred yards separating the two opposing lines. Twice the Texans crashed against the adobe wall and each time were repulsed by the canister and heavy rifle fire laid down by the Yankees on its other side.[33]

The Confederates had no better success assaulting the Union left on Artillery Hill. But on the Union right, the Texans slowly pushed back the remnants of Company I along with the handful of troops Slough risked sending to shore up his flank. By 4:00 p.m., the Confederates gained a vantage point just above Pigeon's Ranch, which enabled them to fire into the infantry and artillerymen gathered behind the adobe wall. The rebels began to kill or wound the Yankees below them. Sensing that the Union center was wavering under this fire, Scurry launched his final assault against the adobe wall.[34]

Capt. John Ritter and Lt. Ira Claflin, the commanders of the federal batteries behind the adobe wall, watched as the Texans above their position picked off their men and horses. Fearing that the new rebel charge now closing on the adobe wall would overrun their guns if they remained any longer, Ritter and Claflin ordered their artillerymen to limber up and fall back. The two Union batteries' withdrawal rendered the federal line untenable. Slough ordered his troops to retire three-quarters of a mile to the east of Pigeon's Ranch to form a third defensive line. The rebels halfheartedly tested the Yankee position but Scurry, realizing that his men were exhausted and night would fall soon, called off the attack. The day's fighting at Pigeon's Ranch ended with the Texans in charge of the field of battle.[35]

It was apparently another Confederate victory, although Slough's outnumbered men still blocked the road to Fort Union. That evening, Slough must have wondered what happened to Chivington and his detachment. He had ordered the major to attack the Confederate rear or flank once his troops got behind the rebel force. Instead, Chivington's men had fallen upon the Confederate supply train at Johnson's Ranch. Guided across Glorieta Mesa by Lt. Col. Manuel Chavez of the 2nd New Mexico Volunteers, the federals arrived at the escarpment above Johnson's Ranch in the early afternoon of March 28. Chivington carefully assessed the Confederate encampment below him before ordering his troops down the steep cliffs to attack the supply train. The Yankees quickly overwhelmed the supply train's surprised guard and spent the remainder of the afternoon destroying everything—supplies, wagons, horses, and mules—that the Confederates had left behind. Scurry could not pursue battle the next day without ammunition, powder, food, blankets, or medical supplies. So thorough was the destruction of the Confederate supply train that the rebels had to borrow shovels from the Union burial party to bury their own dead. It was a loss that completely undermined Scurry's success at Pigeon's Ranch and forced the Texans to return to Santa Fe.[36]

The havoc that Chivington's men wreaked at Johnson's Ranch turned the major into the hero of Glorieta Pass. Yet Chivington had disregarded Slough's order to attack the Confederate rear. He knew that Slough's force had engaged the Texans. He had heard the sound of battle in late morning while crossing Glorieta Mesa. By mid-afternoon, after his men had overrun the Confederate encampment at Johnson's Ranch, he had certain knowledge of Slough's predicament from federal soldiers captured during the late morning fight and sent under guard to Johnson's Ranch. A few hours later, a courier dispatched by Slough informed the major that "immediate aid" was needed and ordered him to "advance to support the main column."[37]

Even though he knew the Union troops under Slough were struggling against the numerically superior Texans, Chivington made no effort to support his superior officer. Instead, he allowed his men to remain in the vicinity of Johnson's Ranch for at least three hours during the afternoon of March 28. There seemed to be no sense of urgency to complete the destruction of the Confederate supply train and to hurry to Slough's aid. Finally, as dusk was falling, Chivington ordered his men to climb the cliffs surrounding Johnson's Ranch and cross over Glorieta Mesa to rejoin their comrades late that night.[38]

For "Union," the "gallant" Chivington was the true victor of Glorieta Pass. In a dispatch written to the *Rocky Mountain News* more than a month after the battle, "Union" claimed that Chivington would have easily led the regiment to victory over the "terrible Texans." Slough, on the other hand, allowed his force to be surprised when he permitted the men to fill their canteens at Pigeon's Ranch. The sudden appearance of the rebels caused Slough to lose his "equilibrium," requiring Tappan to organize the defense. "Union" repeated the charge of cowardice he had leveled against Slough in early February. The pseudonymous writer alleged that at the height of the battle, when the Coloradans struggled to repulse the Texans, the regiment's colonel "was so far in the rear that orders could not be obtained from him." Indeed, Slough's "coward heart blanched before the storm, and seeking protection from a stalwart pine, far, *far* in the rear of his command . . . there remained until the battle had been fought and won." It was another vicious attack on Slough.[39]

"Union" had no interest in providing an impartial account of the battle, only in ruining Slough's reputation. In fact, Slough did well commanding his outnumbered troops. He never panicked despite facing a considerably larger force. He assessed the tactical situation accurately shortly after the battle began and effectively positioned his men in strong defensive lines throughout the day. Even locating his command post on Sharpshooters Ridge, a decision that "Union" considered spineless, demonstrated sound sense because it provided an excellent vantage point over much of the Union line. His tactical skill prevented the Texans from overrunning his men and, coupled with Chivington's fortuitous capture of the Confederate supply train, stopped the Confederate advance to Fort Union. As Capt. Richard Sopris wrote after the battle, "We have saved this Territory and perhaps Colorado by coming here. Colonel Slough deserves a great deal of credit for our success."[40]

Slough did not command the 1st Colorado much longer. The night after the battle at Pigeon's Ranch, he decided he had achieved the objective of harassing the enemy and ordered his men to return to Kozlowski's Ranch. The next day, March 29, Capt. William Nicodemus rode into Kozlowski's Ranch and presented Slough with Canby's unequivocal order to return to Fort Union. Despite the desire of Slough's officers and men to pursue the rebels, now without sufficient ammunition to wage battle, the 1st Colorado's commander had no choice but to obey.[41]

When the federal troops arrived in Bernal Springs on March 31, Slough unexpectedly announced his intention to resign as colonel of the Colorado volunteers. Ovando Hollister believed that Canby's instructions to return to Fort Union gave the 1st Colorado's colonel no option but to step aside. As Hollister saw it, Slough's resignation was the "necessary consequence" of an order that Hollister considered a "disgrace to obey" because it prevented the federal troops at Kozlowski's Ranch from completely destroying the Texans. Slough was "incensed" about Canby's unnecessarily cautious approach to protecting Fort Union and concluded that he could not serve under the conservative career officer. Driven by his impetuous nature, Slough decided that resignation was his only recourse.[42]

Historians have argued that Slough resigned not because he was angry that Canby reined in his command but because he feared that his superior might censure or even court-martial him. He had left Fort Union on March 22 stripped of its men and artillery despite Canby's instructions to "leave nothing to chance" in defending the fort. Although his troops had upended the Confederate plan to capture Fort Union, Slough may have worried that Canby would still blame him for leaving the fort without a "reliable garrison." The overly cautious commander of the Department of New Mexico might resolve to discipline the 1st Colorado's colonel for his liberal interpretation of orders. Slough had been disgraced when he lost his seat in the Ohio legislature. He may have reasoned that resigning his command would forestall censure or court-martial and prevent another personal humiliation.[43]

Slough's ambition cannot be overlooked as a factor in his resignation. Two brief comments from contemporary newspapers suggest this possibility. A loyal New Orleans newspaper, the *Daily Delta*, reported on June 19, 1862, that Slough had resigned his command because there was "no prospect of anything more active than garrison duty in that quarter." A similar notice in the *Cincinnati Daily Enquirer* claimed that with the 1st Colorado's posting to Fort Craig, "such a life [would be] too inactive to suit [Slough]." For an ambitious man, anxious to rise in the wartime army, duty on the frontier would have been intolerable. Slough understood that returning east held much greater promise for advancement than remaining at a dusty territorial fort.[44]

The most astonishing explanation for Slough's abrupt resignation—the one that he offered—was his fear that his own soldiers would kill him. "Union" reported a rumor to the *Rocky Mountain News* that Slough resigned because his men fired at him during the battle at Pigeon's Ranch. Almost a year later, Slough confirmed the rumor in a letter to Samuel Tappan. Tappan wrote Slough on December 28, 1862, asking his old colonel if he was aware that soldiers had plotted to kill him during the harsh march over Raton Pass. Slough replied that he did not doubt the truth of Tappan's story. He admitted that friends in Denver warned him about threats to assassinate him. He also said that one of the 1st Colorado's companies fired a volley at him during the Pigeon's Ranch engagement. "I resigned the Colonelcy," Slough wrote Tappan, "because I was satisfied that a further connection would result in my assassination." He added that he believed that men "high in rank and command"—in other words, Maj. John Chivington—had instigated the plot to kill him.[45]

One historian of the New Mexico campaign claims that men from Company I, still smoldering over the baggage wagon dispute, fired at Slough after their bloody fight in the arroyo. But Company I was positioned in the wooded and rocky slopes above Pigeon's Ranch during this stage of the battle and would not have had a clear shot at Slough on Sharpshooters Ridge. Slough may have believed that an errant volley during the confusion of battle was directed at him. More likely, he decided that a tale of attempted assassination was a more honorable explanation for his resignation than ambition or disgust with Canby or fear of court-martial. All these emotions probably played in Slough's decision.[46]

His withdrawal from command paved the way for Chivington's promotion. On April 13, 1862, the 1st Colorado's officers and men petitioned Colonel Canby to commission Chivington as the regiment's commander. Canby agreed and advanced him over Lieutenant Colonel Tappan. Capt.

Ned Wynkoop, the officer who drafted the petition requesting that Slough order the 1st Colorado to New Mexico, replaced Chivington as the regiment's major. Capt. Jacob Downing was promoted to major in November 1862.[47]

Canby finally ventured north from Fort Craig on April 1, uniting with Chivington and his men thirteen days later at Carnuel Cañon, fifteen miles east of Albuquerque. The combined Union force totaled 2,400 men. The Confederate Army of New Mexico had evacuated Albuquerque the day before Canby and Chivington joined forces. The rebels had only ten days' rations in the Albuquerque depot and almost no ammunition; Brigadier General Sibley understood that his depleted brigade would be no match for the federal soldiers marching from both the north and the south. Retreat to the safety of Texas was his only option. By mid-July 1862, remnants of Sibley's brigade arrived in San Antonio, Texas, where they had embarked nine months earlier on their calamitous invasion of New Mexico Territory.[48]

John Slough had left Colorado Territory two months earlier. The *Rocky Mountain News* reported that the volunteer military officer, newly returned to civilian life, left Denver by stagecoach on May 6, 1862. Slough's military career was not over. He had been successful fighting Sibley's Texans in northern New Mexico. Now he headed east, where, with a new commission, he would face a more formidable opponent: Stonewall Jackson's Virginians.[49]

Part IV

VIRGINIA

10

####### ∞∞∞∞∞

The Defense of Harpers Ferry

JUST THREE WEEKS AFTER HE LEFT DENVER, BOUND FOR CINCINNATI and apparently a civilian's life, John Slough re-entered the war in Virginia as a brigadier general. Despite Maj. John Chivington's plotting to oust him from command, Col. Gabriel Paul's anger at his insistence that he outranked the veteran officer, and Col. Edward Canby's displeasure that he left Fort Union undermanned, the War Department saw fit to promote Slough and ordered him to Harpers Ferry, Virginia.

How Slough obtained his brigadier's star is unknown. Perhaps Arabella Slough resorted to her family's influence in Washington. Secretary of War Edwin Stanton had cultivated the friendship of United States Supreme Court justice John McLean during the 1850s, and although McLean died in 1861, Arabella may have used her uncle's name to push her husband's advancement. The *Rocky Mountain News* implied Arabella's involvement with its observation about Slough's promotion: "One of the stepping stones to fame and fortune now-a-days is to get married into a distinguished family." Intending to belittle the former colonel of the 1st Colorado, the *News*'s imputation that Slough's promotion depended on his wife's connections was likely the truth.[1]

Slough arrived in Harpers Ferry on May 28, 1862, amid frantic preparations for an expected attack. For three days, trains had been disgorging troops that the War Department rushed to the town's defense. Assured by Stanton that Slough was "a bold and able assistant," Slough's superior, Gen. Rufus Saxton, placed him in command of a newly organized brigade and ordered him to ready his troops for battle. Saxton knew there was no time to waste. The enemy was less than a day's march away.[2]

A small Confederate army, under the command of Maj. Gen. Thomas J.

"Stonewall" Jackson, had caused the frenzied reaction in Harpers Ferry. Since the beginning of May, Jackson's troops had conducted a seemingly miraculous campaign in the Shenandoah Valley. They had gone on the offensive to prevent thirty-five thousand Union soldiers under Gens. John C. Frémont and Nathaniel Banks from joining the Army of the Potomac's drive to capture the Confederate capital, Richmond. After a hard-won victory over a portion of Frémont's army at McDowell, Virginia, Jackson turned his army's attention toward his other adversary, Nathaniel Banks. The Union commander had advanced deep into the Shenandoah Valley in pursuit of Jackson, but found his army vulnerable with the transfer of one of his divisions to Maj. Gen. Irwin McDowell's Army of the Rappahannock. Banks withdrew his remaining troops to a more defensible position, he believed, in Strasburg, Virginia. Jackson's "foot cavalry" followed. Screened by the massive Massanutten Mountain, the Confederate infantry raced down the Luray Valley and overwhelmed the federal garrison at Front Royal on May 23. Only twelve miles lay between them and Banks's depleted force at Strasburg.

Banks refused to believe that the rebel army had traveled so far and so fast, but as his headquarters received repeated reports of the setback at Front Royal, he finally grasped that the elusive Jackson was close at hand. In order to avoid disaster from an enemy on his flank, he decided to withdraw his army posthaste down the valley to Winchester. The retreat afforded Banks and his men little safety. On May 24, Jackson's cavalry smashed the Union rear guard and wreaked havoc on a portion of Banks's wagon train. The next day at Winchester, the larger Confederate army turned Banks's right flank, broke the Union line, and forced the Yankees to flee pell-mell northward across the Potomac River into Maryland. Suddenly Maryland, Pennsylvania, and Washington, DC, appeared threatened.[3]

Even before the rout at Winchester, the War Department grasped that the weak federal garrison at Harpers Ferry left Maryland and Pennsylvania open to invasion and the nation's capital exposed to attack. On May 24, the day that Banks's army fled Strasburg for Winchester, Secretary of War Stanton ordered Brig. Gen. Rufus Saxton to assume command at Harpers Ferry. He discovered a garrison of 2,500 to 3,000 men "in a state of great demoralization," five companies of cavalry in "shocking condition," and no artillery whatsoever. It was a force totally ill-prepared to resist the advance of Jackson's

Brig. Gen. Rufus Saxton successfully defended Harpers Ferry against Thomas J. "Stonewall" Jackson's Valley Army in late May 1862. The town's defense was Slough's only combat experience as a brigadier general. Source: Library of Congress Prints and Photographs Division, LC-DIG-cwpb-06589.

battle-hardened veterans. Frantic, Saxton telegraphed the War Department for reinforcements. During the next few days, Stanton dispatched troops and two brigadier generals, James Cooper and John Slough, to Saxton's aid.[4]

The three generals had a formidable task protecting Harpers Ferry and slowing Jackson's advance. The town nestles on a point between the confluence of the Potomac and Shenandoah Rivers in western Virginia (now West Virginia). Directly across the Potomac in Maryland rises 1,300-foot Maryland Heights; if Confederate artillerists captured the heights, they could use the prominence to bombard Harpers Ferry mercilessly. To the southeast, on the other side of the Shenandoah, stands Louden Heights, a ridge as imposing as Maryland Heights. A third elevation, known as Bolivar Heights, marked the western outskirts of 1862 Harpers Ferry. Garrisons charged with defending the town could fortify Bolivar Heights, but if the defense went poorly, the soldiers would find themselves pushed into the town with the Potomac and the Shenandoah at their backs.[5]

Saxton, an 1849 graduate of West Point who taught artillery tactics at the Academy, understood that the successful defense of Harpers Ferry depended on securing the high ground with cannon. After sending the War Department several telegrams begging for artillery, he received two batteries of light artillery as well as three heavy Dahlgren guns from the Washington Navy Yard. He located the heavy guns, one weighing five tons, midway up Maryland Heights and named the emplacement "Battery Stanton" in honor of the secretary of war. Situated high over Harpers Ferry, the battery could fire shells accurately over a mile and command the approaches to the town.[6]

The artillery's arrival in Harpers Ferry occurred not a day too soon. Two days after the Confederates sent Banks's division fleeing from Winchester, the Richmond War Department ordered General Jackson to "demonstrate" against Harpers Ferry, an action that would signal to federal officials Jackson's intention of turning his army toward Washington, Baltimore, and Philadelphia. Jackson ordered his old brigade, now commanded by Brig. Gen. Charles S. Winder, to march to Charlestown, Virginia. Early on May 28, the Stonewall Brigade left Winchester for Charlestown. From there, the Confederates could march to Harpers Ferry in a few hours.[7]

The previous evening, two companies of the 1st Maryland Cavalry (federal) tangled with a few rebel horsemen on Louden Heights. Suspecting that Jackson's forces were converging on Harpers Ferry, Saxton ordered a reconnaissance in force toward Charlestown on May 28. The Union troops entered Charlestown without opposition, but after passing through the village, they encountered Winder's Stonewall Brigade approaching from the southwest. Two Union cannon opened on the rebels. Winder's battery returned the Yankee fire, and after a ten-minute bombardment, the nervous and untested federal troops broke ranks and ran "in great disorder, throwing away arms, blankets, haversacks, etc." The Confederates chased the retreating Yankees almost to Harpers Ferry, but Winder called off the pursuit when he realized that a large number of Yankees were entrenched on Bolivar Heights. From the Union lines, Saxton could see "clouds of dust in various directions" and knew that a rebel force of considerable size—perhaps Jackson's entire army—had arrived.[8]

Jackson, along with most of his Valley Army, joined the Stonewall Brigade outside Harpers Ferry on May 29. He decided to toy with the federals defending the town, believing that the rebels' appearance might frighten the Yankees into abandoning their positions for the safety of Maryland.

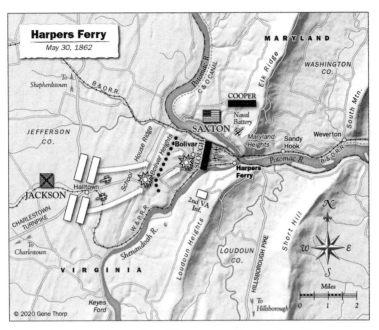

Attack on Harpers Ferry, May 30, 1862. Map by Gene Thorp.
Source: Courtesy of Cartographic Concepts, Inc.

When the Confederate commander sent the 2nd Virginia to occupy Louden Heights, Saxton realized that if the rebels also captured Maryland Heights, they could turn the guns of Battery Stanton on the helpless Yankee forces strung between the Potomac and the Shenandoah. Saxton decided to abandon his trenches on Bolivar Heights. He sent Slough's brigade to Camp Hill, three-quarters of a mile to the east of Bolivar Heights, while ordering Cooper's brigade to protect Battery Stanton on Maryland Heights. Saxton's decision to withdraw to Camp Hill significantly shortened his defensive line while enabling Battery Stanton to shell any troops approaching Camp Hill from Bolivar Heights. By Friday morning, May 30, the new Union line was established.[9]

The mere presence of the rebels unnerved some of the Union troops. Col. William Maulsby's Maryland Home Guard had been ordered to watch over the commissary and quartermaster stores in Harpers Ferry. When Saxton ordered the troops on Bolivar Heights to withdraw to Camp Hill, the Marylanders feared the worst. Believing that the Union force was in retreat, they decided that their responsibility as Home Guards was to protect Maryland, and they fled Harpers Ferry for their home state.[10]

Unlike Maulsby and his hapless Home Guards, Slough quickly exerted control over his brigade. He had commanded troops in battle, an experience that Brigadier General Cooper did not share and that earned Slough the "post of honor" on Camp Hill. Saxton believed that Jackson would attack Camp Hill on May 30 and entrusted the newly minted brigadier with the Union's key defensive position. Any rebel attempt to take Harpers Ferry and rout the federal forces would have to go through Slough's brigade.[11]

Long after dark on May 30, Confederate infantry climbed across Bolivar Heights and halted in a ravine three hundred yards from Camp Hill. A ferocious thunderstorm erupted as they waited for the order to attack. The scene must have been dramatic. Saxton recalled that "vivid flashes of lightning illuminated at intervals the grand and magnificent scenery" and peals of thunder drowned out the roar of cannon. While Battery Stanton lobbed shells at the Confederates awaiting the order to attack, Slough's men used the flashes of lightning to fire on anything that moved outside their trenches. The rebels never charged, withdrawing after an hour. The next morning, a Union reconnaissance discovered that they had abandoned the area altogether.[12]

Jackson probably never intended to assault Camp Hill. He had learned a few days earlier that a portion of Irwin McDowell's Army of the Rappahannock had moved westward toward the Shenandoah Valley, while John C. Frémont's troops had entered it at New Market, Virginia. Jackson abandoned Harpers Ferry to confront the federal forces rushing to trap his army. Aided by Maj. Gen. Richard Ewell's division, Jackson defeated Frémont and Brig. Gen. James Shields's forces at the battles of Cross Keys and Port Republic on June 8 and 9, 1862. Ten days later, Jackson's troops ended their illustrious Valley Campaign, joining Lee's Army of Northern Virginia for the Seven Days battles that drove the Army of the Potomac away from Richmond.

With Jackson gone, Saxton asked to be relieved of his command. Maj. Gen. Franz Sigel replaced him on June 1. Slough continued to lead his brigade, consisting of about 2,700 men from New York, Maryland, Delaware, and the District of Columbia. Three days after assuming command, Sigel ordered him to move his brigade to Winchester. Slough and his men remained there until June 17 when they marched to Middletown, Virginia. Slough's brigade saw no action in the weeks following their defense of Harpers Ferry.[13]

During this period, the *Cincinnati Daily Enquirer* reported favorably on an impromptu speech Slough gave after a regimental band serenaded him and General Sigel. Speaking before a crowd in Winchester that undoubtedly included secessionists, Slough seemed to advocate for peace—a position held by many Democrats during the war—until he reminded his audience that protecting the Constitution demanded commitment to the war effort. He thanked the band for their music, but advised them that the sweeter sounds of hearth and home could not be savored again "until the nation heard that sweetest word of all—'Peace.'" "Let us have the Union," he continued, "which has made us all that we are, all that we have been, and all that we hope to be. Peace, peace, peace was a great objective—an overpowering one, but the supremacy of the laws and the Constitution must be supported at all hazards and at all cost of blood and treasure." His words reflected his lifelong devotion to the Constitution and the rule of law and served as the strongest expression of his dedication to the Union cause.[14]

The newspapers also recounted an incident that reveals Slough's attitude about the appropriate relationship between white soldiers and enslaved Black people. General Sigel had noticed Winchester's filthy condition and ordered men from Slough's brigade to take shovels in hand to remove manure and offal from the city's streets. To the soldiers' annoyance, several Black people, "the property of secession residents [of Winchester]," watched them work. Slough objected that his men had to clean the streets when Black people could have been impressed to do the offensive task. That evening, he complained to Sigel about this "outrage on the rights of the common soldier." Slough believed that as Black people were best fit for the lower forms of labor, they should have cleaned the streets. How Sigel responded is unknown.[15]

On June 26, Lincoln combined the forces in western Virginia under Sigel, Banks, and McDowell into the Army of Virginia and named Maj. Gen. John Pope as its commander. Slough's brigade, still encamped outside of Middletown, was assigned to the new army's second corps, second division. His peer during the defense of Harpers Ferry, Brig. Gen. James Cooper, now led the second division. Cooper had been a Whig during the 1850s and John Pope, a staunch Republican, may have preferred Cooper's politics over Slough's well-known affiliation with the Democratic Party. More importantly, Cooper had received his brigadier's commission in May 1861, a full year before Slough became a brigadier. Whatever the reason for Cooper's promotion, the situation must have rankled the Cincinnatian. Slough believed that his performance at Glorieta Pass and Harpers Ferry trumped Cooper's seniority and that he should command the division. Unable to accept Cooper as his commanding officer, he asked to be relieved of duty on July 1.[16]

Choosing to resign a second time from field command was an ill-considered decision, one that likely limited Slough's advancement in the wartime army. If he had remained in the field, he might have burnished his reputation as a combat officer and won a division command. Both the War Department and General Saxton considered him a capable officer. Assistant secretary of war Peter Watson had wired Stanton on May 29 that "General Slough has made a favorable impression on us all," reassuring the secretary of war that he had been right to promote the unknown officer from Colorado Territory. General Saxton gave "great credit" to Slough and Cooper in his after-battle report for their "untiring exertions during the five days and night siege." Eastern newspapers also spoke favorably about Slough, mentioning his victory in New Mexico Territory whenever they reported his brigade's maneuvers in the Shenandoah Valley. The *Cleveland Daily Leader*'s correspondent praised him as "the man who marched the celebrated Colorado regiment eight hundred miles into New Mexico, and turned the tide of affairs in that territory." The *Sun* of New York reminded its readers that Slough forced the rebels out of New Mexico after "cutting his way through the Texan ranks." The *New York Times* concluded that the results of Slough's leadership at Pigeon's Ranch had been "to render the enemy without subsistence, demoralize and compel them to evacuate New-Mexico." In their accounts, Slough was the hero of Glorieta Pass.[17]

While the Eastern newspapers lavished praise on Slough, the *Rocky Mountain News* continued to malign the former colonel of the 1st Colorado Volunteers. On June 7, the *News* published Captain Downing's dispatch about the battle at Pigeon's Ranch in which Downing, writing as "Union," observed that Slough's "coward heart" caused him to seek shelter "*far, far* in the rear of his command." In July, the *News* repeated Downing's accusations of cowardice. An article titled "Gigadier Brindle Slough" questioned the *Philadelphia Press*'s assertion that Slough performed well in the Shenandoah Valley. It claimed that he had pulled the wool over the eyes of "Eastern people" because they considered him a "brave and efficient officer." To the contrary, "it is well authenticated that he acted the part of a coward in New Mexico, and his qualifications as an officer in camp are notoriously poor. . . . Like an ass with the lion's skin on, he cannot remain long concealed under the eye of the master, Sigel." A few weeks later the *News* again accused Slough of cowardice during the engagement at Pigeon's Ranch and complained about his decision to retreat at the end of the day's fighting. If General Sigel failed to see the mettle of Slough, the article's author concluded, it was because "the brush in the rear is too thick for the 'missing man' to be seen."[18]

The competition for promotion within the volunteer army lay behind the *Rocky Mountain News*'s attacks on John Slough. The path to a brigadier general's commission was narrow, especially for officers in the Far West, and the *News* willingly published derogatory articles about Slough in order to advance the career of its favorite, John Chivington. When Slough resigned as colonel of the 1st Colorado, the newspaper advocated for Chivington's elevation to the regiment's command, mocking Slough's second-in-command, Lt. Col. Samuel Tappan, as a "conceited popinjay," and eventually for Chivington's promotion to brigadier general. The *News* assured its readers that "The Colonel [Chivington] still remains the favorite of the Colorado Tigers, who, with many in the Territory, think he deserves the position of Brigadier General of Colorado; as by his bravery, fidelity, and energy, he has, if merit is rewarded, justly won it."[19]

Chivington coveted a brigadier general's commission but feared that only one officer from Colorado Territory would earn it. He saw two men as his competitors: Slough and Col. J. H. Leavenworth of the 2nd Colorado Volunteers. On June 25, 1862, Chivington wrote the Reverend Hugh Fisher, a Kansas abolitionist, asking Fisher to lobby two United States senators for his promotion. He reminded Fisher that both Slough and Leavenworth were untrustworthy Democrats. He called Slough a "Lecompton Democrat" and derided Leavenworth as a "Democrat of the woolly type" and "the meanest old whore monger and drunkard in the mountains." Echoing the claim made by the *Rocky Mountain News*, Chivington boasted that all the men in the 1st Colorado and half of the men in the 2nd Colorado strongly supported his promotion to brigadier general and "three fourths of the people of Colorado would endorse it heartily, and of this I am not mistaken."

Chivington used the same derogatory language in his letter to Fisher that Downing used as "Union," suggesting that the two men collaborated in drafting "Union's" correspondence with the *Rocky Mountain News*. In his June

7 recounting of the New Mexico campaign, "Union" argued that by keeping the 1st Colorado in Denver, Slough and Acting Territorial Governor Weld conspired to help "the drunken Weld" win a seat in Congress. He smeared Slough again when he wrote the *News* ten days later to complain that a Colonel Collins from Santa Fe—and not the "noble" Chivington—had claimed responsibility for destroying the Confederate wagon train at Johnson's Ranch. He linked Collins, "a strong Buchanan Democrat," to Slough, "of Kansas border ruffian notoriety," and implied that neither man could be trusted as loyal Unionists. The similar wording used by Downing (as "Union") and Chivington—Weld and Leavenworth were both "drunkards" while Slough was a disloyal "Kansas border ruffian" and "Lecompton Democrat"—suggest that Chivington and Downing plotted together to forward their promotions by impugning Slough's reputation. Labeling Slough a Democrat, however, was insufficient to impede his career; after all, Lincoln had already appointed Democrats as generals. But the charge of cowardice would scuttle any officer's chances at advancement. Chivington calculated that rumors of Slough's cowardice, made by "Union" and published in the *Rocky Mountain News*, would find their way into Eastern newspapers and destroy Slough's career in the Union army.[20]

The Eastern newspapers failed to print the accusation. Chivington's plotting did not lead to a general's commission nor did it ruin Slough's reputation. Instead, on August 25, 1862, Secretary of War Stanton and Maj. Gen. Henry Wager Halleck, general-in-chief of all Federal forces, anxiously summoned the Cincinnati brigadier to the War Department. Troops pouring through occupied Alexandria, Virginia, on their way to battle Lee's Army of Northern Virginia had turned the port city into a lawless and unlivable place "beyond the control of the provost marshal there." Halleck and Stanton told Slough that Alexandria "had caused them a great deal of trouble & they wanted to be rid of it." They appointed him Alexandria's military governor, directed him to restore order to the city, and promised him "whatever force should be necessary to accomplish that end." With orders in hand, Slough left the secretary of war and the general-in-chief and immediately took the ferry downriver to Alexandria.[21]

11

⬦⬦⬦⬦⬦⬦

"Disorder and Vice Had Been the Rule"

JOHN SLOUGH ENTERED A CITY UNDER "A REIGN OF TERROR" WHEN he stepped off the Alexandria ferry. As he walked the seven blocks from the waterfront to his new headquarters on South St. Asaph Street, he passed hundreds of intoxicated soldiers, many dead drunk and lying in the street. Stragglers from both the Army of the Potomac, newly returned from the failed Peninsula Campaign, and the Army of Virginia, soon to be bloodied at the Battle of Second Manassas, crowded the docks and sidewalks. Military discipline was totally absent. Soldiers whooped and hollered in the streets, shouting obscenities and firing their weapons in the air. Many drank cheap whiskey obtained from ubiquitous liquor sellers. Some sought the pleasures offered by the city's streetwalkers and houses of ill repute, while others fought with their fellow soldiers. The least savory robbed unwary citizens or broke into private residences to steal whatever they could find. The provost guard—the Civil War's equivalent of today's military police—made little effort to arrest drunkards or return malingerers to their regiments. According to a Union captain, "the fiends of hell" had been loosed in the city. The lawlessness Slough experienced commanding the 1st Colorado hardly compared to the anarchy he now faced.[1]

Alexandria was a pleasant and prosperous river port during the 1840s and 1850s, benefiting from a good natural harbor on the Potomac, expanding industry, and an active slave trade, but by the time Slough arrived in August 1862, the war had wrecked its economy and ruined its peacetime tranquility. It became the first occupied Southern city when seven thousand Union soldiers invaded its quiet streets during the early morning of May 24, 1861. In the months that followed, reinforcements poured across the Potomac River bridges to construct fortifications around Alexandria, making it a critical link in the defenses of Washington, and to establish regimental camps throughout the surrounding countryside. A Maine soldier, writing to his family in summer 1861, described the Virginia side of the Potomac River as "one continuous encampment." In the city itself, Union officers commandeered private residences, abandoned by rebel sympathizers who had fled south, while their troops overwhelmed its neighborhoods. The sheer number of soldiers destroyed the graceful charm that typified antebellum Alexandria. They stripped the adjacent farms of produce and livestock, confiscated furniture and other household items, vandalized empty buildings, and dismantled fences for firewood. "An undisciplined mob," complained a correspondent to the *Washington Star*, "take what they please and destroy what they do not want."[2]

Vice flourished among so many men away from the constraints of home and with too much time on their hands. During the first winter of occupation, the number of saloons in Alexandria increased more than six-fold. Prostitutes prowled the streets, their trade with soldiers "relatively unrestricted." The city's condition horrified a Massachusetts soldier; he observed that the city was "full of Jews and prostitutes; as nasty a moral sink as was ever moulded [*sic*] in Europe." A New Hampshire soldier agreed: "Of all the nasty looking holes that I ever saw, Alexandria is the very worst."[3]

The city had three military governors before Slough's arrival, but none exerted much control or lasted more than a few months. Sixty-year-old Gen. William R. Montgomery assumed command as Alexandria's first military governor in August 1861, but, claiming exhaustion, resigned his position six months later. Col. Egbert L. Viele briefly succeeded Montgomery until charges of drunkenness and abuse of authority forced him to stand down. Col. Edgar M. Gregory, who had been Viele's provost marshal, served as acting military governor from April 1862 until Slough's appointment in August. Montgomery, Viele, and Gregory attempted to enforce military discipline. They established curfews, regulated the sale of alcohol to soldiers, and sought to limit soldiers' interactions with civilians. None of the three had the ability or resolve to maintain a well-ordered military government. It was, however, the horde of troops passing through Alexandria's streets in August 1862 that overwhelmed the city's military administration and led Stanton and Halleck to dispatch Slough to restore order.[4]

Slough wasted no time in squelching the disturbances that roiled the city. He had seen in Denver the havoc that drunken and disorderly soldiers could wreak and had no intention of allowing them to rule in Alexandria. Immediately upon his arrival, he ordered troops to clear the city of hundreds of soldiers who had strayed from their units without permission. That evening and throughout the night, patrols forced wayward soldiers to return to their regiments at the point of a bayonet. Early the next morning, squads again moved from house to house to collect any soldiers that had eluded the previous night's search. Provost guards dragged drunken and unconscious men from underneath the wharves to prevent their drowning at high tide. The *Alexandria Gazette* described the malingerers as they sullenly marched back to their camps, "some endeavoring to elude the vigilance of the guard to make their escape, some muleishly [*sic*] holding back, some pushing forward, headlong, and some resigned to their fate, going on heedless of the confusion . . . enacted around them." By noon of Slough's first day in command, the streets were cleaned of stragglers.[5]

Alexandria's new military governor quickly issued a series of orders intended to maintain control over soldiers and civilians. On August 26, he imposed a strict curfew. All soldiers were required to be in their quarters by 9:00 p.m., all places of business closed by 9:30, and all citizens at home by 10:30. Any person found in the streets after 10:30 faced arrest and confinement. Slough also closed all establishments selling liquor and outlawed its sale to soldiers. Two days later, he prohibited the discharge of firearms within the city limits.[6]

His orders had an immediate effect. The *Baltimore Sun* reported on August 29 that more than sixty barrels of ale and malt liquor had been destroyed, whiskey and champagne bottles confiscated, and the city's saloons closed. The newspaper approvingly noted that neither officers nor enlisted men could purchase alcohol. A correspondent for the *Philadelphia Inquirer* reported that "Drunkenness and rowdyism have ruled the roost here for several days, and it is now at an end."[7]

Alexandria's respite from "drunkenness and rowdyism" did not last long. Thirty miles west, Robert E. Lee's Army of Northern Virginia was humiliating John Pope's Army of Virginia at the Battle of Second Manassas. Neither side gained a decided advantage during the initial fighting, although Stonewall Jackson's corps bloodily repulsed repeated attacks launched by Pope on August 29. The next day, as Pope again assailed Jackson's position, Maj.

Gen. James Longstreet unleashed his twenty-eight thousand Confederate soldiers on the federals' undermanned left flank. The attack crushed Fitz John Porter's Fifth Corps, routed the Union army, and forced the Yankees to retreat to Washington.

As the defeated Union forces filled the forts and camps around Alexandria, Southern sympathizer Anne Frobel commented that "one dense mass" of men covered the surrounding hills, while the *Alexandria Gazette* noted that "mounted and foot soldiers are everywhere to be seen." With the army came the stragglers, soldiers who had strayed from their units and the control of their officers. Large numbers of them wandered aimlessly on King Street. The *Gazette* reported that the southern part of Alexandria was "especially *harried* by stragglers, they asserting that there 'is no guard and they intend to do as they please.'" Citizens living in that neighborhood complained that they had to shut their doors and windows despite the summer heat to block out "the horrid blasphemy and obscenity that were shouted in their ears by stragglers." Houses were again invaded and their contents stolen.[8]

Slough knew that he had insufficient troops to curb the growing disorder. On September 1, he warned Halleck that the city was in danger of reverting to chaos. He grumbled that his command consisted of "new troops, convalescents, and stragglers" and estimated that he needed two regiments for fatigue duty, patrol, and guard duty. He informed the general-in-chief, "It requires here at this time a considerable force to preserve order, to collect stragglers, and prevent the demoralization of passing troops."[9]

Remembering his pledge to provide Slough with the necessary troops to maintain order, Halleck recommended to Maj. Gen. George McClellan that he provide an adequate force to police Alexandria. But the Army of Northern Virginia invaded Maryland on September 4 and McClellan, responsible for the pursuit of the Confederate army, ignored Halleck's suggestion that Slough's force "not be taken away, unless there is an absolute necessity for it." McClellan, whose incessant demands for more troops had earned Halleck's disdain, saw the "absolute necessity" of assigning every available soldier in the Washington defenses to his command. He could not afford to detach any manpower for duty in Alexandria if Lincoln, Stanton, and Halleck expected him to defeat the powerful Army of Northern Virginia.[10]

Slough wrote Halleck's office again on September 12. This time he requested a single regiment. Without it, he worried, "Alexandria will soon be in the control of the drunken stragglers." He was not crying wolf. Guards assigned to Alexandria's commissary were not able to protect its supplies from stragglers' raids. Halleck angrily wrote Slough's superior, Maj. Gen. Nathaniel Banks, demanding that the raids be prevented. In turn, Banks ordered Slough to take immediate measures to secure the stores.[11]

Slough received his reinforcements, the 19th Connecticut Volunteers, on September 18, but was disappointed that the regiment offered only "raw and undisciplined troops." To make matters worse, the 19th Connecticut was ordered to replace the larger 33rd Massachusetts. Slough once more appealed directly to Halleck. He urged that both the 33rd Massachusetts and the 19th Connecticut remain in Alexandria to prevent stragglers from overrunning the city.[12]

On September 17, the day before Slough argued to keep the 33rd Massachusetts in Alexandria, the Army of the Potomac pummeled Lee's Army of Northern Virginia at Antietam Creek but failed to destroy it during the day-long battle. Lee withdrew his battered army the next night across the Potomac and into the safety of the Shenandoah Valley. With the Confederate invasion of Maryland ended, the 33rd Massachusetts was able to remain in Alexandria. Commanding both the 33rd Massachusetts and the 19th Connecticut, Slough had 2,038 officers and men available for duty, a sufficient force to reassert control over his jurisdiction. Anne Frobel noticed the change when she went to church on September 28. "The town seemed entirely cleared of soldiers," she wrote in her diary. "I have not seen it so quiet since [the start of] the war, it seems the military governor there has banished them all." Calm had returned to Alexandria.[13]

With the stragglers gone, other challenges occupied Alexandria's military government. The chaos that warring armies caused in the northern Virginia counties afforded enslaved people the opportunity to escape their bondage and flee to Alexandria, Arlington, and Washington. They began arriving in spring 1862, as the Army of the Potomac marched up the James River Peninsula toward Richmond. By early September, the *Alexandria Gazette* observed that the city was "full of 'contrabands'"—the term applied to enslaved people who sought refuge within federal lines—and estimated that the military authorities had assumed relief for as many as 750 men, women, and children.[14]

The refugees owned virtually nothing as slaves, left their masters without any possessions, and arrived in Alexandria destitute. The authorities initially housed them in buildings abandoned by Southern sympathizers. By the summer of 1862, the military had either commandeered, or speculators had bought, most of the vacant properties in the city. Rents soared for the handful of Alexandria's unoccupied spaces, forcing the city's newly arrived freed people—"freed" by virtue of their initiative and the Union army's presence—to build shanties with whatever materials they could scavenge. Housing conditions quickly deteriorated.[15]

On September 19, 1862, Mayor Lewis McKenzie wrote Secretary of War Stanton to request that the army's quartermaster in Alexandria build barracks for the city's Black refugees. Stanton forwarded McKenzie's letter to Slough, who assigned Provost Marshal John C. Wyman to review the letter and recommend a course of action. Wyman replied that although many Black people in Alexandria lived in crowded and unsanitary conditions, the provost marshal's office could resolve the housing shortage without additional construction. The threat of smallpox, however, caused Wyman to revise his recommendation. On October 21, he submitted plans to Slough for building barracks that would help mitigate the unhealthy circumstances in which the refugees lived. Slough sent Wyman's plans up the chain of command, and within a week the quartermaster general of the army, Montgomery Meigs, ordered that barracks be constructed.[16]

Meanwhile, a formidable advocate for Alexandria's Black population had arrived in the city. Julia Wilbur left Rochester, New York, to serve as an agent of the Rochester Ladies Anti-Slavery Society and to distribute relief to the growing number of freed people around Washington, DC. Well-known in Rochester's abolitionist circles, she was an unmarried, forty-seven-year-old teacher who believed that her virtue and Christian morality especially suited her to advocate for freed people and to provide aid to the needy. Her convictions led her to clash repeatedly with Slough and his subordinates over the treatment of Black people in Alexandria.[17]

Wilbur first traveled to Washington, where she met with George Baker, the treasurer of the National Freedman's Relief Association for the District of Columbia. He informed her about the sufferings of newly escaped slaves in Alexandria and suggested that she devote her relief efforts to them. She arrived in Alexandria on October 28, 1862, and immediately inspected a building sheltering sick Black refugees. There she witnessed scenes of deprivation

Julia Wilbur battled
Slough's administration in
Alexandria, Virginia, over its
treatment of black refugees.
Source: Courtesy of Quaker
& Special Collections,
Haverford College, Haver-
ford, Pennsylvania,
ID mc1158_06_04_001.

that would become familiar as she worked with the city's freed people. She wrote in her diary that night that she saw "people in filth & rags—a dead child lay wrapped in a piece of ticking—in another room, a dead child behind the door. Oh, what sights! What Misery! No doctor—no medicines—only rations & Shelter."[18]

She spent her first week in Alexandria visiting impoverished Black people living in the city's dilapidated buildings. On November 6, she entered a tenement housing three women and thirteen children, some sick and lying on the damp floor. The building, she wrote, was all "crevices & vents" and offered little shelter to its inhabitants. She then visited the Slave Pen, a structure that in antebellum Alexandria had confined slaves waiting to be sold and now served as a jail for disorderly soldiers and housing for Black refugees. In it she found twenty women and children huddled around a small fire in one room. It was more than she could bear.[19]

She decided to pressure the authorities to provide adequate shelter for the refugees. Gen. James Wadsworth, the commander of the Department and Defenses of Washington, had warned her about General Slough. A

Republican, Wadsworth did not trust the conservative Cincinnati Democrat and told Wilbur that Slough would not support her efforts to assist Alexandria's freed people. Wilbur did not waste time appealing to Slough or anyone not sympathetic to her cause. On November 7, the day after her visit to the Slave Pen, she wrote Abraham Lincoln, "in behalf of suffering humanity," to request that barracks be constructed for seven hundred freed people living in "the old slave pen & . . . in several tenements that can hardly be called a shelter." She was not above flattering the president. She told Lincoln that she was "appealing to a kind heart & I come as a child to its father to ask for help in behalf of the most wretched of God's creatures."[20]

Slough had concerns other than a Northern abolitionist lady begging the president for barracks. Smallpox had erupted in Alexandria. Although the disease sickened white civilians and soldiers, it devastated Alexandria's freed people as it rapidly spread through their squalid, unsanitary, and overcrowded neighborhoods. In November, 185 Black people died of smallpox, and by early December, city authorities reported 800 cases and fifteen burials a day. Slough delegated to Provost Marshal Wyman the responsibility of quarantining new cases. Wyman ordered Dr. Charles Culverwell to vaccinate the city's Black population and to isolate all persons exhibiting symptoms of smallpox. He also commandeered Clermont, the home of Confederate navy commodore French Forrester, for use as a smallpox hospital. Despite these efforts, Wyman informed Slough on November 29 that smallpox continued to rage among the city's Black people. He told Slough that the large number of refugees living in whatever space they could find made the disease's containment impossible. In his opinion, barracks appeared to be the best means for impeding its transmission.[21]

Slough responded promptly to Wyman's urgent report. He transferred Dr. J. E. Dow from the army's convalescent camp to the provost marshal's office to aid in the vaccination campaign. He extended the requirement for vaccination to all troops under his command. And he again requested that barracks be built even though Quartermaster General Meigs had ordered their construction more than a month earlier.[22]

When Secretary of War Stanton learned about smallpox in Alexandria, he realized that the epidemic threatened thousands of soldiers in the city's hospitals and nearby camps. He had read Wyman's report that linked the spread of the disease to the lack of suitable housing for Black refugees. On

December 9, he questioned Quartermaster General Meigs about the delay in the barracks' construction. Despite his reputation for bullying, Stanton's intercession with Meigs did little to speed their completion. Neither Slough's nor Wyman's recommendations, nor Stanton's involvement, nor Wilbur's petition to President Lincoln hastened their construction. They were not completed for three more months.[23]

The pestilence continued unabated for weeks. "Much sickness prevails in our midst," Henry Whittington wrote in his diary on December 12, "and we doubt not but that the filthiness of the City & the large numbers of soldiers sick in the various Hospitals, have had much to do with the mortality now prevailing throughout our City." Julia Wilbur observed in late December, "I think it is all over & around us." The military authorities responded by searching houses for unreported cases. Anne Frobel was appalled that infected persons were "taken off to the horrid hospitals, where they are packed in, men, women, and children, Black and white indiscriminately, where there is little, or no care taken of them, and the most of them die." With the limitations of nineteenth-century medicine and public health, little could be done. The epidemic persisted until the disease finally ran its course in the spring of 1863.[24]

• • •

Slough's first months as Alexandria's military governor were overwhelming. He spent long hours at his headquarters attempting to lift the city from chaos to some semblance of order; the *Philadelphia Inquirer* praised him as "untiring" in his efforts. Perhaps exhausted and wishing to leave Alexandria, he wrote his new commanding officer, Maj. Gen. Samuel Heintzelman, to ask about the probability of remaining in his current assignment. Heintzelman chose to ignore the letter, leaving Slough's question about transfer unanswered. Despite his position's challenges, Slough could take comfort that his family had joined him at his house on South St. Asaph Street. The general and his wife attended parties together. At holiday time, they enjoyed two Christmas trees that Julia Wilbur asked the quartermaster to trim for Slough's children. Arabella joined a committee of "Union" ladies in Washington to plan Christmas dinners for sick and wounded soldiers. She and two other women assumed responsibility for soliciting funds and organizing holiday meals for Alexandria's military hospitals. The general's wife raised

$600 for Christmas dinner at the McVeigh House Hospital a few blocks away from the family's residence.[25]

The holidays afforded Slough little respite from his military duties. On November 26, he received orders from General-in-Chief Halleck to serve as a judge at the court-martial of Maj. Gen. Fitz John Porter. Porter had been arrested the previous day and charged with disobeying a lawful order and misbehavior in front of the enemy. The alleged offenses occurred during the fighting at Second Manassas. Porter, who was George McClellan's protégé and favorite subordinate, had performed well during the Seven Days battles. But when his 5th Corps was assigned to the Army of Virginia in August 1862, he found himself reporting to a commander whom he scorned, Maj. Gen. John Pope. It was his contempt for Pope that proved his undoing. Shortly after Pope assumed command of the Army of Virginia, Porter wrote letters calling him an "ass" and predicting that "Pope would be whipped" in the upcoming campaign. His apparent withholding of troops during critical moments at Second Manassas seemed to be the action of a general who wished for his commander's failure.[26]

Pope knew about Porter's churlish comments and needed a scapegoat for the disaster at Second Manassas. Moreover, Secretary of War Stanton calculated that by destroying Porter's career, he could wound his enemy and Porter's champion, George McClellan. Given the general's attractiveness as a presidential candidate, hurting "Little Mac" would have a desirable political result for Lincoln's secretary of war. Stanton carefully selected the nine judges to ensure a guilty verdict. Several judges, like David Hunter, Silas Casey, and Napoleon Bonaparte Buford, shared an intense antipathy toward McClellan. Two judges, Rufus King and James B. Ricketts, had performed poorly at Second Manassas and needed the diversion that the court-martial would provide. James A. Garfield, who became president in 1881, was the protégé of Stanton's ally, secretary of the treasury Salmon P. Chase. The ninth judge had been Brig. Gen. W. W. Morris, but when Morris questioned the legality of the trial, Stanton replaced him with John Slough.[27]

That the court found Porter guilty is not surprising, given its composition, even though commentators at the time expected the general to be exonerated. On January 21, 1863, the court handed down its guilty verdict, cashiered Porter from the army, and disqualified him forever from holding any office in the United States government.[28]

In this sketch of Maj. Gen. Fitz John Porter's court-martial by Alfred Waud, Slough sits at the center of the judges' table and Porter stands to his left. Source: Library of Congress Prints and Photographs Division, LC-DIG-ppmsca-21411.

Historians have suggested that Stanton chose Slough as one of the court-martial judges because Slough needed the secretary of war's support to be confirmed by the Senate as a brigadier general. According to their theory, Stanton coerced Slough's guilty verdict by holding out the promise of advancement. In fact, Stanton had proposed Slough's promotion six months before Porter's court-martial. On May 26, 1862, the day Slough arrived in Harpers Ferry, Lincoln approved Stanton's recommendation that Slough be promoted to brigadier general, but the Senate failed to confirm his promotion. Stanton again recommended the Cincinnatian to Lincoln on December 23, 1862, a month before the court found Porter guilty. Given the timing of Stanton's recommendations, he probably did not use the promise of advancement to pressure Slough to vote as he wanted. Nonetheless, Slough understood the value of the secretary of war's influence, and even though Fitz John Porter regarded the general as "friendly" during the trial, it is not hard to imagine that Slough considered Stanton's good will when casting his vote.[29]

Alexandria's licensed liquor dealers and restaurant owners, locked in a bitter struggle with Slough over his prohibition of liquor sales, vehemently opposed his Senate confirmation as a brigadier general. In late November 1862, Slough issued General Order No. 4 prohibiting both the sale and the gift of liquor to soldiers and civilians. Anyone found guilty of disobeying the regulation, the order stated, would be arrested and the person's supply of liquor confiscated. Because General Order No. 4 threatened to devastate their trade, the restaurant owners and saloon keepers met with Slough to request that he grant them the same privileges as liquor dealers in Washington and Georgetown. Slough was unmoved by their petition. He replied that the previous failure of liquor dealers to abide by regulations plus the need to maintain discipline among the large number of troops camped nearby compelled him to deny their request. He reminded them of Alexandria's disordered condition when he arrived the previous August and drew the conclusion that liquor's prohibition was "an imperative military necessity."[30]

Slough's difficulties with the 1st Colorado blinded him to the need for compromise on the issue of liquor sales. Offended by his haughty manner and peremptory rejection of their proposal, the liquor sellers decided to use more extreme measures to protect their business interests. In early February 1863, when Alexandria's new provost marshal, Lt. Col. Henry H. Wells, tightened the enforcement of General Order No. 4, the hotel proprietors and restaurant owners attempted to force Wells's hand by closing the city's eating establishments. They calculated that the new provost marshal would relent once officers could no longer procure a meal in the city. Wells responded by telling them that he would not "abate one iota" in the enforcement of the liquor regulations. The liquor dealers' committee then placed an advertisement in the *Alexandria Gazette* calling for residents' testimony that Slough's administration had hurt their businesses. They planned to forward the complaints to Stanton and Congress in order to ruin Slough's chances at promotion.[31]

On February 20, 1863, Alexandria liquor dealers J. P. L. Westcott and Samuel Heflebower sent Stanton a printed, three-page complaint about Slough's prohibition of liquor sales. The two men claimed that Slough had issued General Order No. 4 "from personal feelings, and not from a desire to discharge the duties of his office upon principles of equity and justice." They asserted that because he permitted the smuggling of liquor into the city, General Order No. 4 had failed to prevent the sale of illegal spirits by unlicensed vendors. According to Westcott and Heflebower, the order ruined the livelihood of the city's licensed liquor dealers and "swept away . . . the savings of a life-time of honest toil and labor."[32]

Six members of the United States House of Representatives asked Stanton on February 24 to investigate Westcott's and Heflebower's charges. Slough promptly responded to the liquor dealers' allegations in a report delivered to Stanton on February 27. He began his defense by noting that Westcott had been found guilty of violating the liquor regulations on several occasions and that Heflebower was known to be disloyal, even though he had taken the Oath of Allegiance. He charged that the two men intended, by their allegations, to sway the Senate against confirming his rank as brigadier general. In that event, Slough predicted, a "less vigilant and scrupulous" officer would be appointed Alexandria's military governor.[33]

Slough reminded Stanton that when he arrived in Alexandria, he found "crime, disorder, and drunkenness everywhere" and the military authority unable to control a "drunken, large armed mob." Only "by the enforcement of stringent and sometimes prohibitory orders" had he been able to restore peace. Fortunately, he told the secretary of war, Maj. Gens. Banks, Heintzelman, and Halleck, and even Stanton himself, had approved of his liquor regulations. "With the orders rigidly enforced," Slough argued, "crime, drunkenness, and disorder disappear—with a relaxation or modification they become rampant." As a result, he continued to oppose "the disposition of liquor in the city by any person to citizen, officer, or soldier."

Slough attached to his report thirteen letters of support from officers under his command, government bureaucrats, and local merchants. Twenty-one officers from the 19th Connecticut Volunteers, the regiment assigned to Alexandria during Lee's invasion of Maryland, attested that the city was "exceedingly well-governed" and that Slough was "very resolute" in his determination to suppress the sale of liquor. Alexandria postmaster W. D. Massey wrote Slough, "not withstanding our city has been swarmed with pickpockets and cutthroats from other places, there never was better order or less drunkenness in Alexa[ndria] than at present time. . . . This I conceive is owing to the faithfulness of your administration." Capt. F. C. Tapley, from the Quartermasters' Transportation Office, observed that "the City has become a place of safety and quiet, and is only kept so by the stern uncompromising exertions of Genl. Slough." Provost marshal Henry H. Wells, assistant provost marshal William Winship, commander of the provost guards R. R. Meredith, and staff officers Capts. Rollin C. Gale, Davis J. Rich, and William McLean Gwynne all attested to the military governor's competence and character. They described him as "an officer and a gentleman," "an honorable high minded soldier," an "efficient officer," and a successful administrator. Slough had earned the respect of his officers in Alexandria for his efforts in restoring order to the city.[34]

Assistant secretary of war Peter Watson informed Slough on March 9 that Stanton found Slough's report "satisfactory" and approved the general's ongoing efforts to prohibit the sale of liquor. Three days earlier, President Lincoln had endorsed Slough's nomination as a brigadier general of volunteers and sent his name to the Senate along with the names of twenty-nine major generals and ninety brigadier generals. Within a week, the Senate confirmed his promotion. Undeterred by his struggles with the 1st Colorado or by being passed over for division command in the Army of Virginia, Slough had performed brilliantly in governing Alexandria and had won Stanton's trust, the Senate's vote of confidence, and his confirmation as a brigadier.[35]

Slough's fellow officers and the "loyal residents" of Alexandria celebrated the general's accomplishments at a ceremony the evening of March 28, 1863. It was a festive occasion. The committee in charge of the event had decorated a room in Alexandria's Post Office with American flags and portraits of George Washington, wreathed with evergreen sprigs. A platform draped with the American flag was raised for Arabella and other ladies attending the event. At 8:00 p.m., Provost Marshal Wells stood to present Slough with a ceremonial sword. He recounted how "disorder and vice had been the rule" in Alexandria before Slough's appointment, but now, Wells asserted, no city in the North was more orderly. Alexandria had been transformed under the general's leadership.

Wells also noted that the Union victory at Pigeon's Ranch had occurred exactly one year earlier, rendering the ceremony's date "an appropriate time to present this token of their respect and admiration, which they hoped would be handed down to his children's children." He read the sword's inscription, "Presented to Brigadier General John P. Slough by his friends, as a token of their appreciation of his fidelity and zeal in the discharge of his responsibilities as military governor of Alexandria, Virginia, March 1863," and presented it to his commanding officer.

The sword and scabbard were magnificent. The blade, made of Solingen damask steel inlaid with gold, was engraved with battle scenes. Diamonds, pearls, and amethysts ornamented the sword's gold-plated hilt. The largest amethyst had the letter "S" engraved on it. Slough's friends had spent $700 (about $13,000 today) on the gift, a generous expression of their admiration.

Slough thanked Wells for the gift and, referring to the provost marshal's mention of Pigeon's Ranch, said, "You have taken occasion to refer to that day on which this is the first anniversary. That night and this one are the two happiest occasions of my life. The first one, when I stood at the head of my troops, I felt I had achieved a victory over the foes of my country; and tonight, I think, when I look at this testimonial, I have achieved another over your hearts. Gentlemen, you will, therefore, accept my thanks for this sword, and be assured that it will be as free from defending an unholy cause as the blade is spotless from stain." It was a rare moment in his life, one in which he received the warm acknowledgment of his friends and admirers.[36]

He had accomplished much in the seven months since he stepped off the Alexandria ferry. Living conditions for the city's freed people were slowly improving; three barracks had been erected capable of housing fifteen hundred refugees. A new hospital camp for convalescent soldiers replaced the old "Camp Misery," where, during the winter of 1862–1863, sixteen thousand convalescents, stragglers, new recruits, and paroled prisoners of war suffered without adequate shelter, clothing, food, or firewood. And he had saved a city on the brink of anarchy. Soldiers no longer wandered its streets, drunken and disorderly, but now observed a relative quiet in their camps. Even with its heavy wartime burden, Alexandria had become, in Capt. William Gwynne's words, "safe for a lady to walk the streets."[37]

Slough still had enemies in Alexandria despite the approbation of his officers and many of its leading citizens. The city's liquor sellers continued to scheme against him. Julia Wilbur and other abolitionists objected to their Washington friends about his administration's treatment of previously enslaved Black people. And Alexandria's many Confederate sympathizers remained a potential force for discord. In February, assailants set upon Slough but fled when he drew his revolver. The city held perils, both political and personal, for its military governor. Slough had risen to a position of power and responsibility, while his enemies awaited the chance to pull him down.[38]

12

Enemies within the Lines

ALEXANDRIA HAD BEEN DELIVERED FROM THE "FIENDS OF HELL" thanks to John Slough's strict governance, but the city was hardly a paradise. Filth was everywhere during the winter of 1863. Its sidewalks, gutters, and alleys overflowed with rotting garbage and manure left not only by its residents but also by the thousands of soldiers and horses thronging its streets. An anonymous letter written to Alexandria's mayor in February 1863 warned that the city's unsanitary condition promised an outbreak of disease, and it reproached the municipal authorities for ignoring the public's health. Like other military governors across the occupied South, Slough had to assume responsibility for Alexandria's cleanliness lest its filth contribute to sickness among the troops. He ordered residents to remove trash and manure from their homes, stables, outhouses, and outbuildings and threatened them with fines for allowing waste to accumulate.[1]

Slough also directed the provost marshal's office to rid the city of prostitution by ordering any person "not engaged in an honest calling" to leave Alexandria upon pain of arrest and imprisonment. Streetwalkers and "fancy women" still tempted soldiers a month after the military governor instructed them to quit the city. On May 21, 1863, the *Alexandria Gazette* reported that any woman working the streets would be fined six dollars and ordered to leave the city within twenty-four hours. More than prostitution, however, Slough was determined to eliminate the evils caused by drunkenness. When he learned that liquor sales had resumed during his absence for the Porter court-martial, he blamed the provost marshal, John Wyman, and replaced him with Lt. Col. Henry Wells.[2]

Julia Wilbur was not pleased with this appointment. She considered Wyman a friend of Alexandria's freed people and blamed Slough for his removal. To her dismay, she found Henry Wells to be less pliable than John Wyman. During their first meeting, she asked Wells for increased assistance for Alexandria's Black people. When the new provost marshal resisted her pleas, she broke down in tears, saying that she had devoted "heart & soul & substance" to caring for the previously enslaved refugees. Wells was not moved. He condescendingly told her that she was an "excellent woman" but reminded her that only "when you get shoulder-straps on & are made provost marshal" could she assume his responsibilities.[3]

The basis of their disagreement was the government's practice of charging freed people a few dollars a month to live in government-provided quarters. Both Slough and Maj. Gen. Samuel Heintzelman, commanding general of the Department and Defenses of Washington, believed that providing relief to newly freed Black people dampened their desire to attain self-sufficiency. Slough encouraged refugees in Alexandria to build homes so that they might achieve "a thrifty and prosperous condition," and he expected those needing government housing to pay rent. Wilbur challenged this policy. She doggedly struggled with the military authorities so that Alexandria's freed people, especially women with families, and the aged, sick, and infirm, did not have to pay for the provisions, fuel, and lodgings they received from the government.[4]

Wilbur may have disliked Provost Marshal Wells, but she despised Albert Gladwin, Alexandria's acting superintendent of contrabands. Gladwin was a forty-six-year-old white Baptist minister sent to Alexandria in October 1862 by the American Baptist Free Mission Society. The two relief agents' relationship soured shortly after meeting because Wilbur disliked the Baptist minister's haughty and condescending manner toward African Americans. To her horror, Gladwin gained Slough's trust. Like the military governor, Gladwin firmly believed that relief fostered dependency and that newly freed Black people needed prodding to gain self-sufficiency as quickly as possible. Wilbur and Gladwin fought over aid to Alexandria's Black people, and by early 1863 she was confiding in her diary how much she hated working with him. "Mr. G[ladwin] has vexed me very much today," she wrote in her January 22 entry. "I try to possess my soul in patience."[5]

She decided to lobby officials in Washington against Gladwin's permanent appointment as superintendent of contrabands. On March 24, 1863, she wrote Stanton that the freed people's barracks—three buildings with

Rents charged to refugees housed in Alexandria's Freedman's Barracks became a major point of contention between Julia Wilbur and Slough's superintendent of contrabands, Albert Gladwin. Source: Library of Congress Prints and Photographs Division, LC-DIG-ppmsca-34821.

lodgings for fifteen hundred persons—had been completed. Unfortunately, she informed the secretary of war, the current practice was to "extort from the Contrabands in Alex[andria]$17.00 a year in rent for these rude barracks," an injustice she believed neither Stanton nor Lincoln could condone. She then attacked Gladwin as Alexandria's acting superintendent of contrabands. "There is a want of system & order here that hinders the accomplishment of much good that might otherwise be done," she asserted, "and with all proper deference I would say that an efficient & capable superintendent is very much needed here. He should be a *humane* man; he should be large-minded & thoroughly conscientious; one who believes that these people can be elevated & improved; not one who habitually speaks of them as 'thievish, deceitful, ungrateful, dishonest,' a people 'whom you cannot teach any more than you can horses.'" As if Stanton might fail to grasp the object of her invective, she pointedly stated that Gladwin was "altogether unfit for Superintendent of these people." A week later, she wrote Stanton's assistant secretary, Peter H. Watson. She complained again that freed people had to pay rent for their lodgings, attacked Provost Marshal Wells as unhelpful, and characterized Gladwin as incompetent.[6]

Meanwhile, the secretary of the Rochester Ladies Anti-Slavery Society, the organization that sponsored Julia Wilbur, wrote Lincoln about the disturbing treatment of Black refugees in Alexandria. Anna Barnes complained to the president that Union soldiers frequently punished Black men and women housed in Alexandria's Slave Pen with ice cold "shower baths." The humiliation the naked freed women felt before the white soldiers horrified her more than the breathtaking pain inflicted by gallons of cold water poured over their heads. She also warned Lincoln about Gladwin, a "brutal man" who was "smoother than butter to superiors, but harder than iron to the defenseless." Lincoln referred her letter to Stanton, who passed it down to Slough. After being asked by Slough to investigate, Provost Marshal Wells assured the military governor on April 11 that the use of shower baths on Black women had been discontinued. He also reminded Slough that the conflict between Gladwin and Wilbur hinged on the issue of relief and self-sufficiency. To Wells, Wilbur seemed intent on securing "the largest possible grants" for the refugees regardless of the cost to the government. "I am compelled to say," he concluded, "that while respecting Miss Wilbur's goodness of heart, and broad benevolence, I regard her as an interfering, and troublesome person."[7]

The next day, Wells replied to Barnes and Wilbur's accusations in his formal report. He assured Slough that he had always encouraged Julia Wilbur to meet with him whenever she had a concern and that he faithfully investigated any complaint she lodged with the provost marshal's office. He also denied that he told her that freed persons living in the barracks had to pay rent; in truth, he said, impoverished, sick, and infirm refugees were accommodated without charge. He informed Slough that he supported Gladwin's work with the refugees and concluded that Wilbur's and Barnes's negative opinion of the superintendent was "entirely without cause or foundation."[8]

Managing the flood of Black refugees was uncharted territory for both military authorities and relief workers in Alexandria. From Julia Wilbur's perspective, the government had an absolute responsibility for the well-being of former slaves; refugees should receive relief without question. Gladwin, Wells, and Slough, on the other hand, believed that charity fostered indolence and considered Wilbur's efforts on behalf of Alexandria's freed people as "indulgent and destructive." At the bottom of this disagreement was a profound distaste, influenced by mid-nineteenth-century gender norms, for the roles each side assumed in their relationships with Alexandria's Black population. Wilbur considered it inappropriate that men like Gladwin dealt closely with freed women because men tended to treat them with "coarse familiarity." She was convinced that a respectable, moral society demanded that only Christian women, from good backgrounds and demonstrating the best of intentions, should work with refugee women.[9]

But in a society that relegated women to subordinate roles, men dominated Alexandria's relief efforts. Gladwin saw Wilbur's activities as undermining both his official and masculine authority; he complained that in opposing him, she demonstrated a desire to wear "men's clothing." Wells and Slough also belittled her attempts to assume responsibilities that they believed were better left to officers and gentlemen. Slough felt that Julia Wilbur and other women engaged in refugee relief had done good deeds, but that "it too often occurs that these ladies in a mistaken zeal act as if they would usurp the whole power of the Military Governor." He would not allow Wilbur, however good her intentions, to encroach on his authority as Alexandria's military governor or his responsibilities as a man.[10]

Alexandria sheltered three thousand freed people by early 1863. Employment was plentiful for those who could work. Blacks found labor on the wharves and in the city's hospitals and laundries. They worked for the army as teamsters and as laborers on the military railroads. Others washed clothing for soldiers or hired themselves out as servants to officers and their families. Slough himself employed a Black man as his personal servant. According to the *Alexandria Gazette*, former slaves received "just what they needed—protection, plenty of work at a fair price, and punctual payment." But the newspaper's rose-colored assessment overlooked the exploitation Black people experienced. Employers frequently cheated them of their wages and the federal authorities reduced their pay arbitrarily. Col. George Bell, for example, cut the wages of free Black people working on Alexandria's docks to help pay the wages of newly arrived refugees. Slough's policies may have driven previously enslaved persons to "self-sufficiency," but Alexandria's African American population still had to struggle for subsistence.[11]

By late spring 1863, Black men had a new opportunity for employment: serving as soldiers in the Union army. Lincoln had issued the Emancipation

African American men, both free and recently enslaved, found
employment unloading Union army supplies from ships docked at Alexandria's
Quartermaster's Wharf. Source: Library of Congress Prints and
Photographs Division, LC-DIG-ppmsca-33620.

Proclamation on January 1, 1863. The proclamation provided for the enlistment
of Black men in the army and navy and declared slaves "forever free" in those
states in rebellion. Although the War Department formally sanctioned the
creation of the United States Colored Troops on May 22, 1863, federal authorities had already begun planning for the enlistment of Black soldiers. In early
May, General Heintzelman asked Slough about recruiting troops from the
many freed people living in Alexandria. Slough replied that he could recruit
a brigade and put them immediately to work building fortifications. In his
world, manual labor was the only appropriate occupation for Black recruits.
He also sent Heintzelman a list of white officers he considered suitable to
lead African American soldiers and suggested that "troops of African descent"
be assigned to posts in the Defenses of Washington, where their exposure to
white troops would be minimized. Slough never recruited any Black soldiers.
A few days after he proposed raising a brigade of African American soldiers,
events in war-torn northern Virginia suddenly consumed his attention.[12]

On May 24, 1863, three weeks after Lee's Army of Northern Virginia
overwhelmed the Army of the Potomac at the Battle of Chancellorsville, an

anxious Julia Wilbur wrote in her diary that Alexandria expected an attack by forty thousand rebels. Unsubstantiated rumors about the rebels' presence fueled her fears. No movement had been detected among the corps of the Army of Northern Virginia. Since their triumph at Chancellorsville, Lee's troops had not left their fortifications at Fredericksburg, Virginia. But Secretary of War Stanton, concerned that the Confederates intended to raid the capital, ordered general-in-chief Henry Halleck to ready the Defenses of Washington for a rebel assault.[13]

Stanton worried that Maj. Gen. Jeb Stuart, the Army of Northern Virginia's aggressive cavalry commander, might overrun Washington in a surprise attack. A raid by Confederate Maj. John S. Mosby's Partisan Rangers on the Orange and Alexandria Railroad, forty miles from Alexandria, had unsettled the military authorities. Although Mosby had forty-eight men with him, not Julia Wilbur's forty thousand, the foray was sufficiently close to Alexandria for the War Department to take emergency action against a possible assault on the city's vast military establishment. By 1863, Alexandria's value to the Union war effort far exceeded the forts and camps that encircled it. It had served as the Union army's gateway for invasion since July 1861 and the Battle of First Manassas. Regiment after regiment poured through the city on the way to northern Virginian battlefields while the wounded from those battles returned to its thirty hospitals. Its river wharves and railroad connections enabled Alexandria to serve as the Army of the Potomac's supply depot. The United States Military Railroads funneled fourteen hundred tons of supplies daily down the Orange and Alexandria Railroad to feed, clothe, and arm the thousands of soldiers encamped around Fairfax Court House, Centreville, and Manassas Junction. A surprise attack by Confederate cavalry on Alexandria's sprawling storerooms, stables, corrals, and wood lots would prove disastrous to the Union cause.[14]

Anne Frobel noted in her diary on May 30, 1863, that "Gen. Steward [*sic*] is now said to be hovering near [Alexandria] with fifty thousand men." Alexandria's military authorities responded to the rumor with frenzied activity. Slough employed white and Black laborers to erect earthworks west of the city and to sink heavy timbers in the city's thoroughfares to block access to the army's warehouses. Wagons chained together barricaded the streets against attack by Stuart's horsemen. Slough also ordered his entire command, some 2,000 to 2,500 men, to sleep with their rifles at hand. Despite these efforts, the military governor feared he had insufficient resources to repel an attack. He recommended that the employees of Alexandria's Commissary and Quartermaster Departments be issued arms and ammunition and requested that an additional battery be deployed for the city's defense. General Heintzelman refused to supply more guns to Alexandria. Instead he advised Slough to position his one battery centrally so that it could be readily moved to any point of attack.[15]

Besides placing his soldiers on alert, positioning his few cannon, and erecting barricades to prevent rebel horseman from charging down its streets, Slough sought to bolster Alexandria's defenses by suppressing those Southern sympathizers who remained in the city. Two-thirds of Alexandria's prewar population had fled by 1863, but the federal authorities still worried that its remaining residents harbored Confederate spies or saboteurs. Provost Marshal Wells warned Slough that the large number of rebel sympathizers in Alexandria "would actively cooperate with the enemy and their thorough knowledge and complete organization would render them more dangerous than any organized military force of the same strength." Slough decided that the presence of Southern sympathizers in his jurisdiction could no longer be tolerated. On May 31, he requested permission from General Heintzelman to drive beyond the Union lines all men and women suspected of disloyalty to the federal government. Heintzelman concurred with the measure but only for "the most virulent of this class of the population."[16]

Union commanders considered the wholesale expulsion of Southern sympathizers from occupied territory as a drastic and unwise measure during the war's first year. Many Northerners believed that a conspiracy among the Southern slaveholding elite had fomented secession and that the overwhelming majority of Southerners remained Unionists at heart or, at worst, lukewarm supporters of the Confederacy. As a result, early Union policy held that by treating the civilian population with respect, Southerners would realize the grievous mistake of secession and pressure their politicians to rejoin the Union.[17]

With the Confederate victories in spring and summer 1862 and the increasing resistance of civilians in occupied areas, the federal authorities realized that a conciliatory policy toward Southern citizens had failed. "As the toll [of Union casualties] mounted," observes historian Steven Ash, "the distinction between enemy soldiers and hostile civilians appeared less and less meaningful." Practices unheard of in 1861, including using expulsion to force Southern sympathizers to abandon their homes, farms, and businesses, became more common. With the promulgation of General Orders No. 100 in April 1863, Union commanders had clearer guidelines for the treatment of rebel sympathizers. Officers could now "expel, transfer, imprison, or fine the revolted citizens who refuse to pledge themselves anew as citizens obedient to the law and loyal to the government."[18]

Slough and Provost Marshal Wells adopted the practice of exiling rebel supporters shortly after President Lincoln signed General Orders No. 100. Southern sympathizer Anne Frobel complained in her May 15 diary entry that "every now and then we hear of some poor body being sent outside the lines." A few days later, she noted that Wells had the "names of a hundred families who are now under constant espionage," and that "some times one or two in a family, some times the whole, sometimes a small boy, sometimes a young lady ... [are] taken away outside the lines."[19]

Fearing Confederate provocateurs within Alexandria, Slough suggested a new extreme in the treatment of the city's Southern sympathizers: the wholesale deportation of its known disloyal population. On June 18, he forwarded to Heintzelman a list of rebel sympathizers targeted for exile to Southern territory. Four days later, Heintzelman endorsed the removal of disloyal persons from Alexandria. As soon as he had the War Department's concurrence, Heintzelman told Slough, he would issue the necessary orders. Within the week, Secretary of War Stanton approved Slough's proposal to rid Alexandria of its rebel population.[20]

New movement by the Army of Northern Virginia gave added impetus to Slough's plans. On June 3, the first of Lee's divisions left their Fredericksburg camps and marched westward toward the Shenandoah Valley. From there, shielded by the Blue Ridge Mountains, the Confederate army marched northeastward, down the valley toward Maryland and Pennsylvania. By June 27—the day Stanton ratified Slough's plans to deport the disloyal citizens of Alexandria—Lee, riding with Lt. Gen. James Longstreet's First Corps, entered Chambersburg, Pennsylvania. Troops again poured through Alexandria as Maj. Gen. Joseph Hooker, who had commanded the Army of the Potomac since late January 1863, sought to counter Lee's northward movement. Julia Wilbur noticed trains full of soldiers steaming into Alexandria on June 16 and June 17. "Such commotion," she wrote in her diary. "So much excitement I can't work, so much noise, too." By June 27, she noted that she had never seen the city's streets "so lively" with "hundreds of men" at work on barricades to avert the Confederate raids expected nightly.[21]

Slough attempted to reassure the city's nervous residents by claiming that the fortifications around Alexandria would secure it from attack. Nonetheless, he proceeded with his plans to exile those suspected of disloyalty. On June 30 and July 1, Provost Marshal Wells notified persons on Slough's sympathizer list that failure to "make satisfactory proof of your loyalty to the Government of the United States of America" within forty-eight hours would result in their removal to City Point, Virginia, the federal port closest to Confederate territory. Any person refusing to take the Oath of Allegiance, Wells ordered, had to bring their baggage to the Prince Street dock on July 6 so that the authorities could inspect, inventory, and approve the possessions they would carry into exile. The following day, July 7, they would board a steamer at the Prince Street dock "so to be sent South."[22]

Wells's order affected more than two hundred individuals and families living in Alexandria. Some avoided the threat of exile by taking the Oath of Allegiance. Those who refused spent the first days of July frantically determining which prized possessions and necessities they would carry with them—each family was allowed only one hundred pounds of baggage—and either selling the remaining items or storing them in friends' houses. "They broke up their homes and scattered their goods," Anne Frobel bitterly noted. To her, the order was another wrong "perpetrated on the poor defenseless people by the yankees."[23]

July 6 was a miserably rainy day. Those ordered to report arrived at the Prince Street dock in a heavy downpour but found no federal authorities to receive them. They trudged the four blocks from the dock to the provost marshal's office in hopes of gaining instructions, only to discover that the order had been deferred for three days. The dispossessed citizens appeared again at the government wharf on July 9. Anne Frobel, who had come to town that day from her home at Wilton Hill, witnessed a heart-rending scene at the Prince Street dock. "The streets were thronged and packed," she wrote, "with one dense mass, of weeping and wailing humanity. Fathers and mothers, little children and big children, the old, and the young . . . all going they know not where." As they prepared to board the steamer, a rumor spread through the crowd that the War Department had rescinded the order.

Soon, an officer confirmed the whispers. Men removed the baggage already loaded on the boat and the crowd dispersed to their homes as if the order for banishment had never been written.[24]

Rebel diarist Henry Whittington raged against the callousness of the federal authorities. He surmised that Slough and Wells concocted the entire scheme to intimidate residents into taking the Oath of Allegiance. It was, he wrote, "one of the greatest acts of tyranny ever perpetuated in our midst." When Julia Wilbur heard that the order had been rescinded, she caustically noted in her diary, "Too bad." From her perspective, rebels deserved to be exiled.[25]

Secretary of War Stanton had indeed countermanded the order to send Alexandria's disloyal citizens south. Perhaps he felt that Slough had sufficiently intimidated the city's Southern sympathizers. More likely, he no longer feared their collusion with an invading Confederate army. Six days earlier, the Army of the Potomac defeated the Army of Northern Virginia at Gettysburg, Pennsylvania, and although Confederate troops remained on northern soil, Lee's second invasion had clearly failed. A year later, when Jubal Early's Confederate army literally swept to Washington's northwestern outskirts, Slough did not succumb to the fear of civilian insurgency that had gripped him during late May through early July 1863. Whatever the reason for Stanton's retraction of Slough's plan, Slough had learned that a strong hand could cow rebel sympathizers.

After its defeat at the Battle of Gettysburg, the Army of Northern Virginia retreated to approximately the same position it occupied in early June 1863 before embarking on its invasion of Pennsylvania. With the Confederate army again camped south of the Rappahannock River, Union commanders charged with protecting Washington, DC, turned their attention to other responsibilities. John Slough received orders to oversee the backlog of court-martial trials that had accumulated during the recent crisis. He served as the court's president for ten weeks in Washington and heard scores of cases before returning to Alexandria on October 14. The Army of Northern Virginia had been probing the Army of the Potomac's position around Centreville, Virginia, during the first weeks of October, and Slough's superiors wanted Alexandria's military governor to "give his personal attention to his command during the movements in front."[26]

While presiding over the courts-martial, Slough wrote Stanton about his old nemesis, John Chivington. The chief justice of the Colorado Territorial Supreme Court, Benjamin F. Hall, had learned during a grand jury investigation that Chivington and others had conspired to murder Slough so that Chivington could become colonel of the 1st Colorado. When Slough learned about the plot from Hall, he wrote Stanton to withdraw his recommendation for Chivington's promotion to brigadier general. "I thought Col. Chivington a good officer and worthy of the appointment," Slough informed the secretary of war, "but recent information convinces me that instead of being a proper person for promotion he is totally unworthy of it." He asked the secretary of war to discipline Colonel Chivington and promised to devote himself "to rid the service of this unworthy officer." He probably never acted on this vow. Chivington himself destroyed any chance at promotion when, a year later, he ordered the massacre of peaceful Cheyenne and Arapahos at Sand Creek, Colorado Territory.[27]

The War Department called Slough back to court-martial duty on January 16, 1864. He had pleased Stanton with his service during the trial of Maj. Gen. Fitz John Porter and the two men had become warm friends. Stanton now wanted his trustworthy subordinate to sit on another politically charged court-martial. The surgeon general of the United States army, Brig. Gen. William A. Hammond, had fallen afoul of Stanton's wrath and stood accused of conduct unbecoming an officer.[28]

The secretary of war had many reasons to dislike his chief medical officer. Lincoln had overruled Stanton, who recommended a prewar friend and physician, when he appointed Hammond surgeon general in late April 1862. Stanton particularly disliked Hammond's ties to the influential United States Sanitary Commission, an independent organization that the secretary of war resented for its meddling in the army's Medical Department. Perhaps most damning was Hammond's friendship with Stanton's great enemy, Maj. Gen. George B. McClellan. With McClellan's emergence as the leading contender for the 1864 Democratic presidential nomination, Stanton attempted to purge the War Department of McClellan's friends, including Hammond. In the final analysis, the two men simply could not tolerate each other. "Stanton found Hammond insufferable," writes one historian of Hammond's career. "His [Hammond's] persistent demands, his inability to take No for an answer, and his unwillingness to play the political game made it impossible for the two to work together."[29]

As surgeon general, Hammond initiated reforms that improved the deplorable care given to Union soldiers, but many traditionalists within the hidebound Medical Department found Hammond's innovations too radical and his efforts to weed out incompetent surgeons presumptuous. As complaints poured into the War Department about the surgeon general's reforms, Stanton appointed a commission to investigate claims of wrongdoing within Hammond's Medical Department. He named Andrew Reeder, the former governor of Kansas Territory, to lead the investigation. Stanton knew that Reeder would prejudge the surgeon general. While stationed at Fort Riley, Kansas Territory, in 1854, Hammond had testified that a land development scheme, in which Reeder was deeply involved, was corrupt. Reeder never forgave Hammond for the attack on his character and determined to uncover every charge of malfeasance against him, whether true or fictitious.[30]

In August 1863, Stanton dispatched the surgeon general to New Orleans to review medical affairs in the South Atlantic and Gulf Departments. In Hammond's absence, the secretary appointed his personal physician, Dr. Joseph Barnes, as acting medical chief. Having been stripped by Stanton of his authority, Hammond naively wrote Lincoln requesting either a court-martial or a court of inquiry so that he could restore his reputation. Lincoln obliged him with a court-martial.[31]

The trial began on January 19, 1864. The charges against Hammond were based on alleged irregularities in the Medical Department's purchase of supplies and Hammond's insensitive handling of a subordinate's removal. Like Fitz John Porter, he expected to be vindicated, but his optimism was unfounded. Stanton had thoroughly laid the foundation for conviction. He appointed John A. Bingham as the trial's judge advocate general; Bingham relied heavily on Reeder's negative investigative report and became increasingly hostile toward Hammond as the trial progressed. As for the court-martial's other judges, Stanton chose officers like John Slough whom he could trust or officers who had grudges against Hammond. The trial lasted for several months, and by its end Hammond knew his case had no hope. The court took only two hours to find the defendant guilty. Lincoln confirmed the sentence and Hammond left the service in disgrace on August 18, 1864.[32]

While Slough was serving on the Hammond court-martial, the Joint Committee on the Conduct of the War decided to review Alexandria's military administration. Congress had created the Joint Committee on December

10, 1861, with wide powers to investigate army affairs. When questions arose in Congress in early 1864 about the imposition of fines and jail sentences in Alexandria, the committee's members turned their attention to Slough's administration of the city's military government. Slough understood that the committee posed a serious threat to his army career. It had conducted rigorous, and sometimes politicized, investigations into the Union army's leadership, even imprisoning officers that fell afoul of its agenda. Men who underestimated the committee's powerful members did so at their peril.[33]

Slough believed that the committee's inquiries originated with the liquor sellers' false allegations against him. That the Joint Committee would initiate an investigation on rumors spread by Alexandria's liquor merchants seems improbable. Stanton had already dismissed their complaints after reviewing Slough's February 1863 reply to Westcott and Heflebower's accusations. But committee members like Radical Republicans Benjamin Wade and Zachariah Chandler would have responded to Northern reformers troubled about the treatment of freed people in Alexandria. The *New York Times* reported on February 16, 1864, that the Joint Committee was "not charmed with Gen. Slough's government of contrabands," while the *Cincinnati Daily Enquirer* denied that the committee would find Slough to be "oppressive to the contrabands under his authority." Wade and Chandler likely listened to the concerns of their abolitionist allies about Alexandria's Black people rather than the complaints of Southern liquor dealers.[34]

Julia Wilbur had many acquaintances among the North's most prominent abolitionists; most likely her communications with them prompted the Joint Committee to investigate the treatment of Alexandria's refugees. She continued questioning Slough's administration of contraband affairs throughout 1863. He had formally appointed Albert Gladwin as superintendent of contrabands in May, a decision she bitterly rued. She and her colleague, Harriet Jacobs, a reformer well-known in abolitionist circles and a former slave herself, decided to rally support among Northern relief associations for Gladwin's removal.

Wilbur spent the summer of 1863 recuperating from the demands of work at her home outside of Rochester, New York. On August 20, she met with the members of the Rochester Ladies Anti-Slavery Society to review her work, including her struggles with Gladwin. That night, she wrote in her diary that the members were "indignant that a man like Mr. G[ladwin] is tolerated in [that] city." Meanwhile, Jacobs was corresponding with her supporters about Gladwin's "persistent practice of crowding families into the barracks, charging them exorbitant rents, then punishing those unable to pay." The *Weekly Anglo African*, a prominent New York African American newspaper that followed Jacobs's work, joined the attack on the superintendent, claiming that he skimmed a portion of the rents to supplement his income.[35]

Wilbur and Jacobs were not alone in the battle against Slough's superintendent of contrabands. Dr. Samuel Shaw, Alexandria's assistant surgeon for contrabands, had complained to his superior, Dr. J. G. Bigelow, about Gladwin's "course of tyranny and oppression" in threatening sick and destitute refugees with eviction if they failed to pay their rent. When Bigelow ignored his complaint, Shaw and two other physicians wrote the Freedmen's Relief Association of Washington on July 30, 1863, charging that Gladwin used threats to manage Alexandria's freed people. As the three physicians had anticipated, the Freedmen's Relief Association filed a formal complaint against Gladwin with the secretary of war.[36]

Anna Barnes and Julia Wilbur's letters to Lincoln and Stanton had instigated a War Department review of Slough's refugee policies in March 1863. The Freedmen's Relief Association's complaint against Gladwin led to a second review five months later; this time, Slough assigned his aide-de-camp, Capt. William Gwynne, to investigate. In his October 1 report, Gwynne dismissed the three physicians' accusations as "very much exaggerated, if not *untrue.*" He had found the refugees' barracks to be clean, comfortable, and in good condition and he could find no instance of a destitute, elderly, or sick person being forced to pay rent. Most importantly, he believed that Gladwin's efforts had reduced the reliance of Black people on government support, thereby minimizing their expense. As for Julia Wilbur and Harriet Jacobs, Gwynne dismissed their efforts as "meddling." Slough forwarded Gwynne's report to the War Department with his own endorsement of Albert Gladwin. "I commend the policy inaugurated by Mr. Gladwin," he wrote, "of as soon as possible making them [the refugees] self-dependent, rather than that policy which intermeddling, would-be philanthropists would inaugurate."[37]

While the Freedmen's Relief Association's charges did not lead to Gladwin's removal, Wilbur's and Jacobs's communications with their sponsors increased outside scrutiny of his work. On December 10, 1863, representatives from the Rochester abolitionist community visited several buildings occupied by Alexandria's freed people. "They are very indignant," Wilbur wrote in her diary, "that [the] Gov[ernment] sh[ould] rent such buildings. Mr. G. came before we left & was mighty mad that they had seen these." The next day, the New York Commission of Friends toured the refugees' lodgings, much to Gladwin's "discomfort." Finally, on January 7, 1864, Benjamin Latham and Henry Dickinson, prominent New York Quakers involved in relief efforts, visited Alexandria to inspect the government's facilities for refugees. After their tour, the two men met with Slough to discuss his administration's treatment of freed people. Appalled by what they saw, any of these reformers could have voiced their displeasure to their Radical Republican friends in Congress, leading to the Joint Committee's investigation of Slough's governance.[38]

On February 12, 1864, the Joint Committee convened its hearings into the military administration of Alexandria, Virginia. The members first questioned Capt. John C. Wyman, who had been Alexandria's provost marshal from September 17, 1862, until February 1, 1863. Although Slough had sacked him for lax enforcement of the liquor prohibition, Wyman did not use the hearings to even the score. When the committee questioned why so many civilians complained about Slough's administration, the captain replied that "the foundation of the movement was simply a disposition to retaliate upon him [Slough] for having interfered with what they considered their legitimate business," the sale of liquor. Wyman also insisted that the treatment of Black refugees in Alexandria "reflects great credit on the government." He confirmed that the policy of requiring rent payments encouraged many freed people to build their own homes where they now enjoyed "many comforts." At the same time, the government provided "liberal provisions" for the aged and the infirm. Wyman concluded his testimony without damaging the military governor before the Joint Committee.[39]

The committee joined Slough and Gladwin the next day to inspect the condition of Alexandria's freed people and resumed its hearings on February 16 with Slough's testimony. The members treated the brigadier general respectfully, and Slough answered their questions with ease. He recalled his arrival in Alexandria in August 1862 when "the sale of liquor was the prolific source of all the trouble." He then fielded a range of questions about his administration. He discussed the punishment of persons found guilty of breaking the liquor regulations. He insisted that all fines had been applied appropriately toward city improvements and other administrative expenses.

He testified that the keepers at the Slave Pen resorted to the shower bath punishment rarely and only on "drunken, disorderly & troublesome" prisoners. Most importantly, he proudly informed the committee that his policies toward the city's freed people had resulted in a fourfold reduction in the numbers on relief.[40]

Slough carefully told the members what they wanted to hear. He asserted that his commanding officers, Stanton, and even Lincoln, had approved of his liquor regulations. He reminded them that using fines to pay for administrative expenses saved the government money. And he assured them that many of Alexandria's freed people were "now in a thrifty & prosperous condition." Recognizing that the misappropriation of fines was potentially the most serious allegation against his administration, Slough finished his testimony by presenting the bids he had solicited for the repaving of King Street and promising the members a list of all the fines that had been collected. None of the committee's members seemed to doubt his word or question his actions. Slough, for his part, controlled his temper even though he could have misperceived the committee's investigation as an attack on his reputation.

Three more witnesses testified before the committee: property clerk Charles Travis on February 18–19, aide-de-camp Capt. William Gwynne on February 19, and provost marshal Lt. Col. Henry Wells on February 22. All three men endorsed Slough's competency as Alexandria's military governor. The committee questioned Travis and Gwynne closely about the disposition of confiscated liquor. Travis assured the members that appropriate legal proceedings accompanied all confiscations, that officers with access to liquor did not supply civilians, and that the officers associated with the military governor's office or the provost marshal's office never appropriated spirits for their personal use. Gwynne testified that confiscated liquor was mainly used for medicinal purposes by the city's military and general hospitals and by regimental surgeons. He seconded Travis's statement that liquor was never distributed to officers for private use.[41]

The last witness to testify—Lt. Col. Henry Wells—perhaps knew Slough the best. For more than a year, he had worked closely with Slough, first as the general's executive officer and Alexandria's provost marshal and more recently as provost marshal for the Department and Defenses of Washington south of the Potomac River. Wells did not temper his remarks about the military governor. He admitted that Slough made more enemies than friends because his manner was "not very gracious or pleasant" but "a little haughty & curt." Nonetheless, he could not recall a single instance of conflict between Slough and Alexandria's citizens other than the controversy over the sale of liquor. It was the liquor sellers, Wells claimed, who sought to undermine Slough through accusations addressed to Stanton. As for Julia Wilbur and Harriet Jacobs, they too complained but only because they wanted to wrest the care of the city's freed people from the proper authorities. In each instance, Slough's superiors had supported the military governor against his detractors.[42]

Wells only saw improvements since Slough's appointment. Drunken and lawless soldiers no longer rampaged in Alexandria's neighborhoods. Fines levied against the liquor sellers helped clean and pave its streets. Proper management had improved conditions within the Slave Pen. And contrabands enjoyed better treatment in Alexandria than in other refugee centers. The result, Wells concluded, was that "Alexandria is today the most quiet [and] orderly city of its size in the United States." With Wells's glowing testimony, the Joint Committee ended its investigation into Alexandria's military administration.

The testimony taken by the Joint Committee vindicated Slough and his military government. Two months after the hearings, Sen. Zachariah Chandler submitted the committee's report to the Senate. It completely exonerated Slough. The members had determined through their investigation that "the administration of General Slough has been characterized by energy, discretion, and a careful regard for the peace and good order of the community over which he was appointed and deserves . . . the commendation of the military and civil authorities of our government."[43]

Slough had defeated his enemies and silenced his detractors. The liquor sellers' campaign to derail Slough's administration lost all its impetus and quietly disappeared. Julia Wilbur never again complained to President Lincoln or Secretary of War Stanton about Albert Gladwin or the treatment of refugees in Alexandria. And the possibility of censure by the Joint Committee no longer threatened Slough's career. Despite Alexandria's proximity to Washington's overwrought political atmosphere—a proximity that might have overwhelmed a less capable administrator—Slough's skill as Alexandria's military governor had earned the Joint Committee's admiration.

13

∞∞∞∞∞

"Why Then Am I Kept Here So Long?"

BRIG. GEN. JOHN STARKWEATHER HOSTED A LAVISH SUPPER AT HIS Washington residence the evening of April 21, 1864. Among the many military and civilian guests, he invited his colleague, John Slough, to dine. Slough had much to celebrate. The day before, the Joint Committee on the Conduct of the War had released its report commending him for his work in Alexandria. Meanwhile, the testimony in the Hammond court-martial was nearing its conclusion and Starkweather, one of the trial's judges, invited the court's members to enjoy a respite from the tedious proceedings. Maj. John Bingham, the trial's judge advocate, and Maj. Gen. Richard Oglesby, the court's president, along with Generals Ketchum, Greene, Paine, Morris, Howe, and Slough—all judges at the Hammond trial—gathered at Starkweather's home to relax and socialize.

The guests drank punch and conversed as they awaited supper. The week's newspapers offered them little war news to discuss. They may have talked about the latest Union failure, a joint army-navy expedition floundering on the Red River in Louisiana. Or the conversation may have turned to Lt. Gen. Ulysses S. Grant, newly called from the west by Lincoln to command all the Union armies. At 9:00 p.m., the guests entered a flag-draped dining room to sit down at a table "spread in a manner that would have excited the admiration of the most fastidious epicure." The men enjoyed a leisurely meal of several courses—likely oysters, soup, a fish course, several meat entrees, side dishes of salad and vegetables, finishing with sweets and coffee—before the obligatory after-dinner round of brandy, cigars, and speeches. It was early morning before the snifters had been drained, the last toast given, and the guests departed.[1]

For the first time since his arrival in Alexandria, Slough could enjoy leisurely meals with friends and other pleasurable diversions. He visited the Russian fleet, anchored in the Potomac during its December 1863 friendship tour; Slough drank to the "great bond of Union between Russia and the United States." A month later, he joined a large crowd of Alexandrians to cheer as the "Panorama of the Southern Rebellion" unveiled painting after painting of Union heroes and their victories. And he attended the closing festivities at the US Sanitary Commission's "National Fair" held in Washington in March 1864. The fair's commissioners invited Slough and other general officers from the Washington area to hear Maj. Gen. Daniel Sickles's address the final night of the exposition. President Lincoln also offered a few remarks.[2]

The newspapers covering Slough's attendance at these functions made no mention of Arabella. They named only Slough and his staff officers, so it is possible that Slough visited the Russian fleet, the "Panorama of the Southern Rebellion," and the Washington "National Fair" without his wife. John and Arabella's family had grown to three boys and one girl by early 1864: nine-year-old Willie, seven-year-old John, five-year-old Sallie, and two-year-old Martin. Although they lived on South St. Asaph Street in Alexandria, Willie and John played with Tad Lincoln in the White House when their father had business in Washington. The two older boys entered Alexandria's St. John's Academy in fall 1864. On at least one occasion, Slough had to discipline them for fighting with other boys. Whether the general was a strict disciplinarian or a father indulgent of his children's misbehavior cannot be ascertained. With just census records, brief newspaper comments, and a few stories handed down to Slough's great-granddaughter, only the barest picture of the Slough family can be drawn. Nothing more is known.[3]

We can be certain, however, that Slough's ambition and devotion to duty focused him on his military, rather than his familial, responsibilities. Ongoing threats to Alexandria's safety occupied his time during early 1864. At times, Confederate guerrillas attacked the Orange and Alexandria Railroad within a few miles of the city. Slough dispatched troops on January 27 and March 19 to chase them away from the tracks and to guard Alexandria's approaches. Smallpox also threatened the city's residents during the winter months. As it had the previous year, the disease spread quickly through the city's refugee population. Slough ordered Alexandria's medical officers and physicians to report all new cases. He also directed Dr. Christian Hines, the city's chief medical officer, to inoculate any resident requesting vaccination; those too poor to pay were inoculated for free. African Americans stricken with smallpox were admitted to the Contraband Hospital and Claremont Hospital—two former residences of rebel sympathizers—or to L'Overture Hospital, which opened in February 1864 to care for Black soldiers and civilians.[4]

Despite the availability of hospital care, Julia Wilbur still found fault with the medical treatment of Black refugees. She complained that the sick confined at the Contraband Hospital lacked proper nourishment and adequate clothing. "They have no bread, only poor flour & worse corn meal," she wrote in her diary, and the surgeons "seem indifferent to their wants." Yet, she admitted, the medical authorities had made progress in the care of the sick. Slough had replaced Dr. John R. Bigelow, who had medical responsibility for the city's freed people, with Dr. Edwin Bentley. Wilbur credited Bentley with improvements at Claremont Hospital. "As far as I can learn," she reported to the Rochester Ladies Anti-Slavery Society, "the patients are now properly cared for, and all fare alike." More importantly, the 1864 outbreak numbered one-quarter of the previous winter's cases; improvements in refugee housing along with Slough's campaign to vaccinate Alexandria's population, both Black and white, undoubtedly contributed to the reduction in smallpox.[5]

By July 1864, Wilbur began to comment positively in her diary about the circumstances of Alexandria's freed people. After she had stopped at several homes and a school one day, she wrote, "Things look more comfortable than I ever saw them before. Quite hopeful." She acknowledged a few days later that many freed people now "live very nice & comfortable" and that "many do very well." Even though Wilbur still complained about impoverished refugees, Slough could claim some responsibility for the progress she saw. He had provided the destitute with housing, the sick with hospitals, and the young with space for schools. He had even seized property for use as a "Contrabands' Cemetery," a space Wilbur grudgingly admitted was "as good a place as they could get." He had provided a safe, orderly city in which formerly enslaved men and women could find employment, build their own homes, and raise their families. But for all Slough's efforts, the successes that Alexandria's freed people enjoyed resulted from their own resilience and resourcefulness. Their determination to lead productive, self-sufficient lives improved their circumstances far more than the federal government's intervention or relief workers' charity.[6]

Administering a well-ordered city continued to demand Slough's attention during the first half of 1864. His determination "to secure a degree of cleanliness in the city that may prevent epidemic disease" led to new regulations requiring Alexandria's civilians and soldiers to dispose of garbage and manure at a specific site south of town and to remove dead animals for prompt burial. He ordered the destruction of the city's brothels and the banishment of its prostitutes because "many deserters from this army are assisted by women of ill-fame of this city." He continued to prohibit liquor sales to soldiers, although the city's increasing security enabled him to permit its sale to civilians. In notices published in the *Alexandria Gazette*, he allowed "all loyal and respectable hotel, saloon, and restaurant keepers" to sell malt liquor upon posting a $1,000 bond and taking the Oath of Allegiance.[7]

In part, Slough could thank Ulysses S. Grant for the quiet that prevailed in Alexandria. Grant launched his Overland campaign on May 4, sending the Army of the Potomac into a series of extremely costly battles at the Wilderness, Spotsylvania, North Anna, and Cold Harbor. The Union army lost fifty-five thousand men during six weeks of brutal fighting. Grant stripped the regiments from the camps surrounding Washington, Arlington, and Alexandria to fill his depleted ranks. He also established his army's base at City Point, Virginia. As supplies for the Army of the Potomac filled City Point's wharves and warehouses, Julia Wilbur noticed that "not so much business" occupied Alexandria's waterfront. The city's once busy streets emptied of soldiers and wagons.[8]

By early July 1864, Slough had become bored with his responsibilities and impatient for new opportunities. After twenty-two months as Alexandria's military governor, he realized that "nothing is left for me to do but mere matters of form." He wrote Secretary of War Stanton on July 8 to request a new assignment. He began his lengthy letter—more than five pages—by stating that he entered military service "actuated by the desire which has not been dimmed of contributing whatever of energy and capacity I possess toward the work of crushing this unholy rebellion." He reminded Stanton of his accomplishments: his rapid promotion from captain to colonel to brigadier general in ten months, the recognition he had earned for "gallant

& meritorious service in New Mexico and Harpers Ferry," and the approval the president, the secretary, and the Joint Committee on the Conduct of the War had shown for his performance in Alexandria. He complained that other officers, "inferior in all that is necessary to constitute the successful military man," enjoyed positions of more responsibility. "Why then," he asked, "am I kept here so long?" He requested "respectfully, yet urgently" to be transferred to command of a district or department, preferably in the Far West. If Stanton could not grant his request, he proposed that he resign on July 24, the third anniversary of his entry into service.[9]

Slough's timing could not have been worse. Two days before he wrote Stanton, fifteen thousand rebels under Maj. Gen. Jubal Early splashed across the Potomac into Maryland. Opposing the Confederate army was a makeshift force of some seven thousand men commanded by the unreliable Gen. Lew Wallace. Early's men pushed the Yankees aside on July 9 at the Battle of Monocacy and headed toward Washington, DC. The Confederate army entered the city's outskirts on July 11 and halted five miles northwest of the White House. Because Grant's Overland campaign had denuded Washington of troops, only "convalescents, militia, and a few odds and ends of army units" protected the city from Early's soldiers. With the rebels on the verge of entering the capital, Stanton had no time to consider Slough's petition nor Slough to press his demand.[10]

The few troops under Slough's command were rushed into Washington's defenses, leaving Alexandria vulnerable to attack by even a small force of Confederates. Henry Whittington described the city's anxious state: "The excitement this evening has increased to a panic in our city," he wrote, "and all the employees of the government, including the American citizens of African descent, were being drilled & the outskirts of the city were blockaded by wagons." The crisis prompted Alexandria's civilian authorities to consider enlisting a Home Guard. The Board of Aldermen and the City Council requested that Slough enroll males between the ages of sixteen and fifty years "so as to be ready for effective service at the earliest practicable moment, for the defence [sic] of the city." On July 12, the loyal citizens of Alexandria convened at Liberty Hall to organize a Home Guard; about sixty men volunteered. Slough did not need to resort to them. Jubal Early was not able to push his exhausted troops to attack the capital before the Army of the Potomac's 6th Corps filled its defenses. The Confederate commander realized that his men could not breach the newly manned fortifications and ordered them to withdraw. His army returned to Virginia on July 13, ending the latest threat to the capital city.[11]

Stanton ignored Slough's appeal for a new command while Early's Confederates advanced against Washington. Yet even after the threat receded, the secretary did not respond to his friend. In exasperation, Slough wrote Col. E. D. Townsend, assistant adjutant general at the War Department, on July 30, 1864, six days after his threatened date of resignation. He enclosed a copy of his July 8 letter to Stanton, asked for a reply to its contents, and pompously ended his letter, "If I am not to be permitted to participate more prominently than I am here in the effort to crush the armed rebellion, I desire to make a record for my posterity that will exhibit to them the fact that I desired a more active and responsible position and made efforts to attain it." His letter went unanswered.[12]

Stanton suspected that Alexandria's military governor did not possess the temperament for departmental command despite his success as Alexandria's military governor. Slough's tendency to perceive insults, his "haughty & curt" manner, as Lieutenant Colonel Wells had described him to the Joint Committee, and his propensity to act impulsively made him a potential liability to the Lincoln administration. He had tangled with Maj. Gen. Joseph Hooker in June 1863, when Hooker was mobilizing the Army of the Potomac to stop Lee's invasion of Pennsylvania. Without consulting his superiors, Slough told Col. Horatio Sickel, commanding officer of the 2nd Brigade, Pennsylvania Reserve Corps, to ignore Hooker's order to report to Gen. Samuel Crawford's division. Sickel's brigade fell under Slough's command. Slough did not report to Hooker and, in matters concerning his troops, refused to recognize Hooker's authority. When the major general learned that Slough had countermanded his order, he angrily wrote General-in-Chief Halleck to demand Slough's arrest for insubordination. Halleck quickly informed Hooker that no more troops, including the 2nd Brigade, could be pulled from the Defenses of Washington. There the dispute ended, although Halleck and Stanton must surely have noted Slough's unilateral decision to disobey a superior officer's order.[13]

Four months later, Slough became embroiled with Capt. Carroll Potter, a staff officer to Slough's direct superior, Maj. Gen. Christopher Augur. Slough took offense when Potter criticized him for failing to report on a situation beyond his command. Slough lashed out at Potter and then had to justify his angry reaction to Augur. He told his commanding officer that he believed Captain Potter had censured him without Augur's authorization and that he responded "as most officers would have done under the circumstances." On reflection, he realized that Potter did not mean any "disrespect or censure" and asked Augur to ignore anything "offensive" he might have said. Despite his backpedaling, Slough's hot-headed response to a perceived attack on his authority made him appear unduly contentious.[14]

Slough involved Major General Augur in another dispute with a subordinate only two weeks before his letter to Stanton requesting a new command. On June 25, 1864, he asked Augur for instructions on how to handle a "conflict of authority" with Col. W. H. Browne of the 2nd Brigade, Vermont Reserve Corps. No more information exists in the National Archives about this disagreement. How Augur responded to Slough or whether Stanton heard about his dispute with Colonel Browne is unknown. But we do know that Stanton fielded complaints spurred by the liquor sellers' campaign against Slough; listened to charges by Julia Wilbur, Harriet Jacobs, and other reformers about the treatment of freed people in Alexandria; recognized the seriousness of the Joint Committee's investigation; probably was aware of Hooker's demand that Slough be arrested for insubordination; and possibly knew about the general's quarrels with other officers. These were more than enough reasons for Stanton to question his suitability for higher command. The secretary of war ignored his request for a new assignment and Slough remained in Alexandria for another year.[15]

The military governor's duties were not trivial even though Slough claimed that "mere matters of form" occupied his time. Responsible for the management of a Southern city less than ten miles from the capital, he exerted control over Alexandria's order and cleanliness, retained jurisdiction over its freed people, supervised the military police and patrols, performed the civil duties of a military governor, and commanded the troops assigned to the city's defense. He also had responsibility for guarding the Orange and Alexandria Railroad, which ran west from Alexandria through Springfield, Burke's Station, Fairfax Station, and Union Mills before connecting with the Manassas Gap Railroad at Manassas Junction, Virginia. Along these two railways ran the trains that supplied Union Gen. Phil Sheridan's campaign in the Shenandoah Valley during late summer and fall of 1864.[16]

Slough's initial assignment covered the first five miles of tracks leaving Alexandria, but on September 28, 1864, Major General Augur placed him in charge of guarding the Orange and Alexandria Railroad the entire distance to Bull Run Creek. Augur assigned Slough several regiments to protect the railroad; watch over its many bridges, water tanks, and stations; and maintain the telegraph wire that ran alongside the tracks. The short distance between Alexandria and Bull Run Creek—only twenty-seven miles—belied the difficulties Slough faced in defending the railway. Confederate Lt. Col. John Mosby's Partisan Rangers operated at will in the Virginia countryside through which the Orange and Alexandria and the Manassas Gap Railroads ran, and no number of Yankee regiments could prevent Mosby's men from wreaking havoc on the supply trains or the soldiers who guarded them.[17]

During October, Mosby's troopers attacked up and down the two railroad lines. His men first hit the Manassas Gap Railroad. Within a week, they fired on a construction train outside of Gainesville, Virginia, tore up the tracks at Salem, shelled the Union camp at Rectorville, and derailed a train at White Plains. Having disrupted the Manassas Gap Railroad in a matter of days, the rebel guerrillas turned their attention to the Orange and Alexandria Railroad. On October 12, they attacked the train guard posted at Burke's Station and probed the picket lines outside of Alexandria. Four days later, they sabotaged the tracks at Fairfax Station and struck again at Burke's Station.[18]

Slough decided that heavy-handed measures were needed to halt the guerrillas' depredations against the Orange and Alexandria Railroad. He received permission from headquarters to force Southern sympathizers to ride the trains as hostages. On October 17, seven secessionists from Alexandria and three rebel prisoners acted as human shields, riding in the boxcars of two trains. Anne Frobel railed against this uncivilized action. The Yankees, she wrote in her diary, "seized up all the gentlemen, all about the town, all the old men (for there was no other there)—the decrepit, the lame, the maimed, the halt, and the blind, and put them on the cars to protect them, and there these old men were kept night and day, in all kinds of weather, traveling up and down, up and down, for weeks and months." Frobel angrily exaggerated the time that Slough used Alexandria's secessionists and captured rebel soldiers to deter attacks against the railroad. Hostages rode the trains until Mosby's partisans left the area two weeks later.[19]

On November 6, Slough reported "all quiet along the line of the railroad."
He had arrived in Manassas Junction the previous day to supervise troops
engaged in taking up the tracks. Phil Sheridan's army had destroyed Jubal
Early's Confederates at Cedar Creek, and, aside from guerrilla activity, the
Yankees had ended armed resistance in the lower Shenandoah Valley. No
longer needing the Manassas Gap Railroad to supply Union troops in the
valley, Halleck ordered Augur to tear up the tracks, remove the telegraph
wires, and recall the train guards. Slough oversaw work details at Manassas
Junction until Augur and his staff decided that the railroad's destruction
had been accomplished. Sixteen miles of the Orange and Alexandria line
remained between Alexandria and Union Mills, but with the number of
military trains greatly diminished, Mosby and his men no longer considered
the railroad a worthwhile target.[20]

With the tracks destroyed and Mosby's troopers gone, Slough returned
to Alexandria on November 14. He immediately learned that squabbling
had erupted between Julia Wilbur and his superintendent of contrabands,
Albert Gladwin, over Gladwin's efforts to evict her from the rooms she
used to distribute clothing to refugees. It was not the first time the two had
fought over space. In March 1864, Gladwin tried to force Wilbur and Harriet
Jacobs to occupy undesirable rooms in the Contraband Hospital, a space
where the women feared the "sick, the dying, & the dead . . . would haunt
us." Wilbur threatened to appeal Gladwin's decision to Slough, whereupon
Gladwin cried, "Oh! I don't want you to go to Gen. Slough, don't do that" and
backed down. Now, with Slough absent at Manassas Junction, Gladwin again
decided that Wilbur should vacate her rooms so that he could put them to
"better use." Wilbur had to move to new, less desirable space, but Gladwin's
ongoing vendetta against her proved his undoing. Slough had tired of his
pettiness, and when Gladwin became embroiled with US Colored Troops
stationed in Alexandria, Slough decided to remove him.[21]

Alexandria's superintendent of contrabands had overseen the burial of
freed people since January 1864, when Slough seized property on South
Washington Street for use as a "Contrabands' Cemetery." Gladwin considered Black soldiers no different than the contrabands he supervised. Because
long-standing custom did not permit the interment of Black people with
white people, he directed that men who died at L'Overture Hospital, the
facility dedicated to the United States Colored Troops (USCT), be buried in

the Contrabands' Cemetery. The practice irritated Black soldiers recuperating at L'Overture Hospital. They served in the Union Army, shared "equally the dangers and hardships in this mighty contest," and believed that they deserved "the same rights and privileges of burial in every way with our fellow soldiers, who only differ from us in color." War had changed these men, many of whom had been once enslaved, and they knew they merited the honor of a soldier's burial.[22]

Their anger boiled over on December 27, 1864, when Gladwin stopped the funeral procession of USCT Private Murphy to insist that his remains be carried to the Contrabands' Cemetery. Gladwin arrested the African American driver of the hearse when he refused to follow the superintendent's order. That evening, a petition circulated among the wards at L'Overture Hospital; 443 USCT soldiers signed the document. They avowed that "we are not contrabands, but soldiers in the U.S. Army," whose bodies deserved to "find a resting place in the ground designated for the burial of the brave defenders of our countries [sic] flag." The United States government could not ignore their petition nor the moral authority of their claim. Quartermaster General Montgomery Meigs, who had responsibility for the country's military cemeteries, reviewed the petition and ruled that Black soldiers who died at L'Overture Hospital would henceforth be interred in Alexandria's Soldiers Cemetery.[23]

Two weeks after the USCT soldiers' petition, Julia Wilbur recorded in her diary that Albert Gladwin had been "disposed." She believed that her long-standing opposition had finally resulted in his dismissal. More likely, Slough took advantage of the opportunity presented by Meig's decision to rid himself of his troublesome superintendent. Julia Wilbur had won her battle against Albert Gladwin, yet left her position in Alexandria only three weeks after his departure. She was exhausted, worn out by her struggles with Gladwin and the federal authorities, by her work caring for Alexandria's most destitute freed people, and by her bitter realization that Black people "must forever be the victim of the white man's cupidity." She moved to Washington to live with her sister and only occasionally returned to Alexandria.[24]

• • •

Slough's chances for promotion to major general faded as the war in Virginia entered its final months. On January 5, 1865, he requested that Stanton acknowledge his "faithful performance of difficult duty for more than two and one half years in one place" by awarding him the rank of brevet major general. As he undoubtedly suspected, promotion was not likely forthcoming. He had missed the fighting, when officers won promotion. He lost that chance in July 1862 when, angered that General Cooper won the division command he thought he deserved, he impulsively asked to be relieved of duty. Only administrative paperwork and the usual regulations for maintaining order remained for Alexandria's military governor. Undermined by his temperament, the recognition Slough craved again eluded him.[25]

The Confederacy was now collapsing into its death throes. The Army of the Potomac was steadily weakening Lee's fifty thousand hungry, ill-clad, and battle-weary troops in the Petersburg trenches. The Union Army of the Cumberland had destroyed the Confederate Army of Tennessee at the Battle of Nashville; the rebels' major army in the West virtually disappeared after this defeat. Maj. Gen. William T. Sherman and his army were rampaging through South Carolina after devastating Georgia and capturing Savannah. With disaster piling upon disaster for the Confederacy, President Lincoln insisted on unconditional surrender when Confederate emissaries proposed an armistice. Precious little hope remained within the Confederacy for victory and independence.

On April 2, the Army of the Potomac finally overwhelmed the dwindling number of Confederate defenders stretched for thirty miles around Richmond and Petersburg. The Union breakthrough forced the Army of Northern Virginia to abandon the Petersburg line. Richmond could no longer be held. That night, as the Army of Northern Virginia began its retreat toward Appomattox Court House, President Jefferson Davis and the Confederate government fled the rebel capital.

When the news of Richmond's fall reached Alexandria on April 3, all the surrounding forts and batteries fired salute after salute in celebration. That evening, a rejoicing throng crowded into the city's market and lined the roofs of the buildings around the square to listen to Slough and Alexandria's civilian leaders hail the great Union victory. The crowd applauded and cheered each speaker. Afterwards, fireworks in several parts of the city delighted revelers.[26]

Lee surrendered the Army of Northern Virginia to Ulysses S. Grant on

Palm Sunday, April 9, and Alexandrians again exulted. "Rousing Union meetings" were held at Alexandria's Liberty Hall and Parker's Theater; some twenty-five hundred residents crammed into the two buildings to celebrate the end of the Confederacy's most formidable army. Slough spoke at Liberty Hall while the loyal governor of Virginia, Francis Pierpont, and Provost Marshal Henry Wells addressed the crowd at Parker's Theater. Homeowners illuminated their residences in celebration. Soldiers' Rest, the Union army's convalescent hospital, had Grant, Sherman, and Sheridan's names with the word "Victory" emblazoned over the front door of its headquarters. Regimental bands gave impromptu concerts for the enjoyment of the merrymakers parading in the streets. On April 11, at twelve noon, a two-hundred-gun salute thundered in front of Slough's headquarters while the city's bells pealed in yet another celebration. Three days later, Slough led the garrison's troops in a victory parade. Loyal Alexandrians were euphoric. They had undergone almost four years of military occupation and now the end of the war was at hand.[27]

Slough had served as Alexandria's military governor for thirty-two months. Like its residents, he welcomed Lee's surrender as the beginning of peace and the return of civilian authority. He informed the city council that around May 1, the military would yield control over liquor sales, the city's sanitation, the arrest and punishment of civilians (except for military offenses), and civil order in general to the local government. He recommended to the councilmen that they continue to prohibit the sale of liquor to soldiers and the city's freed people and suggested that liquor fines be applied to the maintenance of streets and the payment of the police. He also recommended that the civil authorities give "full protection to the persons and property" of freed people—one-half of Alexandria's population was African American by 1865—and that they repeal any distinction between Black and white people in local laws.[28]

Slough had grown weary of his responsibilities as military governor and hoped that peace would bring new opportunities for personal advancement. But Appomattox did not lead to the withdrawal of troops from northern Virginia nor the cessation of military operations. On April 14, conspirators led by John Wilkes Booth set out to murder President Lincoln, Vice President Andrew Johnson, and Secretary of State William Seward. Booth assassinated

Lincoln at Ford's Theater while Lewis Powell grievously wounded Seward after forcing his way into the secretary's home. Only George Atzerodt, charged with murdering Johnson, failed his assignment.[29]

The conspirators' escape after the night's crimes triggered a manhunt through Maryland and northern Virginia that must have appeared as if the war had not yet ended. Even as the president lay dying in a boarding house across from Ford's Theater, the military began its campaign to apprehend the fugitives. Stanton and his commanders reasoned that Booth would probably pass through Alexandria on his way to safe haven among like-minded Southerners. Shortly after midnight on April 15, General Augur warned Slough to prevent all persons from leaving Alexandria. He telegrammed the military governor a few hours later naming Booth as the president's assassin. He ordered Slough to patrol the Potomac's shores from Washington to Alexandria and to prohibit any travel on the river. Meanwhile, Gen. James Hardie forwarded Stanton's instructions to the superintendent of military railroads at Alexandria to stop all southbound trains and to apply to Slough for troops to arrest any unknown person seeking passage.[30]

The authorities' frenzied efforts on April 15 to shut off routes of escape yielded nothing. Booth and his accomplice, David Herold, successfully slipped out of Washington. For the next eleven days, troops combed the Maryland and northern Virginia countryside. Slough and his provost marshal, Capt. W. W. Winship, received orders during those chaotic days to dispatch patrols to aid in the hunt. Finally, on April 26, a cavalry squad caught the fugitives at Garrett's Farm north of Bowling Green, Virginia. Booth was killed and Herold taken prisoner.[31]

Lincoln's death thrust the loyal citizens of Alexandria into deep mourning. Julia Wilbur attended the April 14 victory parade in Alexandria. She remained in the city the next day, unable to leave because of the suspension of all travel. As she walked the streets, she noticed houses draped in black, flags at half-mast, and the continuous tolling of bells. Soldiers forced reluctant Southern sympathizers to place black crepe on their doors. The president's death particularly affected Alexandria's freed people. "Every colored faces [sic] is sad," Wilbur wrote in her diary. "'Uncle Sam' is dead & many seem to know that they have lost a friend. Every cabin, shanty, & shed where they live has something black upon it."

She returned to Washington on April 16 once ferry service resumed between Alexandria and the nation's capital. By then Lincoln's body had been laid in the East Room of the White House, which was draped in black "like a sepulcher." Grieving citizens, both Black and white, paid their respects to the dead president. Wilbur joined the mourners on April 17, quickly passing by Lincoln's corpse, for the crowd was not allowed to pause before the body. She thought Lincoln looked "very white but natural."[32]

Two days later, a large crowd accompanied the solemn procession transporting Lincoln's coffin from the White House, down Pennsylvania Avenue to the Capitol Rotunda. There the president's remains lay in state until Friday, April 21, a week after the assassination, when his body was transported again, this time to Washington's Baltimore and Ohio depot, where a funeral train awaited to take the martyred president back home to Springfield, Illinois. Slough joined the public mourning in an official capacity. Along with Quartermaster General Meigs and several other army and navy officers, he stood watch over Lincoln's body the last day that it lay in state in the Rotunda. The next day, he rode beside President Andrew Johnson's carriage in the funeral procession from the Capitol to the Baltimore and Ohio railroad station.[33]

It was an uneasy time for Americans, especially those who had once been enslaved. The Emancipation Proclamation, the Union army's presence, and the slaves' own determination to be free had ended slavery throughout the South, although the institution would not be abolished legally until the ratification of the Thirteenth Amendment on December 6, 1865. Blacks had gained their freedom, but no one knew what rights, if any, they would obtain with their new status. African Americans worried that the laws that had oppressed them in the old South might be reinstated with the restoration of civil government.

Concerned that Virginia's loyal government had not repealed the antebellum statutes that had sustained slavery, a committee of Alexandria's Black residents gathered on April 28 to draft resolutions addressed to President Johnson. The resolutions expressed their fears that a reversion to civil authority would again subject African Americans to the onerous laws of prewar Virginia. In particular, the document named those statutes that affected the validity of contracts between persons of color, that prevented Black people from obtaining the benefits of an education, and that excluded them from giving testimony in court. The petitioners asked the federal government to protect them "from again coming under the operation of the unjust and oppressive laws." That same evening, the committee wrote Slough, as representative of the Union army that had protected Alexandria's freed people, to request his assistance in preserving their rights. They praised him "for the generally quiet and peaceful manner in which we have, under his administration, been permitted to pursue our own labors, and enjoy our religious, educational, and social privileges." Knowing that Slough had proposed handing over some of his authority to the civil government at the beginning of May, they begged him to remain in charge until revised state laws offered African Americans "the same just and liberal principles of dealing as contemplated by our worthy Military Governor."[34]

Alexandria's freed people's correspondence with Johnson and Slough reflects a profound transition in the relationship between the United States government and African Americans. Four years earlier, at the start of the Civil War, the federal government recognized only white slaveholders; no direct relationship existed between the government and the country's enslaved people. But as Black people sought refuge within Union lines and offered their labor and their lives for the Union cause, they realized that their contributions to the war effort made a compelling case for recognition. The government's relationship with its citizens, they came to understand, should be based on "useful service" and not race or property rights. As historian Chandra Manning explains, Black people could expect the federal government's protection of their rights as "exchange" for the invaluable services they had rendered to the successful conclusion of the war. Alexandria's freed people, who dug ditches and erected barricades, washed uniforms and cooked hospital meals, hauled supplies off ships and loaded them on to military trains, and ultimately enlisted and fought in the Union army, recognized the value of these services when they called on Johnson and Slough to protect their hard-won rights.[35]

Although the relationship between Black people and the United States government had changed, the freed people's letter to Alexandria's military governor was still a surprising correspondence. Throughout his life, Slough had considered Black people to be a subordinate race. His conservative Democratic principles caused Salmon P. Chase to label his beliefs as proslavery in 1857. He vowed during the 1859 Wyandotte Constitutional Convention that Black people, "upon whom Nature's God has stamped inferiority," would never attend the same schools as his children. He protested to Gen. Franz

Sigel in June 1862 when white soldiers had to clean Winchester's dirty streets while Black people relaxed in its doorways. And he had regarded Alexandria's previously enslaved refugees as persons inherently drawn to indolence and dependency who could only attain self-sufficiency through the benevolent intervention of white people. Yet Alexandria's Black people wrote their "Worthy Military Governor," whose "just and liberal principles" had secured them rights of employment, education, and marriage, to request that he continue to defend them against the expected resurgence of oppression.

Slough's attitudes toward Black people did not differ from those of most Northern Americans. His experience with freed people did. He had served capably as Alexandria's military governor and had recognized that an efficient, even-handed administration of laws and regulations created the necessary discipline for turbulent times. The order that his administration achieved had enabled Black refugees, arriving destitute in Alexandria, to find productive labor, build homes, marry, raise families, educate themselves and their children, and worship in their churches. Slough witnessed these successes. More importantly, he watched as Black men enlisted in the United States Colored Troops, some dying in battle and many more from disease, while their surviving comrades demanded that they be treated as soldiers and laid to rest next to their white comrades. His experiences with Alexandria's Black people profoundly changed him. He, like many Union soldiers across the South, could no longer accept the antebellum world in which Black people had no rights whatsoever. He urged Alexandria's white government to repeal the old slave laws, an action that confirmed the good opinion held by the city's African Americans of their military governor.[36]

Slough did not transfer power to Alexandria's civil authorities on May 1 as he had planned. The city again filled with soldiers, now waiting to be discharged from their regiments. Slough reminded the liquor sellers, eager to dispense spirits to the restless and thirsty men, that the sale of alcohol to troops remained prohibited "for Military reasons." Sometime in late May or early June, President Johnson rescinded Alexandria's liquor regulations, a decision that infuriated Slough. He wrote Stanton on June 8 that he feared that his "attempts to discharge my duty as Military Governor will be laughed at . . . by the many who I have had so much difficulty to curtail during the nearly three years I have acted as such." Believing that the resumption of liquor sales in Alexandria stripped him of the power to maintain order, he asked to be relieved of duty. A month later, the War Department granted his request.[37]

On July 7, 1865, Slough's farewell to the "Citizens of Alexandria and Soldiers of its Garrison" appeared in the *Alexandria Gazette*.

> A—to me—pleasant relationship is severed. Believing that my services
> are no longer needed here, I have been, at my own request, relieved of my
> command as Military Governor of Alexandria. I return to my home in the
> Rocky Mountains, there soon, I hope, to resume civil pursuits. If in the dis-
> charge of my duties here I have benefitted you, I am content. I have labored
> for this result. I shall ever remember with pleasurable emotions, my three
> year's [*sic*] sojourn in Alexandria. I now say "Good-Bye" with earnest wishes
> for your happiness and prosperity.

Return "home" to the Rocky Mountains? Not to Cincinnati, where his mother and father still lived, or to Leavenworth, Kansas, where he achieved a degree of success professionally and politically, but to Colorado Territory, which he left abruptly after his life was threatened? It seems like a strange choice, but Slough had hopes for a new opportunity, one that would satisfy his ambition and demanded his presence in Denver.[38]

Part V

NEW MEXICO TERRITORY

14

∞∞∞∞∞

Chief Justice

THE RUMOR SPREAD QUICKLY BY TELEGRAPH: BRIG. GEN. JOHN P. Slough would replace John Evans as governor of Colorado Territory. The *New York Times* first published the political gossip in a brief, two-sentence notice buried in its June 13, 1865, issue. Evans's removal and Slough's fame were sufficiently noteworthy that editors across the country reprinted the *Times*'s announcement; within a week, newspapers from Pittsburgh to Milwaukee to Galveston repeated the rumor.[1]

The news reached Denver before most of the country read it in their newspapers. On June 14, the day after the *Times* reported the change in Colorado's executive, Evans wrote Slough that he had learned that the general would become the territory's third governor. He assured Slough that he was prepared to turn over his gubernatorial responsibilities and generously pledged his assistance in familiarizing Slough with the "condition of the affairs of the office."[2]

Evans had fallen into President Johnson's disfavor as a result of the government's investigation into atrocities committed by John Chivington and his Colorado Volunteers at Sand Creek. Slough realized that the governor's disgrace presented an opportunity for advancement. He lobbied President Andrew Johnson and Hiram Bennet, Colorado's delegate to the US House of Representatives, to become Colorado's next governor. He reminded the president that he had served his country admirably and selflessly during the late war and requested the choice political plum as his reward. Johnson's or Bennet's response must have been encouraging. In his farewell message to the citizens of Alexandria, Slough announced that he would soon return to his Rocky Mountain home to pursue new civic responsibilities.[3]

Despite his optimism, the weeks passed without an appointment. By late

July, Slough decided to visit Denver, hoping that his presence might speed his nomination. He had not been discharged from the army, which raised questions about his trip's purpose. One officer asked his superior how he should respond to the sudden appearance in Colorado Territory of a brigadier general. Slough wrote President Johnson on August 7 to urge Governor Evans's removal. He asserted that Coloradans disliked Evans and added uncharitably that the governor should be removed "for want of executive ability, yea, for imbecility." In Evans's place, Slough suggested that the president appoint "some energetic man of tested executive ability." The insinuation was evident; Slough considered himself the best candidate for the job.[4]

Johnson would disappoint him. On October 17, 1865, he selected Pennsylvanian Alexander Cummings to succeed John Evans. Johnson had brevetted Cummings a brigadier general for his "meritorious service" as superintendent of colored troops in the Department of Arkansas and the president must have considered him the better man for the governor's job. A few newspapers floated a new rumor about Slough. Coloradans were advocating for statehood and the papers reported that Slough would become one of the new state's two senators. But Colorado did not become a state until 1876, and with Cummings's appointment, Slough's dream of returning to his Rocky Mountain home vanished.[5]

Mustered out of the army on August 24, 1865, Slough had to find work when he failed in his quest to become Colorado's governor. He opened a law office at No. 258 F Street in Washington at the end of October, but a new opportunity quickly commanded his attention. President Johnson had decided to remove Kirby Benedict as chief justice of the New Mexico Territorial Supreme Court. Benedict was an alcoholic and his lapses into drunkenness while on the bench could no longer be tolerated. Slough wrote Johnson's attorney general, James Speed, about his interest in the position. "In view of my military service in New Mexico," he assured Speed, "my appointment as Chief Justice of that Territory would be acceptable to its people." The president agreed with Slough's assessment and nominated him as Benedict's replacement. On January 26, 1866, the US Senate confirmed John P. Slough as chief justice of the New Mexico Territorial Supreme Court.[6]

Slough quickly departed for New Mexico Territory. Less than three weeks after the Senate's confirmation, he arrived by Overland Dispatch stagecoach in Junction City, Kansas. From there, he traveled across the plains to pass a few days in Denver before proceeding to Santa Fe. He expected to arrive in the territory in time to preside over the spring district court session.[7]

In 1866, the New Mexico Territorial Supreme Court consisted of a chief justice and two associate justices. The three justices also served as trial judges for the territory's three judicial districts. Slough presided over the busiest district, the First Judicial District, which consisted of seven northern New Mexico counties spread over more than twenty thousand square miles. Upon his arrival in the territory, he promptly went to work. He convened the San Miguel County District Court in Las Vegas, New Mexico, the second week of March, followed by sessions in Taos and Rio Arriba Counties. The *Santa Fe Weekly Gazette* praised the territory's new jurist. It called Slough "an efficient officer" of the court and noted that his performance had earned "the entire satisfaction of [the] litigants and attorneys" he encountered during his first session.[8]

In late April, Slough requested a leave of absence from his new duties. He returned east to gather Arabella and his four children—Willie, John, Sallie, and Martin—possibly reuniting with them in Cincinnati, but more likely in Leavenworth. There, in the Kansas frontier town where he had lived for four years, Slough met the recently appointed governor of New Mexico Territory, Robert Byington Mitchell.[9]

Slough and Mitchell probably knew each other from Kansas Democratic politics. A fellow Ohioan, Mitchell emigrated to Kansas Territory in 1856. He sat in the territorial legislature as a Free State Democrat from 1857 to 1858, attended the Leavenworth Constitutional Convention, and served as the territorial treasurer from 1859 to 1861. Like Slough, Mitchell was a loyal Unionist during the Civil War. He organized the 2nd Kansas Volunteer Infantry, leading the regiment at the Battle of Wilson's Creek, commanded a division at the Battle of Perryville, and saw action as commander of Maj. Gen. George Thomas's cavalry at the Battle of Chickamauga. His multiple wounds forced him from battlefield command after Chickamauga and into administrative positions within the Military Districts of Nebraska and North Kansas. The US Senate confirmed him as territorial governor for New Mexico on January 15, 1866, the day he was discharged from the army.[10]

Slough, Mitchell, and their families left Leavenworth on May 22 to travel together to New Mexico. They arrived in Santa Fe five weeks later. Slough was already familiar with the old Spanish colonial town, but Arabella must

Robert Byington Mitchell
served as New Mexico territorial
governor while Slough presided
over the territory's Supreme
Court. Photograph by
J. H. Leouard, 1866–1869. Source:
Courtesy of the Palace of the
Governors Photo Archives
(NMHM/DCA), Image # 010294.

have been shocked when she stepped down from the stagecoach. Santa Fe
seemed more like an insignificant, dust-blown outpost than the seat of New
Mexico's government. Surrounding its central plaza, planted with alfalfa and
a few hardy cottonwoods to keep down the dust, stood the town's major
residences, commercial enterprises, and public buildings, monotonously
constructed of sand-colored, sun-dried bricks, "long, low, blind buildings . . .
which in both materials and manner resembled the houses built for centuries
by Mexicans, and for centuries before them, Pueblo Indians." The Governor's
Palace, no grander than its neighboring structures, and the parish church
of Saint Francis anchored the plaza. Populating the town were fewer than
five thousand residents.[11]

There were two hotels, the Exchange and the Santa Fe, kitty-cornered on
the plaza, and some traders' shops marked by hand-painted signs, but little
else to engage a lady recently arrived from the nation's capital. There were, of
course, dance halls and poker rooms and saloons. All were built in the territorial style: adobe walls with rough wooden doors, shuttered windows with
no glass, a covered wooden walkway in front of each building. Once outside
the town's center, the streets meandered by small adobe homes interspersed
with cornfields until any trace of human occupation disappeared in the desert.

The United States Army had erected Fort Marcy at the north end of
town shortly after Gen. Stephen W. Kearny's Army of the West wrested

Santa Fe from the Mexicans in 1846. The officers and men garrisoned at Fort Marcy provided some diversion for Santa Fe's residents—a ball held at the Exchange Hotel on July 25, 1866, honored Gen. John Pope—but the town's newspapers published few notices of traveling dramatic companies, concerts, or other entertainments. Saints days, the occasional dance, and the arrival of wagon trains carrying goods from back east provided the town's greatest excitement.[12]

Adjusting to life in Santa Fe must have been challenging for Arabella. She was accustomed to her husband's long hours at work, but had little diversion from child raising and managing the household. Santa Fe's residents were overwhelmingly Hispano—some 80 percent in the 1860s—and their culture defined the town's life. Arabella would have hesitated to form relationships with the Nuevomexicana women, even the wives of Santa Fe's wealthy and powerful Hispano elite. Instead, she enjoyed afternoon tea and engaged in charitable work with the few Anglo women from her social class. Separated from her husband during the district court sessions, she must have found her days long and trying.[13]

Slough resumed his judicial duties a few weeks after he and his family reached Santa Fe. He convened the Santa Fe County District Court on July 23, 1866, in a converted US Army quartermaster storehouse just east of the Palace of the Governors. Although the *Santa Fe Weekly Gazette* again complimented the chief justice, remarking that he presided in a manner "becoming the high position he occupies," tensions existed in his courtroom. Like most Anglos in the territory, Slough disdained the Nuevomexicano litigants who appeared before him. He chose to disqualify several Hispano men from grand jury duty because they could not prove their American citizenship. The lack of citizenship papers had seldom bothered other justices, but Slough's conservative personality, reinforced by his wartime experience within the army's rigid judicial system, made it difficult for him to adapt to New Mexico's more tolerant courtroom practices.[14]

Slough must have also found the court sessions to be unbearably tedious, especially after his service in wartime Alexandria. He had to endure long hours on the bench, listening to case after case, translated from Spanish, of cattle rustling, horse stealing, carrying a deadly weapon, robbery, larceny, and assault and battery. Once he adjourned the Santa Fe County District Court in mid-August, he traveled seventy miles east to convene the San Miguel

County District Court. San Miguel's county seat, Las Vegas, offered nothing to counter the monotony of life on the judicial circuit. The unpleasant town had "not a spire of grass nor a green thing to be seen within [its] limits," only a miserable collection of buildings "not above nine feet high, with flat, dirt roofs, built of adobes and generally plastered with mud." After finishing court in Las Vegas, Slough rode across the high desert plains to another backwater town, Mora, to begin the dreary judicial proceedings for Mora County.[15]

The *Santa Fe Weekly Gazette* praised his work during the fall court session. "He is discharging the duties of his office," it wrote, "to the satisfaction of the people in the [First Judicial] District. He disposes of business properly and impartially." But after five months as chief justice, Slough had grown disenchanted with his judicial responsibilities. He saw an opportunity to return to military command when fair summer weather brought increased raiding by Chiricahua Apache, Cheyenne, and Arapaho warriors in northern New Mexico. He wrote Secretary of War Stanton on August 17, 1866, that "the prospect of a general Indian War of long duration" threatened the territory and suggested he could swiftly organize volunteer troops from Colorado and New Mexico. Slough's request to lead volunteer soldiers came too late; by 1866, the United States government relied on regular army troops to defend the frontier. Stanton, absorbed in Washington politics, had no interest in responding to a mustered-out brigadier general in New Mexico Territory and did not reply to his old friend.[16]

Denied the opportunity to fight Indians, Slough chose to relive his moment of wartime glory by visiting the battlefield at Pigeon's Ranch. He was shocked to see that little more than plain wooden headboards in a hastily arranged cemetery memorialized the Union dead. He had seen the war memorials and military cemeteries being established in the East and decided that the fallen soldiers at Glorieta deserved to be remembered appropriately. When the Legislative Assembly reconvened in early December, he petitioned for improvements to the cemetery. He reminded the legislators that since the end of the war, the country had dedicated numerous cemeteries "to exhibit the gratitude of the people to the untold and frequently unknown dead heroes who saved the Nation." He urged them to enclose the cemetery properly and to erect "plainly inscribed monuments" to the soldiers' memory. "I call upon you to act," he wrote. "I, their late commander, solicit it. Your sister Territory, Colorado, will rejoice at the favorable action. The friends and surviving comrades of the gallant dead desire it. Your constituents expect it, and the mute, yet eloquent graves, demand it."[17]

Rather than address the cemetery's shortcomings, the Legislative Assembly appropriated $1,500 for the erection of a monument in Santa Fe. The bill appointed the chief justice, the territorial secretary, and the territorial treasurer to oversee the appropriation's expenditure. Slough was chosen to lead the work, although William F. M. Arny, New Mexico's territorial secretary and one of the men whose relief efforts Slough had questioned during the 1860 Kansas famine, opposed the chief justice's involvement. Arny's unsuccessful intervention caused hard feelings between the two men that deepened during the next twelve months.[18]

With court recessed until January, the chief justice was able to enjoy his family and friends. On November 22, he officiated at the marriage of Enos Andrews and Kate Steck, the daughter of Dr. Michael Steck, a former superintendent of Indian affairs in New Mexico Territory. The ceremony took place at the Santa Fe home of William W. Griffin, the territory's special commissioner for Indian affairs. A few weeks later, he and Arabella likely attended the Santa Fe Varieties, an amateur performance organized to benefit one of their neighbors, R. P. Canterbury. Slough also attended to spiritual matters. While he was not particularly religious—Julia Wilbur had noted in her diary that he did not attend church in Alexandria—Slough joined other prominent Anglos, including Governor Robert Mitchell, *Santa Fe Weekly Gazette* publisher James Collins, United States surveyor general John Clark, and United States attorney Stephen B. Elkins, to establish the Presbyterian Church of Santa Fe.[19]

The New Mexico Territorial Supreme Court began its annual three-week session in Santa Fe on January 6, 1867. Normally, the court heard few appeals because litigants preferred to forgo the expense and time required to appear before the court. But the January 1867 session was busy; the *Santa Fe New Mexican* reported that Chief Justice Slough and his two associate justices, Joab Houghton and Sidney Hubbell, handled "a large amount of business."[20]

Among the session's many cases, the three Anglo justices decided an appeal with significant implications for Nuevomexicano culture. The practice of peonage, which originated under the Spanish colonialists, was deeply entrenched in the territory. Under peonage, a person bound himself to the service of another person in order to satisfy a debt. Because low wages prevented many *peones* from repaying their obligations, peonage devolved into a form of involuntary servitude. Indeed, many Anglos and Nuevomexicanos saw little difference between peonage and the long-standing practice of enslaving captured Native peoples.[21]

The issue of peonage and involuntary servitude came before Slough, Houghton, and Hubbell during the Supreme Court's January 1867 session. The facts of the case were that Tomás Heredia had fled his servitude to José Maria García. When García had Heredia arrested, New Mexico's Third Judicial District found that Heredia's contract for services was legally valid and ordered Heredia returned to García to complete his term of servitude. Heredia appealed the district court's ruling to the Territorial Supreme Court. The three justices, led by Chief Justice Slough, reasoned that because the provisions of New Mexico's "master and servant" law resembled the old Southern slave codes, peonage must be as restrictive as "Negro slavery." They concluded that the June 19, 1862, act of Congress, which prohibited slavery and involuntary servitude in the territories, as well as the Thirteenth Amendment, outlawed the practice. The justices decided that Heredia had been "illegally restrained of his liberty" by García and ordered him freed.[22]

The court's decision upended a practice that many Nuevomexicanos considered economically beneficial and culturally appropriate. Families throughout New Mexico, including the family of José Francisco Chávez, the territory's delegate to Congress, held peones in bondage. Slough, who wrote the court's decision, crossed many of the territory's richest and most politically prominent Nuevomexicano families by prohibiting their use of peonage.[23]

Slough had remained above politics during his first year as chief justice. He did not attend the territory's Conservative Party meeting on July 21, 1866, nor did he join Governor Mitchell, Attorney General Charles Clever, and his fellow Supreme Court justices Sidney Hubbell and Joab Houghton when they sent a letter to President Johnson endorsing the president's Reconstruction policies and expressing alarm over Radical Republican efforts to undermine his government. But with Mitchell's return to Santa Fe on February 26, 1867, after a three-month leave of absence, Slough became embroiled in a nasty fight between the Democratic governor and the Republican William Arny.[24]

Mitchell had left New Mexico in December 1866 to promote immigration from the States. The territorial secretary should have assumed Mitchell's responsibilities during his absence, but President Johnson's appointment as New Mexico's secretary, Brig. Gen. George P. Estey, chose to remain in Washington, DC, rather than serve in Santa Fe. His failure to arrive in New Mexico left the office in the hands of the existing territorial secretary, William Arny.

With Mitchell on leave, Arny decided to send his own nominations for territorial office to the legislature for confirmation. Among his selections, he replaced New Mexico's current attorney general, Democrat Charles Clever, with a fellow Republican, Stephen B. Elkins. Mitchell recognized Arny's attempt to grab power when he returned to Santa Fe in late February. He annulled the acting territorial secretary's appointments and reinstated Clever as attorney general. Slough initially recognized Elkins as the territory's attorney general, but after Mitchell's invalidation of Arny's appointments, he reversed his decision and acknowledged Clever as New Mexico's chief legal officer.[25]

Because Slough ultimately recognized Clever over Elkins, the territory's Republicans, suspecting that the chief justice was politically aligned with the territory's Democratic governor, began to criticize his performance on the bench. After hearing former chief justice Kirby Benedict complain about Slough and "one very extraordinary decision," Republican John Clark concluded that the chief justice "decides too hastily as a rule and involves himself as a consequence in many absurdities." Clark also disapproved of Slough's "want of courtesy to members of the Bar," while Richard H. Tompkins, a former territorial attorney general, denounced him as "the most overbearing, tyrannical, and unjust judge I ever saw." Theodore Wheaton topped Tompkin's hyperbole by comparing Slough to George Jeffreys, the English "hanging judge," who condemned to death hundreds of rebels after Monmouth's Rebellion in 1685.[26]

In fact, Slough was heavy-handed and patronizing while hearing cases. He had no patience for courtroom behavior he deemed unacceptable. He jailed a Mora County grand juror for lying about his previous jury duty, found a courtroom spectator in contempt for shouting a political slogan while court was in session, and "discharged dishonorably" the president of the Santa Ana grand jury for behavior he perceived to be objectionable. Slough attacked the easygoing and at times unprincipled practices of territorial courts with the same zeal he brought to disciplining the unruly Colorado volunteers and controlling the sale of liquor in Alexandria. His insistence on decorum and respect intimidated the Hispano men called to serve as jurors, and his rigidity won few admirers among the attorneys who appeared before him. Unable to speak Spanish and dismissive of the Nuevomexicano population, Slough could not adjust to a culture that honored family and friends above the rule of law. Nor could the former brigadier general who had served as judge on the Porter and Hammond courts-martial accept the informal atmosphere of frontier courts.[27]

The physical and mental demands of his office also wore on him. He dispensed with another "laborious" caseload during the Santa Fe County District Court's spring session before facing two more months presiding over courts in Mora, Rio Arriba, and Santa Ana Counties. He finally adjourned the First Judicial District's spring session on April 27, 1867; a week later, he opened court in Albuquerque for the Second Judicial District. The district's presiding judge, Sidney Hubbell, had been granted leave to return to the States and, as was customary for New Mexico's territorial judges, Slough assumed Hubbell's responsibilities during his absence. Between his Supreme Court and his District Court duties, Slough heard cases, practically uninterrupted, in five counties over a span of four months.[28]

The unreasonable demands of his office—the burdensome caseload, the difficult and sometimes dangerous travel necessary to hold court across his large circuit, the weeks away from his family and its comforts, and the incomprehensible behavior of jurymen and litigants—undoubtedly affected Slough's dispatch of his duties. His predecessor, Kirby Benedict, had resorted to heavy drinking while serving as chief justice. Slough responded to the challenges of his office by exhibiting his personality's worst characteristics: irritability, rigidity, and impulsivity.

Financial difficulties also added to his stress. New Mexico's chief justices earned $2,500 annually, and Slough's salary was not sufficient to maintain his family in Santa Fe and cover his expenses while holding court in the outlying counties. He had complained to Santiago Hubbell, Associate Justice Sidney Hubbell's brother, that presiding over the Second Judicial District Court during Hubbell's absence "has caused me serious inconvenience and much expense." He owed money to Santiago Hubbell, so in early June 1867 he traveled to Denver to sell property. Unfortunately, hostilities had broken out in north-central Kansas and eastern Colorado as Cheyenne warriors avenged the burning of one of their villages by Maj. Gen. Winfield Scott Hancock's troops. "Hancock's War" frightened potential emigrants to Colorado and dried up investment in Denver real estate. Slough returned to Santa Fe on June 19 without a buyer and empty handed.[29]

Early summer brought a few weeks' respite from the pressures of business and the law. Court did not convene again until late July, which allowed Slough the opportunity for personal pursuits. He and Arabella called on members of Santa Fe's Anglo community; the evening of June 25, for example, they had tea with Governor Mitchell, Surveyor General John Clark, and Inspector General William Marcy. A few days later, Slough and J. Howe Watts, a Santa Fe attorney who had lived in the territory for more than a decade, inspected the Placer gold and silver mines outside Santa Fe. Perhaps the two men considered speculating in the mines' output. The chief justice also umpired the Santa Fe Base Ball Club's game on July 4. Thompson's team squeaked by Thatcher's squad, 23 runs to 22. The *Weekly Gazette* commended Slough's officiating as "very good, and the few, if any, errors of judgment were not noticeable." Perhaps the crowd did not care about the officiating or the score as they "quickly disposed" of a keg of beer during the contest.[30]

The Santa Fe County District Court again had a heavy docket—reportedly 250 actions—when Slough resumed work in late July. Among the everyday cases of "keeping a gaming table," embezzlement, and carrying a deadly weapon, Slough heard his most famous lawsuit, *United States v. Benigno Ortiz*. The case arose when Nuevomexicano settlers purchased lands belonging to the Cochiti Pueblo, southwest of Santa Fe. US Attorney Stephen B. Elkins indicted the Nuevomexicanos because they had violated the 1834 Trade and Intercourse Act, which prohibited the purchase of lands inhabited by those "savage and uncivilized tribes" found "beyond the settlements and on the frontier." The buyers hired Kirby Benedict to defend their interests.[31]

Slough determined that the 1834 Act, extended in 1851 to include New Mexico and Utah, did not apply to the Pueblo Indians. Rather than the "savage and uncivilized tribes" contemplated by the Trade and Intercourse Act, he regarded the Pueblos as "a peaceable, industrious, intelligent, honest, and virtuous people. . . . Indians only in feature, complexion, and a few of their habits." Because Slough did not consider the Pueblos to be a "savage" tribe, he ruled that the Nuevomexicanos had not violated the Trade and Intercourse Act and therefore had legally purchased lands within the Cochiti Pueblo. But he did not limit his findings to the sale of Pueblo lands. He also determined that the Treaty of Guadalupe Hidalgo had conferred United States citizenship on the Pueblos. "They should be treated," he wrote, "not as under the pupilage of the government, but as citizens, not of a State or Territory, but of the United States of America." Slough had argued during the Wyandotte Constitutional Convention that treaties with Kansas tribes granted them United States citizenship. In *United States v. Benigno Ortiz*, the chief justice concluded again that a treaty trumped race in determining a person's citizenship.[32]

Many New Mexicans shared Slough's view that the Pueblos were a "civilized tribe." They bartered with them for agricultural produce, applauded their peaceful and agrarian lifestyle, and considered them to be "models of behavior" for other Southwest Native people. Nor did New Mexicans question Slough's approval of the sale of Cochiti Pueblo lands; after all, opening Native lands to purchase would foster settlement by Anglos and strengthen the territory's economy. What did concern New Mexicans was Slough's decision that the Pueblos were American citizens; if they voted, Native people might affect the outcome of New Mexico's upcoming election.[33]

Campaigning for the territory's fall election had become heated by summer 1867. Charles Clever was challenging José Francisco Chávez to be New Mexico's delegate to the United States Congress. New Mexicans shouted for Clever or Chávez in rallies held throughout the territory, while the Democratic *Santa Fe Weekly Gazette*, backing Clever, and the Republican *Santa Fe New Mexican*, supporting Chávez, traded barbs and insults in front-page editorials.

Slough's ruling in *United States v. Benigno Ortiz* pulled the chief justice into New Mexico's rancorous politics. Claiming that Slough supported Clever, the *Santa Fe Weekly Gazette* argued that his ruling saved "poor" Nuevomexicanos from the heavy fines that Elkins, a Republican US attorney and a "Chávez partisan," wanted to impose on them for occupying Pueblo lands. Meanwhile, in rallies held in Santa Ana and Santa Fe counties, Chávez supporters criticized Slough for his decision in the *Benigno Ortiz* case that recognized the Pueblos' citizenship. And Republican John Clark, believing that the Pueblos would throw their support to Clever, worried that Slough's verdict effectively handed the fall election to the Democrats.[34]

By fall 1867, Slough's support among New Mexicans was wavering. His courtroom demeanor, at times arbitrary and overbearing, troubled members of the Santa Fe bar and intimidated the Hispanos who appeared before his bench. His ruling in *Heredia v. García* alienated the wealthy Nuevomexicanos, who economically benefited from peonage. He angered the territory's Republicans by supporting Charles Clever for attorney general rather than Samuel B. Elkins, and he further upset them by apparently undermining José Francisco Chávez's re-election as territorial delegate with his decision in *United States v. Benigno Ortiz*. His first year as chief justice seemed to repeat previous times in his life. Successful initially in his position, Slough was starting to fail as his difficult personality and rigid adherence to principle estranged friends and emboldened his enemies.

15

Disintegration

Chosen to replace the absent General Espey as New Mexico's secretary, Herman Heath owed his job to the territory's congressional delegate, José Francisco Chávez. Chávez advocated strongly for Heath's appointment because he believed that Heath would be "an invaluable asset to New Mexico Republicans." Heath's political leanings—at least prior to the Civil War—made him an unusual candidate for Chávez's patronage. He had aligned with Iowa's Democrats shortly after his arrival in Dubuque in the late 1850s and led the Iowa faction that supported John C. Breckinridge during the 1860 presidential election. Democratic Senator George Wallace Jones repaid his loyalty by nominating him for the position of Dubuque's postmaster.[1]

Heath proclaimed his allegiance to the South in a letter he wrote Confederate president Jefferson Davis five days before rebel batteries fired on Fort Sumter. "Although a Northern man by birth," he assured Davis, "[I] have never been anything but Southern in my feelings." But Heath was a man who valued advancement over principles. By May 1861, he transferred his loyalty to the Union and organized a company of Iowa volunteer cavalry. His change of heart prompted Senator Jones's son to write his father, "Your pusillanimous friend Heath has turned black Republican.... I loathe & detest and despise a man who has hitherto pretended to be a democrat." One of the men who served with him in the Iowa cavalry, Capt. Eugene F. Ware, described him as "a self-important, dictatorial wind-bag" who "was willing to be a traitor to his country or anything else."[2]

Heath became editor of the *Omaha Republican* at war's end. He attempted to enter Nebraska politics, but the territory's Republicans distrusted him—his reputation as an "adventurer" preceded him—and he failed to achieve office. New Mexico's congressional delegate, however, felt differently about him. Describing Heath as "a gentleman of undoubted capacity and sterling

As editor of the *Santa Fe
New Mexican*, Herman Heath used
the newspaper's columns to condemn
Slough's performance as chief justice
and his public behavior in Santa Fe.
Source: Courtesy of Fold3.

integrity," José Francisco Chávez recognized the value of a high-ranking
territorial official who would be indebted to him. He convinced President
Johnson to nominate Heath as New Mexico's secretary.[3]

Heath did not hesitate in declaring his support for Chávez upon his
arrival in Santa Fe in July 1867. He quickly decided that political power in
the territory rested with the Arny-Chávez faction and dedicated himself to
transforming the faction into a political machine aligned with the Radical
Republicans in Congress. To secure the power and patronage that accompanied mid-nineteenth-century political office, he set about organizing an
effective campaign promoting Chávez's re-election as territorial delegate.[4]

Heath had greater plans than Chávez's re-election. An unfortunate accident suffered by Associate Justice Sidney Hubbell created the possibility of
an open seat among the territory's three jurists. While on leave of absence
back East, Hubbell was badly injured in a steamboat explosion and could
not return to New Mexico until he recovered. If Hubbell's incapacitation
prevented him from resuming his courtroom responsibilities, Chávez and
Heath reasoned, Chávez could lobby President Johnson for a sympathetic
replacement. With Chávez's man on the bench, the Republicans could potentially wrest control of New Mexico's highest courts by forcing either

Slough or Associate Justice Houghton to resign. Heath decided that grumblings about Slough's performance on the bench made the chief justice a vulnerable target.[5]

Hubbell's disability meant that Slough had to return to Albuquerque in early October for the Bernalillo County District Court's fall session. Because some of the District Court's grand jurors had relatives among the accused, he instructed US Attorney Samuel Duncan to advise them that "no matter whether it was their Mother, their Father, or their Brother, they should do their duty without fear, favor, or affection." Several grand jurors ignored Duncan's warning about favoritism, causing the US Attorney to inform Slough on October 14 that they had failed to perform their sworn responsibilities. He and the grand jury's foreman, Santiago Baca, reported that the jurors had refused to find a true bill against two men accused of carrying a deadly weapon despite "clear, plain and uncontradicted evidence." If grand jurors could subvert their oaths, the US Attorney argued, "the people had better do away with them, and save the expense to the county." Slough took Duncan and Baca's information seriously. He called the grand jurors into the courtroom and unceremoniously discharged twelve of them.[6]

The last case Slough heard the day he discharged the grand jurors involved the contested election between Tomás Gutierres and Serafin Ramirez for the office of Bernalillo County's probate judge. Before the trial began, the plaintiff's attorney complained that two jurors had expressed an opinion about the case and therefore should be discharged. When the chief justice agreed to dismiss the two jurors, the defendant's attorney replied by demanding that several more jurors be discharged. The attorneys' challenges soon exhausted the jury pool. Slough was forced to adjourn the day's proceedings so that more jurors could be empaneled.

That night, Slough decided that holding an impartial trial in Bernalillo County was impossible. On October 15, he ordered the clerk of the Probate Court to keep the contested ballots in safekeeping until he could hear *Gutierres v. Ramirez* in his chambers in Santa Fe. He then prematurely ended the Bernalillo County District Court's fall session. He told those in attendance that "perjury and false swearing" had tainted the current jury and that the brief time remaining in the fall session made it impossible to obtain a new jury of "men of integrity and intelligence." Consequently, he concluded, any effort to "continue this Court at this time is folly."[7]

The chief justice's determination to "maintain the supremacy of the law" played into Herman Heath and the Republicans' hands. Kirby Benedict complained that Slough discharged jurors when they "find verdicts which do not suit him," while R. H. Thompkins charged that the chief justice had essentially convicted the Bernalillo County grand jurors of lying under oath, "without any opportunity of defending themselves," when he dismissed them from their duties. John Clark criticized Slough's decision to terminate the Bernalillo County District Court session, "giving as a reason that not only witnesses but Juries were so corrupt that they had no regard for an oath & that in consequence jury trials were ridiculous & farcical & saying many other things of the Mexicans in his usual style." Slough never used the words "ridiculous" or "farcical" when he adjourned the Bernalillo County District Court, but Clark chose to portray him as an overbearing and contemptuous judge. Sensing the possibility of replacing Slough with a more pliable chief justice, New Mexico's Republicans were gathering the necessary evidence to force his removal.[8]

Frustrated by the corruption he saw in New Mexico's judicial system, Slough devoted his time to other, more rewarding activities during the summer and fall of 1867. He had not forgotten his appeal for a suitable cemetery to be located at the Glorieta battlefield. Accompanied by Herman Heath and J. S. Steck, he traveled to Pigeon's Ranch in August to select a "very appropriate and beautiful spot" for the Union dead. The owner of the land ceded the property to the United States, leading the *Santa Fe Weekly Gazette* to predict that the area would soon be enclosed and the remains of the fallen heroes moved there.[9]

The chief justice also spent the summer and fall overseeing preparations for raising a war memorial in Santa Fe's plaza. In a notice published in the *Santa Fe Weekly Gazette*, Slough, Heath, and territorial treasurer Felipe Delgado urged New Mexicans to attend the dedication of the monument's cornerstone on October 24 to demonstrate their gratitude toward the honored dead. The afternoon of the dedication, the city's residents gathered in the plaza and, preceded by a band, walked to the cathedral, where former governor John Evans and a delegation from Colorado joined them. The ceremony began with prayers and music before dignitaries lowered a box of artifacts into the pit intended for the cornerstone. Slough read the box's contents to the crowd: various laws and legislative journals of New Mexico, the names of civilian officials and military officers in the territory, specimens of coins, a copy of the dedication oration, a list of military officers who fought at Valverde and Glorieta Pass, Masonic relics, postage stamps, and the seals of various territorial offices. Sadly, the committee was not able to obtain a list of the Union soldiers who had died in New Mexico and could not include their names in the time capsule.[10]

Governor Mitchell was the day's principal speaker. In a style customary for mid-nineteenth-century orations, he recounted at length the battles of Valverde, Apache Canyon, and Pigeon's Ranch, noting that the "valor, determination, and skill" of the Union troops destroyed the Confederate dream of conquering the western territories. Governor Evans added his remarks after Mitchell finished. He urged the citizens of New Mexico and Colorado to remain steadfast to the principles for which the Union soldiers died: "the principles of unwavering loyalty, liberty, and equal and exact justice to all men."[11]

One unhappy fact marred the cornerstone's dedication. The territorial treasury lacked the funds to complete the monument. Slough, Heath, and Delgado solicited contributions, but they found "a great unwillingness to subscribe" and only raised $200. The legislature had to appropriate an additional $1,800 before the monument could be finished. On June 9, 1868, the thirty-two-foot sandstone obelisk was raised in the center of Santa Fe's plaza. Limestone plaques were fixed to each of the obelisk's four sides. Two of the plaques read "To the heroes of the Federal Army who fell at the Battle of Valverde fought with the rebels February 21, 1862," and "To the heroes of the Federal Army who fell at the battles of Canon del Apache and Pigeons Ranch (La Glorieta) fought with the rebels March 28, 1862 and to those who fell at the Battle with the rebels at Peralta April 15, 1862." As Slough had entreated the legislature in December 1866, New Mexico Territory now had a memorial that remembered "the untold and frequently unknown dead heroes who saved the Nation."[12]

Other civic pursuits occupied the chief justice. Construction of a transcontinental railroad captivated the imagination of Westerners eager for the easy transportation of goods to eastern markets. The Union Pacific Railroad had moved rapidly west during 1866 by taking advantage of the gentle Platte River valley in Nebraska Territory. Although the company's directors chose to lay the railroad's tracks across present-day Nebraska, Wyoming, and Utah, the possibility of a second, more southern "Pacific" route energized promoters in the Southwest.

Slough willingly embraced his responsibilities, as one of New Mexico's leading citizens, to advance the "Pacific" route's development. In May 1867, he attended a convention in Albuquerque to build support for a railroad line. He and several other New Mexican luminaries served as vice presidents of the organizing committee. He also headed the committee that drafted the meeting's resolutions, including one that pledged the delegates to devote "our services, our experiences, our energies, and, if needed, our money to aid in the successful promotion of the great National work." The resolutions were unanimously adopted.[13]

Four months later, another "large and enthusiastic" railroad meeting occurred in Santa Fe. Governor Mitchell gathered the territory's leaders together to confer with Gen. W. J. Palmer, treasurer of the Union Pacific Railroad Company. Slough again helped to draft the meeting's resolutions. The drafting committee produced a document that extolled the advantages of locating a portion of a transcontinental railroad in New Mexico, including the possibility of low elevations for its route, the lack of harsh winter weather (as opposed to the more northern path through the Rockies), and the ready availability of raw materials and cheap labor. Recalling the French invasion of Mexico in the early 1860s, the committee argued that a railroad would help re-establish trade connections with Mexico's northern provinces and "safeguard against any future European attempts at the invasion of this portion of the continent." For these reasons, the committee urged Congress to award the Union Pacific the same aid for a route through Colorado, New Mexico, and Arizona Territories as it had for the railroad line through Nebraska Territory. Slough advocated for the adoption of the resolutions "in a stirring address." At the meeting's conclusion, he joined Secretary Herman Heath, Treasurer Felipe Delgado, Special Commissioner for Indian Affairs W. W. Griffin, US Marshal John Pratt, and former *Gazette* publisher James Collins to work with the Union Pacific in facilitating the selection of the southern route.[14]

New Mexicans anticipated that a railroad would open the territory's mineral and pastoral resources to the country. Although ranching was the predominant industry in New Mexico in the 1850s and 1860s, mineral extraction assumed increasing importance by the late 1860s. The *Santa Fe Weekly Gazette* and the *Santa Fe New Mexican* frequently reported on successful mining ventures, including the Las Cruces, Pinos Altos, and Cimarron mines. In May 1866, prospectors struck gold fifty miles south of the Colorado border in the Moreño district. By summer, some six hundred to eight hundred prospectors were working claims in the area, largely on property owned by one man, Lucien Maxwell.[15]

The chief justice and Governor Mitchell, in their role as promoters of New Mexico's economy, visited the apparently rich Moreño gold mines in fall 1867. The two men spent ten days investigating the diggings and in late November published a favorable report in the *Santa Fe Weekly Gazette*. For those interested in prospecting the region's minerals, they noted the plentiful availability of water, the easily procured supplies at Maxwell's and Abreu's ranches, the abundance of wood to build cabins and mining works, and the presence of copper as an additional source of wealth. Most importantly, the two officials confirmed that those men who applied themselves had profited from their labor; one group of prospectors had already mined $52,000 in gold from their claim.[16]

Beyond promoting New Mexico mining, Slough and Mitchell had an additional interest in the Moreño district. In the same issue that printed the two men's report about the area's gold strikes, the *Weekly Gazette* published an advertisement signed by Slough as the "President and Business Manager" of the "Virginia City Town Company." It announced that Slough, Mitchell, Lucien Maxwell, and others intended to lay out "Virginia City" at the entrance to the Moreño mining region. Four hundred lots would be sold at public auction on January 6, 1868. It noted that the new town would be located near the Willow Gulch mine and other diggings and assured interested parties that based on the town's proximity to the mines, investment in the sites would prove to be profitable. Having arrived too late in both Kansas and Colorado to participate in their early land speculation, Slough now sought his fortune in selling plots of land in "Virginia City."[17]

Before Mitchell and Slough inspected the Moreño mines, Slough had an ugly confrontation that cost him the friendship of Colonel Charles McClure, chief commissary for the New Mexico District. McClure's employee, Joseph Purcell, had warned Slough's nine-year-old daughter, Sallie, about abusing his dogs. Incensed that Purcell had scolded his daughter, Slough upbraided him at the commissary. Using a torrent of obscenities, he told

Purcell that he would thrash him if he talked to his daughter again "in that way." Another commissary employee named Barta suggested that the judge leave the commissary. Slough replied that that he would not be forced to leave a public building, pushed Barta to the ground, and then fought with two army officers as they dragged him out of the commissary. Slough and McClure likely argued over Slough's treatment of the chief commissary's employees, which led to the rift between the two men.[18]

Slough quarreled publicly with another friend, Governor Mitchell, shortly after their return from the Moreño district. During the previous session of the Santa Fe County District Court, Slough had sentenced Guadalupe Mares to prison for selling alcohol to the Pueblos. The *Santa Fe New Mexican* regarded the sale of liquor to Indians as "the great cause of trouble in our territory" and applauded Mares's conviction. The *New Mexican* seldom wrote about the chief justice but in this instance concluded that "Great credit is due to the Hon. John P. Slough for the manner in which he dispatches business, and for the fairness and impartiality of his decisions." Despite the *New Mexican*'s praise, Theodore Wheaton, who had defended Mares, complained that Slough "abused" the jury because he dismissed them without pay when they failed to reach a verdict. Mares decided to plead guilty after a second deadlocked jury. Upon reviewing the conviction, Mitchell pardoned Mares.[19]

Mitchell's pardon infuriated Slough, who saw it as a betrayal, an action that repudiated his belief in the rule of law and undermined his efforts to reform the New Mexico courts. Confronting the governor outside Steinberger's Drug Store in Santa Fe, Slough denounced him in "very loud and boisterous words" for pardoning Mares. Mitchell brushed Slough off, which only angered the chief justice more. Continuing to castigate Mitchell in "terms more forcible than polite," Slough announced that he would resign as chief justice; indeed, one startled onlooker remembered, he told Mitchell to "take the Chief Justiceship and . . . stick it up his Royal Bengal ass." Slough then quickly wrote a letter of resignation and, against the advice of friends, took it to the post office to be mailed to Washington.

That evening, perhaps under Arabella's soothing influence, Slough's anger cooled. He decided to remain as the territory's chief justice. The next morning, he retrieved his letter of resignation from the post office and tore it up.

Territorial Secretary Heath, who now controlled the content of the *Santa Fe New Mexican*, saw an opportunity in Slough's abuse of Mitchell to hurt the chief justice. Reporting on the altercation between the two men, the paper concluded that Slough should have stuck with his resignation and "not further taxed the confidence of men by showing that although he could be rash, yet that he had no nerve to stand up to the position he had taken." Heath's editorial essentially taunted Slough to resign or be considered spineless.[20]

Five days after Slough confronted Mitchell outside of Steinberger's Drug Store, he publicly accosted William F. M. Arny over another perceived insult. The newly elected territorial legislature had convened the morning of December 2, 1867. Normally Slough, as chief justice, would have sworn in the legislators, but the pro-Chávez, pro-Republican body invited Secretary Heath to administer the oath. Slough reacted strongly to the snub; indeed, he believed that Heath and Arny, as the territory's two most outspoken Republicans, engineered the insult.[21]

Slough had known Heath for only five months, but he had been acquainted with Arny since the late 1850s in Kansas Territory. During those years, Arny had been a well-known Kansas Republican, chosen to deliver the Wyandotte Constitution—the constitution that Slough and his fellow Democrats had rejected—to President James Buchanan. Arny was also instrumental in the Kansas Relief Committee, which Slough accused of siphoning donations for its leadership's personal use. Bad blood probably existed between Slough and Arny; at the very least, New Mexico's partisan politics divided the two men.[22]

Arny moved to New Mexico Territory in July 1861 and a year later was appointed territorial secretary. James Collins, Francisco Perea, and other Democrats may have told Slough about Arny's plots to remove Democrats from office while Arny served as territorial secretary. Slough likely knew that Arny had attempted to undermine his campaign to erect a monument for New Mexico's Union dead, and he had witnessed Arny's efforts to replace Governor Mitchell's appointments while Mitchell was absent from the territory. As far as Slough was concerned, Arny was not a man to be trusted.[23]

The afternoon after the swearing-in ceremony, Slough caught up with Arny in the plaza. Accusing the former territorial secretary of plotting against him, he called Arny a liar, "a dirty dog," and "a damned son of a bitch." Slough then turned and walked away, but when Arny shouted after him that he was no gentleman, Slough could no longer contain what little restraint he possessed. He returned to Arny, seized him by the shoulder, raised his left hand as if to strike him, and raged, "I will whip you in two minutes you God-damned son of a bitch." Arny coolly reacted to Slough's threats, reminding him that he was unarmed. Slough thought twice, lowered his hand, and broke off the confrontation.[24]

Arny pressed charges of assault and battery against the chief justice. On December 4, Slough appeared before justice of the peace Abram Ortiz. Arny testified first that Slough had threatened and abused him on December 2. Slough responded by calling several witnesses, including Governor Mitchell and Attorney General Merrill Ashurst, who swore that Arny was a known liar. As he was examining Ashurst, Slough suddenly asked Justice Ortiz if he had been charged a few weeks previously for malfeasance and lying under oath. When Ortiz admitted that he had, Slough vowed that he would not be tried in Ortiz's court, and, with an obscenity, stormed out of the court-room. That evening, John Clark wrote in his diary, "I fear that there may be somebody shot before all this excitement is over."[25]

The same day that Slough appeared before Justice Ortiz, Herman Heath armed himself with a Spencer rifle and went looking for the chief justice because he believed that Slough had slandered his wife. Unable to confront Slough directly about his wife, Heath turned to the columns of the *Santa Fe New Mexican* to denounce the chief justice for attacking Arny. The *New Mexican* described Slough's behavior as "cowardly," "disgusting," and "un-manly" and piously reminded its readers that the newspaper had hesitated to "speak of the many flagrant violations of propriety, manliness . . . and decency" committed by the chief justice. Now, however, when Slough "descends in the scale of manhood, as to exhibit himself upon the public streets of our city, blaspheming, assaulting, and by his coarse, vulgar and consummately low language outrage the ears of the public, we can assure him . . . that our forebearance [*sic*] . . . would be justly construed as a neglect of the first duty of Journalists." Calling Slough's behavior in Justice Ortiz's courtroom "an outrage upon the law and the dignity of the courts," the *New Mexican* advised the chief justice "to moderate his conduct, and descend from his high stilts, and believe this certain fact, that he is no more than other men, and much less than most of them."[26]

Not even the *Cincinnati Daily Gazette*'s denunciations of Slough's assault of Darius Cadwell nor the *Rocky Mountain News*'s criticism of his command of the 1st Colorado had the impact of Heath's words in the *New Mexican*.

He touched every insecurity Slough possessed—his manhood, his courage, his status as a gentleman, his work as a jurist—with unerring accuracy.

Slough could only manage a weak rejoinder. On December 7, he published a notice in the *Santa Fe Weekly Gazette* defending his actions against Arny. He claimed that the *New Mexican*'s account was "not justified by the facts," that he had been excited by the legislature's insult, and that he had used language "more forcible than polite" because he believed that Heath and Arny, "both claiming . . . to be friendly to me," manipulated the legislature into slighting him. He dismissed Heath and Arny, refusing to "lessen my self-respect" by acknowledging them, and he ended his statement entreating, "I regret the excitement which followed my action, and plead an excitable nature and natural indignation at a gross and unnecessary insult as my excuse." Ten years after the Ohio Legislature had expelled him for striking Darius Cadwell and refusing to apologize, Slough continued to blame others and dismiss his own bad behavior. He had not learned the value of a well-phrased mea culpa.[27]

The chief justice's erratic behavior undoubtedly disturbed his friends and delighted his enemies. Contributing to a sense of madness was the ongoing turmoil engendered by the Clever-Chávez race for territorial delegate. Election day disturbances roiled the territory; men with mule whips and drawn pistols intimidated voters in Mora County, while clubbings and shootings occurred in Río Arriba County. Santa Fe barely avoided a riot when a crowd forced judges to count votes that they had previously rejected. Other voting sites experienced similar outbreaks of violence. Political feelings continued to run high after the election. John Clark reported that pro-Clever crowds had expressed "great indignation" toward Herman Heath. Heath worried that "there was a real danger of a mob & assassination" if, in his position of territorial secretary, he declared Chávez elected.[28]

Clever barely won the election, causing Chávez to object that the result was fraudulent. Inexplicably, Secretary Heath signed Clever's election certificate and affixed the territorial seal to the document yet, at the same time, submitted a letter protesting Clever's election. Recognizing his error in signing Clever's certificate, Heath launched into an aggressive campaign, both in the columns of the *New Mexican* and in letters to officials in Washington, to overturn the election's outcome in favor of Chávez.[29]

Chávez's challenge and Heath's reversal led to renewed fighting between the two candidates' adherents. On December 3, leaders of the pro-Clever faction created a committee to investigate the circumstances behind Heath's repudiation of Clever's election certificate. Three committee members met with Slough, who was present when Heath signed the document. Slough informed his visitors that Heath had said that Clever "had really received said majority," and that when he was asked about providing Chávez with his own certificate responded "in a categorical manner" that he would award a certificate to no person other than Clever.[30]

Based on Slough's eyewitness account, the committee concluded that Heath had lied about being forced to sign Clever's certificate. The committee asserted in a set of resolutions sent to the US Congress that Heath had obtained his position through "misrepresentation and fraud" and that he was "politically, morally, and personally unworthy of occupying the high office of Secretary of the Territory." The day after the committee drafted its resolutions condemning Heath, the pro-Clever faction held an "indignation rally" in Santa Fe to protest Heath's meddling in New Mexico's politics. Heath's *Santa Fe New Mexican* reported that participants made "loud, obscene, brutal, and disgusting" speeches and that Slough, along with others "disloyal during the war," attended the rally.[31]

No extant record indicates when Heath learned about the committee's resolutions calling for his dismissal or about Slough's role in their creation. Regardless, the territorial secretary had already initiated his plan to bring down the chief justice. Just after the territorial legislature convened on December 2, Heath approached Senator Jesús María Pacheco about introducing resolutions in the Legislative Council condemning Slough's behavior. After considering Heath's request for several days, Pacheco declined the responsibility. Heath then turned to a more compliant legislator, the newly elected senator from Doña Ana County, William Logan Rynerson.[32]

Rynerson had entered the territory in 1862. He had served with the "California Column" that, like the 1st Colorado, marched into New Mexico to repel the Confederate invasion. After the war, he settled in Doña Ana County, opened a law practice, invested in the Pinos Altos mines, and grew increasingly influential in local business. Rynerson ran for the Territorial Legislative Council in fall 1867 against the pro-Clever candidate, Samuel L. Jones. Doña Ana County probate judge John Lemon declared Jones the winner and awarded him the certificate of election. Unhappy with the outcome, Heath announced that Lemon illegally tallied the votes, declared

Jones's certificate invalid, and issued a new one to Rynerson. The Territorial Legislative Council, heavily weighted with Chávez supporters, conducted its own inspection of the Doña Ana ballots and on December 5 voted to admit Rynerson to the council.[33]

Heath reminded the freshman senator that he had been elected "on our ticket." Rynerson did not wait long to repay the debt. On December 11, he introduced a series of resolutions censuring Slough's actions as chief justice. Six charges covered all the complaints that the Republicans had raised about Slough's judicial conduct: his overbearing and intimidating presence in court, the unjust and arbitrary basis of his decisions, and his practice of fining and imprisoning jurors who failed in their duties. Two charges about his judicial conduct were fabricated. Slough had steadfastly avoided political entanglements, yet the fifth resolution accused him of acting "as the politician rather than the Judge." It is also unlikely that Slough, who had strictly banned alcohol in Alexandria, appeared in court "under the direct influence of ardent spirits." The final five resolutions recounted his "vulgar and blasphemous" assaults on Mitchell and Arny, his December 4 refusal to be arraigned by Justice Ortiz, and his eventual arraignment for assault and battery, "much to the discredit of the bench of this Territory, and to the mortification of the people of New Mexico." For these offenses, the resolutions concluded that Slough must be removed from office.[34]

Slough tried to rally support among his friends and even among Chávez's supporters, but he could not stop the attack on his character and his performance. On Saturday, December 14, the Legislative Council passed Rynerson's resolutions ten votes to two. Herman Heath gleefully predicted that the Legislative Assembly would follow suit early the following week.[35]

• • •

The Exchange Hotel had stood on the southeast corner of Santa Fe's plaza since the early nineteenth century. The inn was known by a variety of names, including "The Fonda," "La Fonda Americana," and the "U.S. Hotel," but had been called the "Exchange Hotel" since the 1850s. It was a single-story adobe building built in the territorial style with a covered porch in front, a railing along the roofline, and a corner entrance next to the mercantile owned by Sigmund Seligman and Charles Clever. Despite its humble appearance, the Exchange Hotel was the "principal stopping point and leading caravansary"

This street scene highlights the Exchange Hotel, Santa Fe's predominant hostelry in the 1860s. Slough's denunciation of William Rynerson in the hotel's billiard room presaged the bloody confrontation between the two men. Street Scene, Old Santa Fe (N.M.), ca. 1856. Source: Courtesy of New Mexico History Museum, Fray Angélico Chávez History Library Graphics Collection 3–16.

between Kansas City and San Francisco and the gathering spot for Santa Fe's prominent citizens.[36]

One can only imagine John Slough's frame of mind when he strode through the hotel's front door the evening of December 14, 1867. In a little more than two weeks, he publicly abused his friend and colleague, Governor Robert Mitchell. He brutally attacked William F. M. Arny—at least according to the *Santa Fe New Mexican*—and stormed out of his arraignment hearing for assault and battery. The *New Mexican* had savaged this "most disgraceful conduct" while the Territorial Council overwhelmingly adopted resolutions decrying his courtroom outbursts, his drunken appearances, his partisan judicial rulings, and his shameful altercations with Mitchell and Arny.

Now, as he entered the hotel's billiard room, he caught sight of his latest enemy, William Rynerson, bent over a table playing billiards. Slough sat down on one of the room's settees and, to no one in particular, began to rant about Rynerson. "There is a strange combination," he said, "but one which you frequently see in the world, a gentleman associated with a damned thief. I allude to that damned, seven-foot son of a bitch playing with Colonel Kenzie. He is a damned lying thief and a coward." But Slough was not through with Rynerson. He continued, "He stole while in the army, stole since he got out, and stole his seat in the Legislature. I here denounce him as a son of a bitch, a thief, and a coward, but the damned scoundrel has not the courage to take it up." With that, Slough strode out of the billiard room.[37]

No one knows if Rynerson heard Slough's insults. Slough had not raised his voice and even though the two men were standing less than twenty feet apart, most witnesses reported that Rynerson did not hear Slough above the room's conversations and noisy billiard play. An hour later, Rynerson entered the store owned by S. B. Wheelock and asked the proprietor what Slough had said. Wheelock told him what he had heard in the Exchange Hotel's billiard room, which did not seem to faze Rynerson much. He parted from Wheelock and headed toward Green's saloon, where the Masonic Lodge chapter was meeting. He bumped into Merrill Ashurst outside of the saloon. He asked the attorney general if he had seen Slough; Ashurst pointed in the direction of Seligman's mercantile, telling Rynerson that he had seen the chief justice there just a few moments ago. Rynerson headed off in the direction of the store, looking to confront the chief justice. Failing to find Slough, he returned to his room in the Exchange Hotel.[38]

The next morning, Sunday, December 15, Arabella and the four Slough children attended services at the Presbyterian Church. It was a special day because the small congregation was dedicating their new building. Slough knew that Arabella would scold him for not attending church, but he had other matters on his mind. He first went to the office of his court's clerk, Peter Connelly, to attend to correspondence. Around 11:00 a.m., he walked over to the Exchange Hotel, had a drink in the barroom, and then visited US attorney Samuel Duncan in Duncan's hotel lodgings. Meanwhile, Rynerson had asked the keeper of the Exchange Hotel's billiard room—a man named Wilder—about Slough's comments the previous evening. Wilder repeated Slough's insults and told Rynerson that Slough was at the Exchange. Rynerson grimly made up his mind to challenge the chief justice about his words.[39]

Slough and Duncan left Duncan's room at 1:00 p.m. when the hotel's dinner bell rang. Rynerson, who was pacing in front of the hotel, caught Slough at the door between the billiard room and the barroom. "You have used language which you must take back," Rynerson told the chief justice coolly and firmly.

Slough took a few steps toward Rynerson and asked, "What did I say?"

"You called me a lying son of a bitch and a thief and I want you to take it back," Rynerson replied, pulling a Colt revolver from underneath his heavy black overcoat. Slough raised his left hand as if to stop Rynerson. "Hold, hold, don't shoot," he warned the senator.

"You must take it back," Rynerson insisted.

His face red, Slough eyed Rynerson closely and said, "I don't propose to take anything back."

Rynerson fired once. With a jerk, Slough's body collapsed on the floor. As he fell, his right hand came out of his coat pocket. A loaded derringer clattered to the floor.

Men rushed to restrain Rynerson, others to aid Slough. One bystander asked the chief justice where he had been hit. "In my side," Slough grunted. "No, I don't think so," the bystander answered. "You've been hit in the hip. You're not badly hurt." Slough shook his head. "I am. Send for the doctor."[40]

Epilogue

Slough knew that his wound was mortal. He lay back on the barroom floor, asked for a cigar, and waited for the doctor to arrive. Two physicians, Drs. Kennon and McKee, rushed to the chief justice's side. Both agreed that little could be done. The bullet had entered the lower portion of his abdomen and pierced his intestines. Death would be the only possible outcome.[1]

That afternoon, US surveyor general John Clark called on Mrs. Slough to offer his services. Arabella asked him to bring Colonel McClure to the house, where the chief justice now lay in considerable pain. Slough had argued bitterly with the colonel in early October, destroying the two men's friendship. He now wanted to reconcile with McClure before he died. Clark persuaded the reluctant McClure to visit the dying man so that Slough could ask his forgiveness.[2]

Slough rested a little more comfortably that evening, but on Monday he began to weaken. Knowing that the end was near, he made out his last will and testament. He died the next morning, Tuesday, December 17, 1867.[3]

Santa Fe buried Chief Justice John Potts Slough on December 18. Citizens draped the buildings around the plaza in black and then turned out in large numbers for the funeral. The *Santa Fe Weekly Gazette* claimed it was the "largest ever witnessed in Santa Fe," while the *Santa Fe New Mexican* expressed hope that "Santa Fe will never [again] be called upon to witness so solemn an occasion." Slough's pastor, the Reverend McFarland, led the funeral service, and then, taking Slough's death as his lesson the following Sunday, filled his sermon and prayers with "admonitions to repentance." Even the *New Mexican* put aside its rancor—at least temporarily—to wish that "this severe dispensation of an all wise Providence, may not, in its influence be lost upon the people, but that every effort may . . . be made to prevent such fearful results in the future."[4]

In an effort to exculpate William Rynerson of Slough's murder, Herman Heath resumed his attacks on the chief justice in the *New Mexican*'s January 14, 1868, issue. The paper blamed "madness . . . which finally drove Judge SLOUGH to his death." It recalled his abuse of Governor Mitchell over Mares's pardon and his rage over the oath of office incident, a slight that would not have aggravated "a man of a better balance of mind." The *New Mexican* reminded its readers that because of his "previously maddened condition," Slough embarked on a course of "abuse, invective, traduction, which finally resulted in the only way known in this country, in such cases, fatally at the hands of a man who dared to resent it." Its analysis was a classic example of blaming the victim, although Slough's increasingly irrational behavior clearly suggests a man, already under stress, breaking down under the attacks of his enemies.[5]

The *New Mexican*'s rival newspaper, the *Santa Fe Weekly Gazette*, saw a conspiracy in the events leading to Slough's death. Persons "inimical to the late Chief Justice" had "concocted" the scheme of passing resolutions "derogatory to his official conduct and private character." The "false, malicious, and ill-natured character of the resolutions chafed the proud and sensitive spirit of the deceased," the newspaper observed, causing "a natural feeling of antipathy to those whom he regarded as his defamers." Regardless of Slough's behavior, the *Weekly Gazette* told its readers that "No cloak of this kind can cover up the fact that he [Rynerson] killed Judge Slough; that he killed him in the Fonda [Hotel]; that he killed him after having deliberated over the matter from six o'clock on Saturday evening until about one o'clock the following day; that he was fully armed and prepared to kill him when he did." Madness had nothing to do with Slough's death; it was premeditated murder.[6]

Newspapers across the country either indicted Rynerson and Heath or blamed Slough for his death. An anonymous army officer wrote the *Ohio Daily Statesman* that Slough was assassinated "for having stated his opinion, and nothing but the truth in the face of his murderer, by calling him a coward and a swindler." For his crime, Rynerson "ought to be publicly branded for murdering a straight forward, good, intelligent man." The *Council Bluffs Nonpareil* came to the same conclusion as the *Daily Ohio Statesman*'s correspondent. In its estimation, Slough had denounced Rynerson "very justly and naturally to his face" and fell victim to Rynerson's Colt "without any blame on his part." Another Iowa newspaper, the *Dubuque Herald*, stated that Heath, "of unfragrant [*sic*] memory hereabouts," was just as culpable as Rynerson.[7]

Other newspapers argued that Slough should have expected nothing less than violence for his outrageous behavior. The *Highland Weekly News*, reprinting an article from the *Marietta Register*, recalled that Slough had had "a quarrelsome disposition, had been in 'hot water' at Santa Fe, for some weeks, quarreled with the Court, with the Legislature, and has met the fate of his perverseness." A Santa Fe resident repeated the theme of just deserts in a letter to the *Daily Kansas Tribune*. Commenting on Rynerson's response to Slough's insults, the *Tribune*'s correspondent wrote, "This is the third or fourth time Judge Slough has used such language to men since I came here, and now he has found his man."[8]

Some newspapers simply blamed frontier violence for the assassination. The *Brooklyn Daily Eagle* classified Slough's murder as "an example of frontier brutality," while the *Detroit Post* stated that the deadly encounter between Rynerson and Slough concluded "in the usual way, in New Mexico, in a bar-room on a Sunday." Perhaps the *Montana Post* came closest to the truth in ascribing blame to the nasty political atmosphere in New Mexico Territory. It wrote, "It appears that in that hot bed of turmoil and interminable broils, Santa Fe, in which all the U.S. officials were more or less concerned, a large amount of personal crimination and re-crimination was indulged on all sides."[9]

Rynerson surrendered to Sheriff José Sena shortly after he shot Slough. Later that afternoon, US Marshal John Pratt took custody of Rynerson and transferred him to the guardhouse at Fort Marcy. On January 3, 1868, he was arraigned before Judge Joab Houghton. The hearing lasted for four days, with multiple witnesses offering essentially the same account of Rynerson gunning down Slough after the chief justice refused to retract his slurs. When the last witness completed his testimony, Judge Houghton remanded Rynerson to jail to await trial on a charge of murder in the first degree.[10]

A more sympathetic judge now assumed responsibility for Rynerson's case. Associate Justice Perry Brocchus arrived in Santa Fe on January 12 to preside over the 1st Judicial District in which the freshman senator would be tried. Brocchus aspired to be the territory's next chief justice and understood that his success depended on Herman Heath and José Francisco Chávez. When Rynerson's lawyers applied for a writ of habeas corpus, he allowed the habeas corpus hearing to become an indictment of Slough's character. Witness after witness described how the chief justice abused juries, witnesses, attorneys, territorial officers, even innocent bystanders with his ferocious temper and vile language.[11]

When this sad litany ended, Brocchus was prepared to exonerate Rynerson. Arguing that the law "looks with compassion on the infirmity of human passion when it suddenly results from a sense of wrong or a deep and poignant sense of wounded honor," the judge concluded that Rynerson "would have been held, in the eye of the law, as well as the sight of his fellow man, guiltless of that degree of crime against society which demands the expiation of death." Brocchus condemned Slough's behavior, even though the chief justice had acted from a similar sense of "wounded honor," but excused Rynerson's crime as one of understandable passion. He consequently ordered Rynerson released on $20,000 bond to await trial.[12]

Republicans cheered Brocchus's ruling. The *Santa Fe New Mexican* printed the judge's opinion in its January 28, 1868, issue along with an editorial that praised the judge as "the people's hope." Stephen Elkins wrote Chávez that Brocchus "rendered a decision that reflects honer [*sic*] upon him as an able judge and pleases everyone," while William Arny reported favorably about Brocchus to his Republican contacts in Washington. If Brocchus had his eye on Slough's old position, his ruling at the Rynerson hearing could not have served him better.[13]

On March 17, Rynerson stood trial in the Santa Fe County District Court. Judge Perry Brocchus presided. The trial's transcript no longer exists and Santa Fe's two newspapers, perhaps viewing the verdict as a foregone conclusion, failed to cover the trial in any detail. After five days of testimony, Brocchus directed the jury's attention to Slough's behavior and dismissed them to the jury room. On March 22, they acquitted William Rynerson of murder in the first degree.[14]

Arabella had left Santa Fe long before Rynerson walked out of Brocchus's courtroom a free man. She and her children boarded a stagecoach on January 6 bound for Kansas. There they bought passage on the Union Pacific Railroad for their return to Cincinnati and home.[15]

Her husband's premature death left her with few fungible resources. She inherited shares in the New Mexico Mining Company worth $800, but not payable for two years, plus shares in gold, silver, and copper mines elsewhere in New Mexico Territory and Colorado Territory. Slough also left her two lots and a brick house in Denver as well as a one-thirteenth share in the Virginia City Town Company, the speculative venture near the Moreño mining district.[16]

Perhaps wary of the dangers he encountered while riding the judicial circuit, Slough had taken out a $5,000 accidental loss of life policy in June 1867. When Arabella attempted to collect the proceeds, the Accident Insurance Company of Columbus refused payment because, it argued, the circumstances of Slough's death fell under several of the policy's exclusions. Arabella sued the insurance company in the Franklin (Ohio) Court of Common Pleas in late 1869. After reviewing extensive testimony about Slough's death, the court ruled that the chief justice "lost his life through an injury affected by violent and accidental means within the intent and meaning of the policy" and awarded the widow the policy's proceeds.[17]

Arabella married Wallace M. Probasco on September 5, 1871, in Urbana, Ohio. Two years later, the couple moved to Massillon, Ohio, where Probasco served as the rector of St. Timothy's Episcopal Church. Unfortunately, the marriage was short-lived. Probasco died of smallpox on March 21, 1877. Shortly after his death, Arabella moved to Washington, DC, along with her four youngest children, Sallie and Martin Slough and Ada and Wallace Probasco. She found employment, perhaps using family connections, with the Department of the Interior. She worked there until 1906, when failing eyesight forced her to resign. Without income, she applied to the Pension Board in January 1908 for an increase in her widow's pension, based on her marriage to the brigadier general. The board awarded her $30 a month. On February 7, 1911, Arabella McLean Slough Probasco died at the age of seventy-four. She outlived John Slough by forty-three years.[18]

By the time the Moreño mines played out in 1904, more than $3 million in gold had been recovered from its works. Despite the mines' riches, Virginia City, the town where Slough hoped to find his fortune, never took root. Although he and his fellow investors gambled that a hundred houses would be built by spring 1868, Virginia City never amounted to more than a store, a post office, and a handful of miners' shanties. Its tiny population abandoned their shacks in 1869 and moved to the more promising camp at Elizabethtown, New Mexico.[19]

Slough's final venture, the Virginia City Town Company, is symbolic of his entire life. As Virginia City's proximity to the Moreño mines promised growth and prosperity, Slough's background—his upbringing in a thriving, upwardly mobile family, his marriage to the niece of a Supreme Court justice, his early ties to the Ohio Democratic Party, and his connection to several of the period's most powerful men—afforded him an auspicious path to financial and professional success. He used these advantages to enter the Ohio House of Representatives at an early age. When the legislature expelled him and Cincinnati's voters rejected him, Slough was forced to seek redemption elsewhere. Just as the hope of riches lured prospectors to the Moreño gold fields, Kansas Territory attracted Slough with opportunities to match his large ambitions.

During the next nine years, Slough moved repeatedly across the continent—Kansas Territory, Colorado Territory, Virginia, and finally New Mexico Territory—in search of advancement. He did not hesitate to grasp new possibilities, even if he had to reinvent himself, and he achieved considerable success for his efforts. When the Kansas Democratic Party no longer embraced the pro-slavery ruffianism of bleeding Kansas, Slough stepped forward to oppose the Lecompton Constitution, to lead the Democratic delegates at the Wyandotte Constitutional Convention, and to run for election as Kansas's first lieutenant governor. He gained Territorial Governor William Gilpin's trust and became the 1st Colorado's colonel; without military experience, he led the Colorado Volunteers to victory at Pigeon's Ranch. While serving as military governor of Alexandria, Virginia, he used his administrative talent to stabilize a town reeling from the disruptive presence of thousands of Union soldiers. Even in New Mexico Territory, he fared well during his first year as chief justice before the pressures of his position and the attacks of his Republican adversaries demoralized his behavior and destroyed his reputation.

Slough never achieved the full measure of success that he desired. Just as Virginia City failed before Elizabethtown's more attractive location, Slough faltered before the fierce competition of other ambitious men he encountered. Some opponents, like Robert Hosea in Cincinnati or J. P. Root and James L. McDowell in Kansas Territory, took advantage of the Republican Party's growing ascendancy during the 1850s to defeat the Democrat Slough at the polls. James Cooper, commissioned a brigadier general a year earlier than Slough, claimed the division command that Slough believed he had earned at Harpers Ferry. And some men—Darius Cadwell, Jacob Downing, John

Chivington, William Arny, and Herman Heath—manipulated his weaknesses or resorted to unscrupulous and dishonest means to advance their own agendas. Slough had many opponents during his life; he defeated some, like the Alexandria liquor sellers, but he lost to many more.

Slough failed in his ambitions not simply because he embraced the Democratic Party or because he faced unprincipled rivals. It was his character flaws that sabotaged his plans. Having been raised by a prosperous father in a city bursting with growth, he expected success and could not easily accept others' accomplishments at his expense. Insecurity may have caused his hypersensitive reactions when he perceived that men questioned his status as a gentleman, his rank as a Union officer, or his position as chief justice. His anger, uncontrollable at times, led him to impulsive decisions that undercut much of what he wanted to achieve. All these failings eventually coalesced into the rage that ended his life. He came close to realizing his ambition for greatness, but in the end, his personal shortcomings thwarted all of his dreams.

Notes

INTRODUCTION

1. *The Squatter Sovereign*, September 12, 1857, 3.

2. Billington and Ridge, *Western Expansion*, 685; see Sandage, *Born Losers*, for a discussion of nineteenth-century American attitudes toward success and failure.

3. Ralph Waldo Emerson, quoted in Cawelti, *Apostles of the Self-Made Man*, 93.

4. According to John Slough's great granddaughter, Carolyn Laceky, the family name rhymes with "plow."

5. *Daily Ohio Statesmen*, May 1, 1868, 1; Moore, *Early History of Leavenworth City and County*, 20; *Columbus Statesman* reprinted in the *Cincinnati Daily Enquirer*, November 20, 1856, 2.

6. For examples of one-sided descriptions of Slough, see Sides, *Blood and Thunder*, 369; Frazier, *Blood & Treasure*, 204; Anders, *Injustice on Trial*, 429–30; Miller, "William Logan Rynerson in New Mexico, 1862–1893," 104; Edrington and Taylor, *The Battle of Glorieta Pass*, 30; and Whitlock, *Distant Bugles, Distant Drums*, 64. Historians have also repeated earlier historians' errors about Slough's life. As one example, in his 1925 book, *Old Santa Fe: The Story of New Mexico's Ancient Capital*, Ralph Emerson Twitchell claimed that Slough's grandfather was a colonel commissioned by George Washington in the Continental Army and his father was a brigadier general. Arie Poldervaart cited Twitchell when he inaccurately described Slough's military family, while Hampton Sides changed Slough's predecessor in the Continental Army to his uncle. Poldervaart, *Black-Robed Justice*, 67; Sides, *Blood and Thunder*, 369. Two recent studies, Phillip B. Gonzales's *Política: Nuevomexicanos and American Political Incorporation, 1821–1910* and Paula Tarnapol Whitacre's *A Civil Life in an Uncivil Time*, offer fuller pictures of Slough's role in postbellum New Mexico politics and Civil War Alexandria.

7. See Gaeddert, *The Birth of Kansas*.

8. Volo and Volo, *Family Life in 19th-Century America*, 67.

1. Ford and Ford, *History of Cincinnati, Ohio*, 80.

2. James, *The Life of Andrew Jackson*, 488.

3. *The Cincinnati Directory for the Year 1829.* There is no record of the names of Mary's parents or siblings. Given the nineteenth-century custom of naming children after parents, it seems reasonable that John Potts Slough was named after Mary's father.

4. Weisenburger, *The Life of John McLean*, 5; *The WPA Guide to Cincinnati*, 14–16.

5. *The WPA Guide to Cincinnati*, 14–16; Blum, "A Devotion in the West," 16.

6. Written correspondence from Carolyn Laceky, November 7, 2014; Poldervaart, *Black-Robed Justice*, 67; *Biographical Annals of Lancaster County, Pennsylvania*, 15–16; Foote, *The Schools of Cincinnati and its Vicinity*, 6.

7. Blum, "A Devotion in the West," 15–16; Ross, *Workers on the Edge*, 6–7; *The WPA Guide to Cincinnati*, 25.

8. *The WPA Guide to Cincinnati*, 58; *Gibbons v. Ogden* (accessed on January 24, 2015) available from http://en.wikipedia.org/wiki/Gibbons_v._Ogden; Ross, *Workers on the Edge*, 12–14.

9. Although Martin had been married for a year, it seems unlikely that the directory listing for Mrs. Slough referred to his young wife. More likely, Martin's father had died sometime before 1829 and his widow lived with her son and supported herself by millinery. *The Cincinnati Directory for the Year 1829.*

10. Mary was born in November 1804 in Belmont County, Ohio, adjacent to present-day West Virginia. She and her parents came to Cincinnati in 1805 (*The Cincinnati Pioneer*, 28). Although not as severe as the cholera epidemic that struck Cincinnati in 1849, the epidemics of the early 1830s killed enough citizens to frighten the populace to stay indoors or to flee the city. Salmon P. Chase, who fought off an attack of cholera in 1832, noted that the "streets are quite deserted" while the Fords, in their history of Cincinnati, recorded that "business was almost wholly suspended . . . the din of the city was hushed, and every day appeared as a Sabbath." Niven, *Salmon P. Chase: A Biography*, 30; Ford and Ford, *History of Cincinnati, Ohio*, 81–84.

11. *The Cincinnati Directory for the Year 1834*; Ross, *Workers on the Edge*, 36.

12. The Cincinnati Directory Advertiser for the Years 1836–7; Weisenburger, *The Life of John McLean*, 159–60; Ford and Ford, *History of Cincinnati, Ohio*, 90.

13. City directories for the period often included hotels and taverns together in the same business listing, suggesting that the two types of establishments commonly shared the same location. *Shaffer's Advertising Directory for 1839–1840*; *The Cincinnati*

Directory for the Year 1842; The Cincinnati Directory for the Year 1843; Ford and Ford, *History of Cincinnati, Ohio*, 90.

14. *The WPA Guide to Cincinnati*, 50–51; Ross, *Workers on the Edge*, 20, 168; Cist, *Cincinnati in 1841*, 290, 292. In March 1841, the Ohio Senate Standing Committee on Privileges and Elections, investigating illegal voting in Cincinnati during the fall 1840 election, deposed Martin Slough because of his coffee house's association with the Democratic Party. *Journal of the Senate of Ohio at the First Session of the Thirty-Ninth General Assembly*, Appendix #1: "Report of the Majority of the Standing Committee on Privileges and Elections, in the Matter of the Contested Seat of George W. Holmes, Esq. from the County of Hamilton, March 4, 1841, 397. *The Cincinnati Daily Enquirer* reported that Martin Slough attended a 15th Ward Democratic meeting in October 1857 and was a delegate to the Hamilton County Democratic nominating convention in September 1863. *Cincinnati Daily Enquirer*, October 13, 1857, 3, and September 7, 1863, 3.

15. *Daily Cincinnati Enquirer*, May 28, 1842, 3. The advertisement ran at least ten times between May 1842 and June 1843. Other prominent Cincinnatians among the advertisement's endorsers were businessmen J. P. Tweed (insurance), W. S. Merrill (chemicals), S. S. L'Hommedieu (banking, publishing, and railroads), F. G. Ringgold (shoe manufacture), J. A. James (printing), and John P. Garniss, father-in-law of Salmon P. Chase. Greve, *Centennial History of Cincinnati*, 600.

16. *Catalogue of the Officers and Students of the Cincinnati College, 1841;* Foote, *The Schools of Cincinnati and its Vicinity*, 6, 9. We can be certain that the Sloughs were Protestant because John's sister Mary attended Wesleyan Female College, a school for women founded by several Methodist ministers in 1842, and Martin's funeral was held at St. Paul's Methodist Church. *The Alumna*, 104; Greve, *Centennial History of Cincinnati*, 680; Cist, *Cincinnati in 1841*, 117–18; Shotwell, *A History of the Schools of Cincinnati*, 494; *The Cincinnati Commercial Gazette*, November 8, 1887, 5; Reid, *Ohio in the War*, 933.

17. According to "An Act, amendatory to the Act incorporating the Cincinnati College," passed by the Ohio legislature in 1846, any adult Ohio male who provided a certificate from the Law Department to two judges of the Ohio Supreme Court would be licensed as an "attorney and counselor at law." The certificate demonstrated that the applicant had been "carefully examined and reported to be qualified to practice . . . by at least five Lawyers of good standing." Charles Gordon Matchette, who attended the Cincinnati Law School in 1855–1856, described a process of questioning by a panel of examiners. Upon passing the examination and receiving his diploma, Matchette appeared the next day before a judge and, certifying that he was at least twenty-

one years old, a United States citizen, and a resident of Ohio for at least one year, was admitted to the Ohio Bar. *Catalogue and Circular of the Law Department of the Cincinnati College, 1846–1847,* 5, 7–8; Charles Gordon Matchette Journal.

18. Charles Gordon Matchette Journal.

19. *Cincinnati Daily Enquirer,* April 22, 1849, 3. During the 1840s and 1850s, the *Cincinnati Enquirer* had five different names: *Daily Cincinnati Enquirer* (1841–1843), *Enquirer & Message* (1843–1844), *Daily Enquirer and Message* (1844–1845), *Cincinnati Daily Enquirer* (1845–1849 and 1852–1872), and *Cincinnati Enquirer* (1849–1852).

20. The city directory for 1851–1852 has John Slough living at his father's house at 256 Main Street, but the 1853 city directory lists him as an attorney at law practicing at 16 Richmond Street. *Williams' Cincinnati Directory and Business Advertiser for 1851–52* and *Williams' Cincinnati Directory, City Guide, and Business Mirror for 1853*; Ford and Ford, *History of Cincinnati, Ohio,* 320; Foote, *The Schools of Cincinnati and its Vicinity,* 23; *Cincinnati Enquirer,* June 15, 1850, 2.

21. *Cincinnati Enquirer,* August 29, 1851, 2; Baker, *Affairs of Party,* 126; Holt, *The Political Crisis of the 1850s,* 134; Powell, *The Democratic Party of the State of Ohio,* 1:96–97.

22. *Cincinnati Enquirer,* March 2, 1852, 2.

23. *Cincinnati Enquirer,* September 16, 1851, 2, October 2, 1851, 2, and April 7, 1852, 2; *Williams' Cincinnati Directory, City Guide, and Business Mirror for 1853*.

24. Arabella had four sisters—Eliza, Sarah, Caroline, and Mary—and one brother, Nathaniel. Her parents lost three other children in infancy or early childhood. William McLean (accessed on February 4, 2015), available from http://freepages.genealogy .rootsweb.ancestry.com/~dmcl/i/i1520.htm; Weisenburger, *The Life of John McLean,* 1–4.

25. Nelson, *Documents Relating to the Colonial History of the State of New Jersey,* xv; John McLean (accessed on February 4, 2015), available from http://en.wikipedia .org/wiki/John_McLean; William McLean (accessed on February 4, 2105), available from http://en.wikipedia.org/wiki/Willam_McLean_(Ohio Politician); *Biographical Directory of the American Congress, 1774–1949,* 1546; Weisenburger, *The Life of John McLean,* 219–20.

26. Weisenburger, *The Life of John McLean,* 180–81, 219–20, 225.

27. Slough enlistment papers (accessed on April 27, 2016), available from www.fold3-com.research.cincinnatilibrary.org/image/320175115; *Notices,* 33.

28. In May 1849, the Cincinnati Pioneer Association held a parade with eighty-four members who had been residents of Cincinnati before 1819, when the city's first charter was granted. Martin Slough was among the eighty-four charter members who participated in the parade to the city council chambers, where they were honored with speeches. *Cincinnati Enquirer,* May 26, 1919, 16.

29. United States Census 1850; Ford and Ford, *History of Cincinnati, Ohio,* 94. The

Slough family status was recognized at their deaths. Many of the nation's newspapers, including the *New York Times*, reported John Slough's death in 1867 (*New York Times*, December 28, 1867, 1). John's sister Mary's death in 1871 merited several pages of remembrance in the 1877 annual of the Wesleyan Female College (*The Alumna*, 38–39). Mother Mary's death in 1878 was noted in Charles Theodore Greve's *Centennial History of Cincinnati* (883). The Slough family has a plot in Spring Grove Cemetery, where Cincinnati's prominent families have been buried since the 1840s.

30. William Slough's age in the 1860 and 1870 censuses suggests that he was born in 1854 or even 1855. But his death record at Spring Grove Cemetery where he is buried indicates that he was born on August 6, 1853. *Williams' Cincinnati Directory, City Guide, and Business Mirror for 1853*; *Cincinnati Daily Enquirer*, March 21, 1854, 2; *M'Arthur Democrat*, January 12, 1855, 2; *Cincinnati Daily Enquirer*, August 28, 1855, 2; United States Census 1860, 1870.

31. Maizlish, *The Triumph of Sectionalism*, 162, 180–81; Holt, *The Political Crisis of the 1850s*, 132.

32. Holt, *The Political Crisis of the 1850s*, 160–61; Holt, *Political Parties and American Political Development*, 284–87; Niven, *Salmon P. Chase: A Biography*, 162–63.

33. Maizlish, *The Triumph of Sectionalism*, 213–14; Niven, *Salmon P. Chase: A Biography*, 163.

34. Maizlish, *The Triumph of Sectionalism*, 189; Foner, *Free Soil, Free Labor, Free Men*, 94; Holt, *The Political Crisis of the 1850s*, 190.

35. Foner, *Free Soil, Free Labor, Free Men*, 239; Maizlish, *The Triumph of Sectionalism*, 205.

36. *Perrysville Journal*, November 10, 1855, 5.

2. "AN ARDENT AND ZEALOUS DEMOCRAT"

1. Baker, *Affairs of Party*, 50.

2. Ibid., 45, 110.

3. Washington McLean, the chair of the Ohio Democratic State Central Committee in 1853 and the owner of the *Cincinnati Daily Enquirer*, was not related to Arabella or John McLean. Niven, *Salmon P. Chase: A Biography*, 372.

4. Quoted in the *Daily Ohio Statesman*, September 16, 1855, 2.

5. *Perrysburg Journal*, November 11, 1855, 5.

6. *Notices*, 34; *Journal of the House of Representatives, 1856*, 1–5.

7. *Journal of the House of Representatives, 1856*, 80; *Daily Ohio State Journal*, January 17, 1856, 2.

8. Governor Chase included in his Inaugural Address the organization and

discipline of the militia as one of the initiatives for the legislature to address. Slough, who had been appointed to the Select Committee on the Militia early in the session, responded with a bill intended to simplify the military laws of Ohio. The bill required all able-bodied white male citizens between the ages of eighteen and forty-five to enroll in the militia. It defined the militia's organizational structure and established each township and ward as a military district. And it stipulated that the militia could only be called out in case of riot, insurrection, invasion, or war. Slough's bill served as the basis of legislation passed in the 1857 session. *Journal of the House of Representatives, 1856*, 65, 141, 146, 309, 322; *Journal of the House of Representatives, 1857*, 159; *Western Reserve Chronicle*, January 30, 1856, 2; *Cincinnati Daily Enquirer*, February 7, 1856, 2.

9. Baker, *Affairs of Party*, 130, 248; Silbey, *A Respectable Minority*, 25, 27; *Daily Ohio State Journal*, April 10, 1856, 2; *Journal of the House of Representatives, 1856*, 527.

10. Of the 131 House or Senate bills that reached a third reading, which was required for a bill's passage, Slough voted with the majority 96 times, about three-quarters of the roll calls. Holt, *The Political Crisis of the 1850s*, 111–18; Maizlish, *The Triumph of Sectionalism*, 162–65.

11. Etcheson, *Bleeding Kansas*, 2–3, 29.

12. Ibid., 39, 46.

13. Nevins, *Ordeal of the Union*, 313, 385.

14. Etcheson, *Bleeding Kansas*, 74–75.

15. Nevins, *Ordeal of the Union*, 408.

16. Niven, *Salmon P. Chase: A Biography*, 176–77.

17. Niven, *Salmon P. Chase: A Biography*, 176, *Journal of the House of Representatives, 1856*, 63–74.

18. *Cincinnati Daily Gazette*, February 7, 1856, 1.

19. *Notices*, 31–32; *Cincinnati Daily Gazette*, February 7, 1856, 1; *Cincinnati Daily Enquirer*, February 7, 1856, 2.

20. Foner, *Free Soil, Free Labor, Free Men*, 108–9; Darius Cadwell from *The Encyclopedia of Cleveland History* (accessed on June 14, 2016), available from http://ech .case.edu/cgi/article.pl?id=CD.

21. The partisan *Cincinnati Daily Enquirer* belittled Cadwell's speech as being "in strict accordance with the wishes of the Governor." *Cincinnati Daily Enquirer*, February 7, 1856, 2; *Journal of the House of Representatives, 1856*, 157.

22. *Notices*, 8.

23. *Cincinnati Daily Gazette*, February 11, 1856, 2.

24. *Cincinnati Daily Enquirer*, February 10, 1856, 1; *Cincinnati Daily Gazette*, February 11, 1856, 2.

25. *Cincinnati Daily Enquirer*, February 10, 1856, 1; *Journal of the House of Representatives, 1856*, 172–73; *Daily Ohio State Journal*, February 9, 1856, 2.

26. *Notices*, 25.

27. Tragically, the boat taking the Garners south sank after colliding with another boat. One of Margaret's children drowned in the mishap. It is said that Margaret rejoiced that another child had avoided slavery through death. Yanuck, "The Garner Fugitive Slave Case," 47–50, 53–59.

28. Debate over Monroe's habeas corpus bill was reported in the *Daily Ohio State Journal*, February 15, 1856, 2; *Cincinnati Daily Enquirer*, February 17, 1856, 1, and February 20, 1856, 1.

29. *Journal of the House of Representatives, 1856*, 320.

30. Niven, *The Salmon P. Chase Papers*, 267; Hagedorn, *Beyond the River*, 112, 216–18; Ford and Ford, *History of Cincinnati, Ohio*, 80; Cist, *Sketches and Statistics of Cincinnati in 1851*, 44.

31. *Daily Ohio State Journal*, February 2, 1857, 2.

32. *Journal of the House of Representatives, 1856*, 351–53; *Daily Ohio State Journal*, March 19, 1856, 2.

33. *Journal of the House of Representatives, 1856*, 537–39; *Daily Ohio State Journal*, April 10, 1856, 2.

34. *Notices*, 33; *Cincinnati Daily Gazette*, February 12, 1857, 1.

3. DISGRACE AND DEFEAT

1. Etcheson, *Bleeding Kansas*, 100–101; SenGupta, *For God and Mammon*, 109.

2. Etcheson, *Bleeding Kansas*, 104–5; Nevins, *Ordeal of the Union*, 435.

3. Nevins, *Ordeal of the Union*, 440–41.

4. *Official Proceedings of the National Democratic Convention Held in Cincinnati, June 2–6, 1856*, 5–6; *Cincinnati Daily Enquirer*, June 3, 1856, 1, and June 4, 1856, 2.

5. *Daily Ohio State Journal*, February 2, 1857, 2; *Cincinnati Daily Enquirer*, July 20, 1856, 4, July 25, 1856, 4, August 1, 1856, 4, and October 19, 1856, 4.

6. Reprinted in the *Cincinnati Daily Enquirer*, November 20, 1856, 2; *The Ashland Union*, December 17, 1856, 2.

7. Ohio's partisan newspapers offered differing explanations of why Slough proposed a resolution seeking per diem payment and mileage during the adjournment. The *Holmes County Republican*, on the one hand, condemned the resolution as a "scheme no better than to propose taking without consideration just so much money from the State Treasury." The *Cincinnati Daily Enquirer*, on the

other, argued that the people of Ohio, through adopting the 1850 state constitution, intended that each general assembly would last for two years, but the Republicans had "eroded" the constitution by voting for adjournment after meeting for only four months. Because the state constitution did not allow for a midsession adjournment, Slough wanted the attorney general to determine if members were entitled to pay for the entire two years. According to the *Enquirer*, "The resolution was *merely one of inquiry*, to test a constitutional point." *Holmes County Republican*, February 12, 1857, 2; *Cincinnati Daily Enquirer*, February 12, 1857, 4; *Journal of the House of Representatives, 1857*, 8, 30–31.

8. "Report of the Select Committee of the House in the Case of Messrs. Slough and Cadwell," Appendix to the *Journal of the House of Representatives, 1857*, 78–83.

9. *Daily Ohio State Journal*, January 14, 1857, 2; *Cincinnati Daily Enquirer*, January 16, 1857, 3; Appendix, *Journal of the House of Representatives, 1857*, 82–83.

10. *Notices*, 11, 14, and 19.

11. *Cincinnati Daily Enquirer*, January 18, 1857, 3; *Journal of the House of Representatives, 1857*, 42–43.

12. *Cincinnati Daily Gazette*, February 7, 1857, 2; *Journal of the House of Representatives, 1857*, 53–54 and 70.

13. Appendix to the *Journal of the House of Representatives, 1857*, 78.

14. *Notices*, 28–29; *Journal of the House of Representatives, 1857*, 58.

15. *Daily Ohio State Journal*, January 22, 1857, 2.

16. *M'Arthur Democrat*, February 5, 1857, 2; *Cincinnati Daily Enquirer*, February 1, 1857, 4; *Cincinnati Daily Gazette*, January 27, 1857, 2, and February 11, 1857, 2.

17. *Journal of the House of Representatives, 1857*, 97–99; *Notices*, 14.

18. *Cincinnati Daily Gazette*, January 30, 1857, 2.

19. *Cincinnati Daily Gazette*, February 2, 1857, 1.

20. Ford and Ford, *History of Cincinnati, Ohio*, 87; *Notices*, 11–12; *Daily Ohio State Journal*, February 4, 1857, 2, and February 6, 1857, 2; *Cincinnati Daily Enquirer*, February 8, 1857, 1.

21. *Daily Ohio State Journal*, January 30, 1857, 2.

22. *Cincinnati Daily Gazette*, February 2, 1857, 1 and February 7, 1857, 2.

23. *Journal of the House of Representatives, 1857*, 99. One Republican representative, Licking County's C. B. Griffin, voted against expulsion. While several representatives felt compelled to explain their vote in the days after Slough was expelled, Griffin kept silent. No newspaper commented on Griffin's break with his fellow Republicans. The author of the *Notices* made no suggestion that Griffin had an independent streak but described him as "well-posted in the matters of State and National policy, and understands the variations and peculiarities of parties thoroughly." *Notices*, 15.

24. *Preble County Democrat*, January 29, 1857, 2; *Cincinnati Daily Enquirer*, January 27, 1857, 4; *M'Arthur Democrat*, February 5, 1857, 2. The *Dayton Empire*, the *Lebanon Citizen*, the *Mount Vernon Banner*, the *Cleveland Plain-Dealer*, and the *Portsmouth Spirit of the Times* all denounced the Republicans' action, articles the *Cincinnati Daily Enquirer* faithfully reprinted (*Cincinnati Daily Enquirer*, February 6, 1857, 2). The Democrats also organized meetings around the state to protest Slough's treatment. A rally was held in Columbus on January 30, another in Zanesville on February 5, and the largest in Cincinnati on February 7. *Cincinnati Daily Enquirer*, January 31, 1857, 4; February 7, 1857, 4; and February 8, 1857, 1.

25. *Cincinnati Daily Gazette*, February 2, 1857, 2; *Holmes County Republican*, February 12, 1857, 2. Newspapers that reported Slough's expulsion included the *Wheeling Daily Intelligencer* (January 30, 1857, 3), the *Daily Nashville Patriot* (January 31, 1857, 3), Washington DC's *Evening Star* (February 2, 1857, 3), the *Daily Dispatch* in Richmond, Virginia (February 2, 1857, 2), the *Raftsman's Journal* in Clearfield, Pennsylvania (February 4, 1857, 3), the *Athens* (TN) *Post* (February 6, 1857, 3), and the *Lewisburg* (PA) *Chronicle* (February 6, 1857, 2).

26. *Journal of the House of Representatives, 1857*, 81–83.

27. *Cincinnati Daily Enquirer*, January 18, 1857, 4, and January 24, 1857, 4; Foote, *The Gentlemen and the Roughs*, 6.

28. *Daily Ohio State Journal*, February 19, 1857, 1; *Cincinnati Daily Gazette*, February 11, 1857, 2.

29. *Daily Ohio State Journal*, February 19, 1857, 1; *Meigs County Telegraph*, February 3, 1857, 1; *Cincinnati Daily Enquirer*, January 27, 1857, 2. The *Holmes County Republican* connected not only Brooks's caning of Sumner but also the killing of Thomas Keating by Representative Philemon T. Herbert to Slough's assault on Cadwell and the Democrats' penchant for violence. Herbert was a Democratic congressman from California. Two weeks before Brooks's assault, Herbert and Keating, an African American waiter at Willard's Hotel in Washington, DC, exchanged punches over Herbert's complaints about his breakfast. Other breakfast diners pulled the two men apart, but Herbert drew his pistol and shot Keating point-blank in the chest. When it was discovered that Herbert came from an Alabama slaveholding family, the abolitionist press claimed that such men as Herbert "contemptuously treated Northern free laborers like slaves." *Holmes County Republican*, February 2, 1857, 2; "Philemon T. Herbert: Breakfast Brawl" (accessed on July 19, 2016); available from http://downfalldictionary.blogspot.com/search/label/Philemon%20T.%20Herbert.

30. *Cincinnati Daily Enquirer*, February 5, 1857, 4.

31. *Cincinnati Daily Enquirer*, February 8, 1857, 1 and 4.

32. Joblin, *Cincinnati Past and Present*, 291–97; *Cincinnati Daily Enquirer*, February

10, 1857, 4, and February 13, 1857, 4; *Cincinnati Daily Gazette*, February 13, 1857, 2, and February 16, 1857, 2.

33. *Cincinnati Daily Gazette*, February 17, 1857, 2, and February 19, 1857, 2; *Cincinnati Daily Enquirer*, February 17, 1857, 4, and February 20, 1857, 4.

34. *Cincinnati Daily Gazette*, February 21, 1857, 2; *Cincinnati Daily Enquirer*, February 22, 1857, 4. Whether the Hamilton County voters rejected John Slough or rejected the Democratic Party in the February 16 special election is difficult to know. In September 1855, Slough had handily won his seat in the Ohio House of Representatives, while a year later in the 1856 presidential election, Hamilton County voters gave Democrat James Buchanan a 2,700-vote margin over John C. Frémont. Slough's seventeen-vote loss to Hosea four months later suggests that the voters rejected the man. Yet the election tide appeared to be turning against the Democratic Party even in 1856. The combined ballots cast for Frémont and Fillmore outstripped those cast for Buchanan. By the 1858 election, a new fusionist party defeated the Hamilton County Democrats. And in the 1860 presidential election, Lincoln carried the city and county over Stephen A. Douglas by more than 1,100 votes. *Cincinnati Daily Enquirer*, October 21, 1856, 4, October 14, 1858, 2, and November 8, 1860, 2.

35. *Cincinnati Daily Enquirer*, February 26, 1857, 2; *Daily Ohio State Journal*, February 24, 1857, 2; *Journal of the House of Representatives, 1857*, 205.

36. *Cincinnati Daily Enquirer*, June 23, 1857, 2, and July 8, 1857, 2; Carolyn Laceky, "John Potts Slough, Frontier Lawyer: Hero, Villain, Victim," unpublished manuscript.

4. A RIGHTEOUS FIGHT

1. Etcheson, *Bleeding Kansas*, 109–10.

2. Nevins, *Ordeal of the Union*, 474; SenGupta, *For God & Mammon*, 115.

3. Shortly after the Pottawatomie Creek murders, Captain H. C. Pate arrested two of John Brown's sons and turned them over to the federal authorities for prosecution. Brown, seeking revenge, led thirty-five Free State militants against Pate's territorial militia, composed mostly of proslavery men, in the Battle of Black Jack on June 2, 1856. Free State forces continued their rampage by descending on proslavery settlements on August 7, 12, 15, and 16. Proslavery militiamen, perhaps as many as four hundred, retaliated by overrunning John Brown's camp at Osawatomie on August 30. During the raid, they killed several Free State men, including one of John Brown's sons. Free State and proslavery forces clashed again on September 13–14 at the Battle of Hickory Point; six Missourians died in the bloodshed. Etcheson, *Bleeding Kansas*, 114, 121–22, 134.

4. *Kansas Constitutional Convention*, 413; Nevins, *Ordeal of the Union*, 484–86.

5. Rawley, *Race and Politics*, 211; Richardson, *Beyond the Mississippi*, 53; Thomas

Ewing Jr. to Judge M. F. Moore, June 1857 (accessed on April 20, 2015), available from www.kansasmemory.org/item/862/text; Thomas Ewing Jr. to Thomas Ewing Sr., July 1857 (accessed on April 20, 2015), available from www.kansasmemory.org/item/866/text.

6. *Cincinnati Daily Enquirer*, May 5, 1858, 3. Carolyn Laceky, in her graduate paper on her great-grandfather, "John Potts Slough, Frontier Lawyer—Hero, Villain, Victim," states that Slough and fellow Cincinnati lawyer William C. McDowell traveled to Leavenworth together in 1857. Other sources, however, place McDowell's arrival in Kansas in 1858. William C. McDowell (accessed on January 26, 2019), available from https://www.kshs.org/kansapedia/william-c-mcdowell/17078.

7. John J. Ingalls to Elias Ingalls, September 23, 1858 (accessed on May 18, 2015), available from www.kansasmemory.org/item/2896/text; John J. Ingalls to Elias Ingalls, October 5, 1858 (accessed on April 20, 2015), available from www.kansasmemory.org /item/2898/text.

8. Moore, *Early History of Leavenworth City and County*, 20.

9. Moore, *Early History of Leavenworth City and County*, 129; *Leavenworth— First City of Kansas* (accessed on October 30, 2015), available from www.legends ofamerica.com/ks-leavenworth; Goodrich, *War to the Knife*, 197; Maria Felt to Thomas W. Higginson, June 25, 1858 (accessed on April 21, 2015), available from https://territorialkansasonline.ku.edu/index.php?SCREEN=show_transcript &document_id=101936SCREEN=search&submit=search&search=Maria%20Felt &startsearchat=0&searchfor=keywords&printerfriendly=&county_id=&topic_id =&document_id=101936&selected_keyword=.

10. Hall and Hand, *History of Leavenworth County*, 120–32, 167; Minor, *Kansas: The History of the Sunflower State*, 80.

11. *Cincinnati Daily Enquirer*, July 8, 1857, 2; Daniel Mulford Valentine diary (accessed on May 20, 2015), available from www.kansasmemory.org/item/208140/text.

12. John J. Ingalls to Elias Ingalls, November 21, 1858 (accessed on May 19, 2015), available from www.kansasmemory.org/item/2935/text.

13. Moore, *Early History of Leavenworth City and County*, 297; *Cincinnati Daily Enquirer*, May 5, 1858, 3.

14. Census records are contradictory about Sarah's place of birth. The 1860 and 1880 censuses list Ohio as her birthplace, while the 1870 census lists Kansas. Genealogies prepared by Gwen Fuller, a descendant of Sarah Slough, and Cheryl Nunn indicate that Hamilton County, Ohio, was Sarah's birthplace. *Cincinnati Daily Enquirer*, November 27, 1857, 3, and December 3, 1857, 2.

15. *The Squatter Sovereign*, September 12, 1857, 3.

16. Nevins, *Ordeal of the Union*, 380.

17. Nevins, *The Emergence of Lincoln*, 138, 162; Etcheson, *Bleeding Kansas*, 145–47.

18. Etcheson, *Bleeding Kansas*, 158, 160; Nevins, *The Emergence of Lincoln*, 1:240.

19. Nevins, *The Emergence of Lincoln*, 1:152.

20. *Daily Ohio State Journal*, January 17, 1858, 1; *M'Arthur Democrat*, January 14, 1858, 2.

21. Among the committee's seven men were George W. Perkins, John A. Halderman, and Edward L. Berthoud, men whom Slough would meet again in Colorado Territory. *Kansas Herald of Freedom*, January 9, 1858, 2.

22. Gaeddert, *The Birth of Kansas*, 27; *M'Arthur Democrat*, January 14, 1858, 2; *Findlay Jeffersonian*, January 28, 1858, 2.

5. FRUITLESS LABOR

1. John J. Ingalls to Elias T. Ingalls, July 5, 1859 (accessed on April 20, 2015), available from www.kansasmemory.org/item/2970/text; Morgan, *History of Wyandotte County, Kansas*, 146–47.

2. Cheatham, "Slavery All the Time or Not at All," 170; Nevins, *The Emergence of Lincoln*, 1:296.

3. Gaeddert, *The Birth of Kansas*, 28; Etcheson, *Bleeding Kansas*, 178; *Leavenworth Constitution* (accessed on December 29, 2015), available from www.kansasmemory.org/item/207410.

4. *Cincinnati Daily Enquirer*, May 5, 1858, 2, and February 17, 1859, 1; *Findlay Jeffersonian*, January 29, 1858, 2; Billington, *America's Frontier Heritage*, 100.

5. *Topeka Tribune*, December 16, 1858, 3.

6. *Kansas Constitutional Convention*, 15.

7. Reprinted in the *White Cloud Kansas Chief*, July 28, 1859, 3.

8. Some days the delegates met in general assembly from eight o'clock in the morning to six o'clock in the evening and then adjourned to conduct their committee work. Throughout the convention, the members complained about the unbearable heat. C. K. Holliday, who had come to Wyandotte to lobby for Topeka as the state capital, wrote his wife on July 14 that the day was "as hot as I think I ever saw it. It is almost difficult to move around." Cyrus K. Holliday to Mary Dillon Holliday, July 14, 1859 (accessed on April 15, 2015), available from www.kansasmemory.org/item/2877/text; Samuel Adams Stinson (accessed on July 22, 2018) available from www.kshs.org/kansapedia/samuel-adams-stinson/17092; William C. McDowell (accessed on July 22, 2018), available from https://www.kshs.org/kansapedia/william-c-mcdowell/17078.

9. *White Cloud Kansas Chief*, July 14, 1859, 2; *Kansas Constitutional Convention*, 40–43.

10. *Kansas Constitutional Convention*, 44.

11. Ibid., 61.

12. Gaeddert, *The Birth of Kansas*, 42; *Kansas Constitutional Convention*, 265–69; *Kansas Herald of Freedom*, July 9, 1859, 2.

13. John W. Forman (accessed on January 13, 2016), available from www.kshs.org/kansapedia/john-w-forman/17061; *Kansas Constitutional Convention*, 287, 492.

14. *Kansas Constitutional Convention*, 324–25.

15. Ibid., 271, 274–76.

16. Ibid., 277, 283–84.

17. Ibid., 169, 178, 302, 342.

18. Ibid., 177.

19. Ibid., 176, 182; *White Cloud Kansas Chief*, August 4, 1859, 3.

20. *Kansas Constitutional Convention*, 180, 182.

21. Ibid., 205–19, 237–38, 253, 263; Samuel Adams Stinson (accessed on July 22, 2018), available from www.kshs.org/kansapedia/samuel-adams-stinson/17092.

22. *Kansas Constitutional Convention*, 115, 119, 130, 141.

23. Ibid., 395–96; 468–69.

24. Ibid., 477.

25. Ibid., 508–11.

26. Ibid., 524–26.

27. Reprinted in the *Topeka Tribune*, August 4, 1859, 2.

28. *Kansas Constitutional Convention*, 526–27.

29. *White Cloud Kansas Chief*, August 11, 1859, 2.

30. John J. Ingalls quoted in Laceky, "John Potts Slough, Frontier Lawyer—Hero, Villain, Victim"; also see the *Emporia Weekly News*, August 13, 1859, 2; *Leavenworth Times* reprinted in the *Topeka Tribune*, August 4, 1859, 2; and the *Kansas Herald of Freedom*, August 20, 1859, 2.

31. *Kansas Constitutional Convention*, 518–19; *White Cloud Kansas Chief*, August 18, 1859, 2.

32. *White Cloud Kansas Chief*, August 18, 1859, 2.

33. *Kansas Constitutional Convention*, 566–67.

34. Thirteen Democrats voted against the constitution. Frederick Brown, Elijah Hubbard, William Perry, and John Wright—all Democrats—either abstained or were absent. All the Republicans except Thomas S. Wright, who was ill and absent that day, voted for the constitution. *Kansas Constitutional Convention*, 568–70.

6. TWO ELECTIONS

1. Wilder, *The Annals of Kansas*, 226.

2. *Topeka Tribune*, November 5, 1859, 2; *Kansas Herald of Freedom*, November 5, 1859, 2.

3. *Emporia Weekly News*, October 29, 1859, 1, and November 5, 1859, 2; *White Cloud Kansas Chief*, December 1, 1859, 2.

4. Samuel Medary to John Halderman, December 10, 1859 (accessed on April 19, 2015), available from www.kansasmemory.org/item/90107/text; *Leavenworth Daily Times*, October 28, 1859, 1; *Leavenworth Weekly Herald*, November 26, 1859, 2; John J. Ingalls to Elias Ingalls, January 2, 1859 (accessed on May 18, 2015), available from www.kansasmemory.org/item/2941/text; John J. Ingalls to Elias Ingalls, June 10, 1859 (accessed on April 19, 2015), available from www.kansasmemory.org/item/2966/text.

5. *Topeka Tribune*, November 5, 1859, 2, and November 26, 1859, 2; *Kansas Herald of Freedom* reprinted in the *Topeka Tribune*, November 12, 1859, 1; *White Cloud Kansas Chief*, November 10, 1859, 2.

6. Brinkerhoff, "The Kansas Tour of Lincoln the Candidate," 295–96.

7. Contemporaries reported that Lincoln arrived in Elwood on December 1, 1859. Fred Brinkerhoff questions that Lincoln could have traveled to Troy, Doniphan, and Atchison, giving speeches in all three towns, on December 2. He theorizes that contemporary records were incorrect and that Lincoln spoke in Elwood on November 30, Troy and Doniphan on December 1, and Atchison on December 2. Brinkerhoff, "The Kansas Tour of Lincoln the Candidate," 299–303; Daniel Mulford Valentine's diary (accessed on May 20, 2015), available from www.kansasmemory.org/item/208140/text; *Leavenworth Weekly Herald*, December 10, 1859, 1; Minor, *Kansas: The History of the Sunflower State*, 80.

8. Samuel Medary to John A. Halderman, December 10, 1859 (accessed on April 19, 2015), available from www.kansasmemory.org/item/90107/text; *Emporia Weekly News*, January 28, 1860, 4; *Leavenworth Weekly Herald*, December 10, 1859, 1.

9. *Emporia Weekly News*, March 10, 1860, 2.

10. Wilder, *The Annals of Kansas*, 242; *Official Proceedings of the Democratic National Convention Held in 1860*, 27–30.

11. Donald, Baker, and Holt, *The Civil War and Reconstruction*, 116–17.

12. *Topeka Tribune*, September 1, 1860, 2; *Atchison Weekly Champion and Press*, September 1, 1860, 2; *Commercial Gazette*, September 8, 1860, 2; *Emporia Weekly News*, September 8, 1860, 2.

13. *Cincinnati Daily Enquirer*, September 15, 1860, 1; *Emporia Weekly News*, September 17, 1859, 2.

14. John's father, Martin, and the author's great-great grandfather, Perry Miller, offer benchmarks to the value of John's personal property. According to the 1860 census, Martin Slough owned personal property worth $3,000 and Perry Miller, who worked as a mate on a Cincinnati steamboat, had personal property worth $100. Slough's fortune barely exceeded that of a steamboat hand. Gambone, "Starving Kansas," 31; *Daily Rocky Mountain News*, December 14, 1860, 3; United States Census, 1860.

15. *Cincinnati Daily Enquirer*, February 20, 1861, 1.

16. Gambone, "Starving Kansas," 32.

17. *Cincinnati Daily Enquirer*, February 20, 1861, 1.

18. West, *Contested Plains*, 280–81.

7. GILPIN'S PET LAMBS

1. Leonard and Noel, *Denver: Mining Camp to Metropolis*, 10–11; Ubbelohde, Benson, and Smith, *A Colorado History*, 7th ed., 61.

2. *The Pike's Peak Gold Rush* by Richard Gehling (accessed on June 1, 2015), available from www.oocities.org/richardgehling/TheMerchandisers.html; Leonard and Noel, *Denver: Mining Camp to Metropolis*, 5–8.

3. Bromwell, *Fiftyniners' Directory*, 3.

4. Slough's letter to the *Cincinnati Daily Enquirer* detailing the devastating effects of the Kansas drought was dated February 13, 1861, and he ended his newspaper advertisement for his Leavenworth legal practice on February 28. The winter of 1860–1861 was unusually cold, with temperatures frequently below zero, so it is unlikely that Slough made the long journey from Leavenworth to Denver in late winter. We can therefore place his likely arrival in Denver sometime during late March or early April 1861. *Cincinnati Daily Enquirer*, February 20, 1861, 1, and February 28, 1861, 4; Minor, *Kansas: The History of the Sunflower State*, 81; Smiley, *History of Denver*, 356–57.

5. Smiley, *History of Denver*, 366; *Daily Rocky Mountain News*, May 29, 1861, 4.

6. Ubbelohde, Benson, and Smith, *A Colorado History*, 78, 80–82; Wharton, *History of the City of Denver*, 75; Dorsett, *The Queen City*, 27–28; Smiley, *History of Denver*, 369.

7. Bloated animal carcasses filled Denver's streets because the town's residents did not want to pay for their removal. Even nine years after Denver's founding, the *Denver Daily* described it as "dirty a town as any one of its size in the country," with "old clothes, bones, and decayed vegetable matter" piled up in its back streets. Dorsett, *The Queen City*, 28, 31, 33–34; Leonard and Noel, *Denver: Mining Camp to Metropolis*, 25; Halaas, *Boom Town Newspapers*, 91; Smiley, *History of Denver*, 335; Wharton, *History of the City of Denver*, 91–93.

8. Dorsett, *The Queen City*, 8–9, 30.

9. William Gilpin (governor) (accessed on June 9, 2015), available from www. wikipedia.org/wiki/William_Gilpin_(governor); Karnes, *William Gilpin*, 253; Bancroft, *History of the Life of William Gilpin*, 60, 62.

10. Karnes, *William Gilpin*, 255–56.

11. "The Reception of Colorado's First Governor," *The Colorado Magazine*, September 1930, 233–35; *Daily Rocky Mountain News*, May 28, 1861, 2, and May 31, 1861, 3; *Weekly Rocky Mountain News*, June 5, 1861, 4.

12. A party from Northern Georgia, led by William Green Russell, helped found Auraria, Denver's rival town on the western bank of Cherry Creek. Denver and Auraria decided to unite in April 1860. Leonard and Noel, *Denver: Mining Camp to Metropolis*, 5–8, 24; Smiley, *History of Denver*, 376–78; Whitford, *Colorado Volunteers in the Civil War*, 38–39.

13. Although the Richmond government signed treaties with the Cherokee, Chickasaw, Choctaw, Seminole, and Creek Nations, scant evidence exists that the Confederacy had enlisted the Arapaho. Nonetheless, the territorial administration in Denver realized that the Arapaho and other tribes in Colorado Territory understood that the withdrawal of federal troops from western forts for duty back east afforded better opportunities for harassing white settlers. Karnes, *William Gilpin*, 259, 275; Smiley, *History of Denver*, 367.

14. *Daily Rocky Mountain News*, September 2, 1861, 2.

15. *Daily Rocky Mountain News*, July 9, 1861, 2; *Colorado Republican and Rocky Mountain Herald*, September 4, 1861, 3; *Weekly Rocky Mountain News*, September 4, 1861, 4.

16. The *Rocky Mountain News* referred to Slough as Colonel Slough well before his commission as commander of the 1st Colorado Volunteer Infantry. *Weekly Rocky Mountain News*, June 5, 1861, 4. Flint Whitlock, in his *Distant Bugles, Distant Drums: The Union Response to the Confederate Invasion of New Mexico*, speculates that Gilpin promoted Slough based on misinformation that either Slough or someone else provided to the governor when the two men first met. Whitlock claims that Slough had led a "remarkably quiet and private life" since his arrival in Denver (which Whitlock inaccurately dates as 1860) and argues that Gilpin must have acted on misinformation given Slough's lack of credentials, military or otherwise. Whitlock, *Distant Bugles, Distant Drums*, 64. In 1863, Gilpin wrote Slough a warm letter to thank him for his service to Colorado Territory. He assured Slough that the territory was safe and prosperous and that the "government to which we [Gilpin and Slough] gave existence . . . is a success . . . and cannot be shaken upon its foundation." Karnes, *William Gilpin*, 297–98.

17. Slough placed notices in the *Rocky Mountain News* announcing the start of the May, June, and July 1861 court sessions, but after his promotion to colonel, he no longer signed the notices of the court sessions. *Daily Rocky Mountain News*, May 29, 1861, 4, June 18, 1861, 2, July 23, 1861, 4, November 19 1861, 2, December 7, 1861, 2.

18. Smiley, *History of Denver*, 269, 271; Hollister, *Boldly They Rode*, 2, 55; *Weekly Rocky Mountain News*, August 14, 1861, 4; Karnes, *William Gilpin*, 276n44.

19. Stanton, "History of the First Regiment of Colorado Volunteers," 6; Sanford, "Camp Weld, Colorado," 47.

20. Cox-Paul, "John Chivington," 127–29.

21. Leonard and Noel, *Denver: Mining Camp to Metropolis*, 18; Enoch, "A Clash of Ambitions," 59; Cox-Paul, "John Chivington," 130.

22. Colton, *The Civil War in the Western Territories*, 44; Sanford, "Camp Weld, Colorado," 46; *Weekly Rocky Mountain News*, September 18, 1861, 2.

23. Tappan to Slough, September 19, 1861, Samuel Tappan manuscripts, Colorado Historical Society MSS 617, FF1.

24. Enoch, "A Clash of Ambitions," 59; Cox-Paul, "John Chivington," 130–31; Tappan to Chivington, January, 23, 1863, Colorado Historical Society MSS 617, FF3.

25. *Daily Rocky Mountain News*, August 19, 1861, 2; Wharton, *History of the City of Denver*, 91.

26. *Colorado Republican and Rocky Mountain Herald*, August 24, 1861, 2.

27. Dorsett, *The Queen City*, 30; *Colorado Republican and Rocky Mountain Herald*, October 3, 1861, 3, and January 23, 1862, 1.

28. *Daily Rocky Mountain News*, August 1, 1861, 2, and October 31, 1861, 3.

29. Ubbelohde, Benson, and Smith, *A Colorado History*, 72–74; Dorsett, *The Queen City*, 32–33.

30. Governor Gilpin returned to Washington, DC, in December 1861 to plead with the War Department to reimburse the merchants and other businessmen holding vouchers. Gilpin successfully pressed his case. The War Department auditor determined that most of the claims were valid and in late March 1862 authorized payments of $375,000. By then, Gilpin's enemies had convinced Lincoln that Gilpin was an inept administrator and should be removed from office. Karnes, *William Gilpin*, 255–56, 290–93; *Weekly Rocky Mountain News*, August 14, 1861, 1.

31. Gallatin's story had an interesting twist involving John Slough. Earlier in the day, when Slough visited the saddlery looking for leather belts for his men, Gallatin had pressed him for the $35 that Slough owed Gallatin's employer, John Landis. Slough reluctantly paid the debt in gold dust. Later that night, after the men from the 1st Colorado had left the saddle and harness shop, Gallatin found the gold dust

missing and assumed that Slough had had his men steal it. Not surprisingly, Gallatin had little good to say about Slough, calling him a "deadbeat." Chivington, "The First Colorado Regiment"; Gallatin, *What Life Has Taught Me*, 19–20; *Colorado Republican and Rocky Mountain Herald*, February 27, 1862, 4.

32. Hollister, *Boldly They Rode*, 40–43.

33. Ibid., 34–35.

34. *Colorado Republican and Rocky Mountain Herald*, January 30, 1862, 2, and February 6, 1862, 1; Whitlock, *Distant Bugles, Distant Drums*, 83–84; *Daily Rocky Mountain News*, December 2, 1861, 3.

35. *Daily Rocky Mountain News*, February 5, 1862, 3.

36. *Colorado Republican and Rocky Mountain Herald*, December 26, 1861, 2.

8. "THE GREAT MOGUL OF THE COLORADO FIRST"

1. Camp Weld's guardhouse always held several enlisted men under confinement. During the first two weeks of October, for example, the regiment's morning report recorded at least three and as many as thirteen soldiers in the guardhouse. By the end of December 1861, with the men drinking too much from either boredom or the Christmas festivities, the morning report's number of men in confinement skyrocketed to seventeen privates and four noncommissioned officers on December 20 and twenty privates and one noncommissioned officer on December 27. Morning Reports, 1st Cavalry, Military Affairs, Roll 1, Colorado State Archives; *Daily Rocky Mountain News*, July 27, 1861, 3; Stanton, "History of the First Regiment of Colorado Volunteers," 8.

2. According to the *Rocky Mountain News*, Slough arrested both Captain Marion and Company G's Capt. J. W. Hambleton, so it is possible that men from both Company K and Company G were involved in the revolt. Both Marion and Hambleton were cashiered in November 1861 for insubordination. *Daily Rocky Mountain News*, November 7, 1861, 3; Chivington, "The First Colorado Regiment"; Hollister, *Boldly They Rode*, 32; Whitford, *Colorado Volunteers in the Civil War*, 49.

3. *Daily Rocky Mountain News*, July 31, 1861, 2, August 24, 1861, 2, and October 31, 1861, 3; Edrington and Taylor, *The Battle of Glorieta Pass*, 6–7.

4. *Daily Rocky Mountain News*, August 29, 1861, 2.

5. Edrington and Taylor, *The Battle of Glorieta Pass*, 9–11; Wright, "Colonel John P. Slough and the New Mexico Campaign, 1862," 89.

6. Frazier, *Blood & Treasure*, 117, 126, 135; 137; Edrington and Taylor, *The Battle of Glorieta Pass*, 15–16.

7. Whitlock, *Distant Bugles, Distant Drums*, 94; Whitford, *Colorado Volunteers in the*

Civil War, 75; *Daily Rocky Mountain News,* January 16, 1862, 2; Smith, "An Exercise in Deception," 24–28, 38–39.

8. Tappan and the officers detached to Fort Wise also did not sign the petition. *Daily Rocky Mountain News,* February 8, 1862, 2; *Weekly Rocky Mountain News,* February 15, 1862, 2.

9. Chivington, "The First Colorado Regiment."

10. *Weekly Rocky Mountain News,* February 7, 1862, 2.

11. *Daily Rocky Mountain News,* February 8, 1862, 2.

12. Ibid.

13. Ibid.

14. *Daily Rocky Mountain News,* February 11, 1862, 2.

15. *Colorado Republican and Rocky Mountain Herald,* February 13, 1862, 2; *Daily Rocky Mountain News,* February 11, 1862, 2; *Weekly Rocky Mountain News,* June 7, 1862, 2.

16. Downing reminisced about his early Colorado days and the New Mexico campaign in newspaper articles published when he was in his late seventies. In none of the articles did Downing bother to mention John Slough or Lewis Weld, although he did take credit for organizing the 1st Colorado. Jacob Downing scrapbook, Colorado Historical Society #211; *Portrait and Biographical Record of Denver and Vicinity,* 1240.

17. When Tappan and Wynkoop turned against Chivington in 1864 after the Sand Creek Massacre, Downing remained loyal to Chivington and served as his legal counsel during the hearings convened to investigate the affair.

18. Halaas, *Boom Town Newspapers,* 16.

19. Halaas, *Boom Town Newspapers,* 38–39; Karnes, *William Gilpin,* 287.

20. *Colorado Republican and Rocky Mountain Herald,* February 13, 1862, 2.

21. *Daily Rocky Mountain News,* February 11, 1862, 2.

22. *Colorado Republican and Rocky Mountain Herald,* February 27, 1862, 4.

23. Whitford, *Colorado Volunteers in the Civil War,* 75; Whitlock, *Distant Bugles, Distant Drums,* 143–44.

24. *Colorado Republican and Rocky Mountain Herald,* February 20, 1862, 3, and March 27, 1862, 4.

25. In a dispatch to the *Rocky Mountain News* describing the 1st Colorado's march to New Mexico Territory and the battles at Glorieta Pass, "Union" reported that Downing denied writing "Union's" February 7 letter, although "Union" slyly added that "he never denied being the author." *Daily Rocky Mountain News,* February 24, 1862, 2; *Weekly Rocky Mountain News,* June 7, 1862, 2; *Colorado Republican and Rocky Mountain Herald,* February 27, 1862, 2; Whitlock, *Distant Bugles, Distant Drums,* 143.

1. Samito, "The Intersection between Military Justice and Equal Rights," 187.

2. *Colorado Republican and Rocky Mountain Herald*, March 6, 1862, clipping in Colorado Historical Society #141, FF #11; Whitford, *Colorado Volunteers in the Civil War*, 77; Whitlock, *Distant Bugles, Distant Drums*, 145–46.

3. Chivington untitled manuscript, Colorado Historical Society #141, FF #65.

4. Chivington's account, written in 1890, is the only record of Company I's mutiny. By then, his involvement in the Sand Creek massacre had ruined his reputation, which may have led him to embellish his role in the 1862 New Mexico campaign. Chivington untitled manuscript, Colorado Historical Society #141, FF #65.

5. Linderman, *Embattled Courage*, 36; Gordon, *A Broken Regiment*, 6, 21–22, 113–17; Foote, *The Gentlemen and the Roughs*, 146–47, 167. See also Garrison, *Mutiny in the Civil War*.

6. Whitford, *Colorado Volunteers in the Civil War*, 101; Hollister, *Boldly They Rode*, 47.

7. *Colorado Republican and Rocky Mountain Herald*, February 27, 1862, clipping in Colorado Historical Society #141, FF #10; Hollister, *Boldly They Rode*, 86.

8. Wright, "Colonel John P. Slough and the New Mexico Campaign," 90.

9. Alberts, *The Battle of Glorieta*, 30–31.

10. Whether Slough accompanied his regiment during the final push to Fort Union is unclear. "Soldier" reported in a dispatch to the *Colorado Republican and Rocky Mountain Herald* that Slough stayed with the men during the march, which "Soldier" described as "severe." Pvt. Charles Gardiner, in a letter written to his mother after the Battle of Glorieta Pass, claimed that Slough "rode ahead" while Ovando Hollister noted that Slough rode in a coach. Chivington, Colorado Historical Society #994 and #141, FF #65; *Colorado Republican and Rocky Mountain Herald*, March 20, 1862, clipping in Colorado Historical Society #141, FF#14; Gardiner, letter, May 3, 1862, 32; Hollister, *Boldly They Rode*, 48–49.

11. Gardiner, letter, May 3, 1862, 32; Hollister, *Boldly They Rode*, 48–49; Alberts, *The Battle of Glorieta*, 32.

12. *Daily Rocky Mountain News*, April 4, 1862, 2; Alberts, *The Battle of Glorieta*, 31; Whitford, *Colorado Volunteers in the Civil War*, 78.

13. Pvt. Charles Gardiner bitterly complained that Slough informed Paul that no rations or accommodations were needed as "his men were all old mountaineers and accustomed to all kinds of hardships & privations." Although some historians have accepted Gardiner's explanation for the lack of provisions, it seems unlikely that Slough actually refused food for his troops. (See, for example, Alberts, *The Battle of Glorieta*, 33.) Aside from Gardiner's letter, no evidence exists that Slough disregarded

his soldiers' well-being. Quite possibly, Paul did not expect the 1st Colorado to travel eighty miles in two days, especially in the middle of a winter storm, and failed to make provisions for the troops. Perhaps Slough, in a misguided effort at graciousness, excused Paul's shortsightedness by saying that his men would be fine. Already angry that Slough had pushed them hard during the brutal final days of marching, the volunteers readily blamed their unpopular commander for the lack of rations and tents upon their arrival. Gardiner, in turn, repeated the rumors he heard when Company A reached Fort Union. Gardiner, letter, May 3, 1862, 32; Hollister, *Boldly They Rode*, 51–52; Chivington, Colorado Historical Society #141, #FF65.

14. Hollister, *Boldly They Rode*, 55–56; Alberts, *The Battle of Glorieta*, 34; Chivington, Colorado Historical Society #141, FF #65.

15. *Daily Rocky Mountain News*, April 4, 1862, 2; Alberts, *The Battle of Glorieta*, 34–35; *The War of the Rebellion*, series I, vol. 9, part I, 645–46.

16. *The War of the Rebellion*, series I, vol. 9, part 1, 649 and 652.

17. Alberts, *The Battle of Glorieta*, 38, 40–41.

18. The theory that Slough decided to use the topographical features of northern New Mexico to his advantage is argued in an unattributed article titled "Colorado's Role in the Civil War" in the Stephen H. Hart Library and Research Center in Denver. Colorado Historical Society #118, FF #28; *Official Records*, series I, vol. 9, part 1, 654; Alberts, *The Battle of Glorieta*, 37.

19. *The War of the Rebellion*, series I, vol. 9, part 1, 652–55.

20. Edrington and Taylor, *The Battle of Glorieta Pass*, 32, 34; Alberts, *The Battle of Glorieta*, 20.

21. Edrington and Taylor, *The Battle of Glorieta Pass*, 42; Alberts, *The Battle of Glorieta*, 42–43.

22. Edrington and Taylor, *The Battle of Glorieta Pass*, 42–43.

23. Alberts, *The Battle of Glorieta*, 49–50; Whitford, *Colorado Volunteers in the Civil War*, 100–101.

24. *The War of the Rebellion*, series I, vol. 9, part I, 531; Alberts, *The Battle of Glorieta*, 67.

25. Edrington and Taylor, *The Battle of Glorieta Pass*, 59–61.

26. Edrington and Taylor, *The Battle of Glorieta Pass*, 63–64; Alberts, *The Battle of Glorieta*, 71.

27. Historians have disputed the size of the Confederate force. Edrington and Taylor argue that Scurry had only 600 effective troops when he left Johnson's Ranch the morning of March 28. Alberts claims that Scurry had at least 1,285 men. Jerry Thompson, in his *Civil War in the Southwest*, places the Confederate force at "over 1,200" men. Given that the Confederates successfully pressured the Union line

throughout the day's battle at Pigeon's Ranch—even though the Yankees had strong defensive positions and better arms than the rebels—it seems likely that the Texans significantly outnumbered their opponents and that the higher estimate is more accurate. Edrington and Taylor, *The Battle of Glorieta Pass*, 132; Alberts, *The Battle of Glorieta*, 196n28, Thompson, *Civil War in the Southwest*, xviii.

28. Edrington and Taylor, *The Battle of Glorieta Pass*, 70–71; Alberts, *The Battle of Glorieta*, 82–84.

29. Alberts, *The Battle of Glorieta*, 46, 86.

30. Ibid., 91–93.

31. Alberts, *The Battle of Glorieta*, 90; Edrington and Taylor, *The Battle of Glorieta Pass*, 73, 130–31.

32. Alberts, *The Battle of Glorieta*, 98, 114; Whitford, *Colorado Volunteers in the Civil War*, 108; Edrington and Taylor, *The Battle of Glorieta Pass*, 78.

33. Alberts, *The Battle of Glorieta*, 114, 116.

34. Ibid., 113–14.

35. Ibid., 119–20, 123.

36. Edrington and Taylor, *The Battle of Glorieta Pass*, 90, 92–94, 102, 105.

37. Chivington document on the First Colorado Regiment, Colorado Historical Society #994; Alberts, *The Battle of Glorieta*, 97; *The War of the Rebellion*, series I, vol. 9, part I, 539.

38. The *Rio Abajo* (New Mexico Territory) *Press* criticized Chivington for waiting two hours on the mesa above the Confederate wagon train before deciding to attack. Quoted in Keleher, *Turmoil in New Mexico*, 181. Alexander Grzelachowski, a former priest who ran a business in Las Vegas, New Mexico, led Chivington's detachment back that night to Slough's forces at Kozlowski's Ranch. Without Grzelachowski's assistance, Chivington's tired men might have stumbled upon the Texans as they tried to rendezvous with their comrades. Edrington and Taylor, *The Battle of Glorieta Pass*, 98.

39. "Union's" dispatch to the *Rocky Mountain News* covered the March 26 engagement at Apache Canyon and the March 28 battle at Pigeon's Ranch. Only two 1st Colorado captains were present at both battles: Company F's Capt. Samuel Cook and Company D's Capt. Jacob Downing. Cook had no reason to besmirch Slough's reputation and, in fact, had been stationed at Fort Wise, two hundred miles away from Denver, when "Union's" first letter appeared in the *Rocky Mountain News* on February 7. Downing, on the other hand, had been at Camp Weld on February 7 and fought at both Apache Canyon and Pigeon's Ranch. His physical presence close to Denver in February and at both battles in late March implicate him as having a hand in "Union's" letters. *Weekly Rocky Mountain News*, June 7, 1862, 2.

40. See Alberts, *The Battle of Glorieta*, 88, 98, 114, 122, and 141, for an assessment

of Slough's performance at Pigeon's Ranch. Colton, *The Civil War in the Western Territories*, 76–77.

41. Arthur Wright, in his study of the exchanges between Canby, Slough, and Paul, dates Slough's receipt of Canby's order to March 31, when the federals had returned to Bernal Springs. Thomas Edrington and John Taylor also place its receipt to March 31 in their book about the battle of Glorieta Pass. But Ovando Hollister mentioned Slough's order for "the backward movement" in his entry for March 29. March 29 seems to be the most likely date as there is no good explanation for Slough's giving up the battle to return to Fort Union except Canby's order. Wright, "Colonel John P. Slough and the New Mexico Campaign," 100; Edrington and Taylor, *The Battle of Glorieta Pass*, 106; Hollister, *Boldly They Rode*, 74.

42. Hollister, *Boldly They Rode*, 86; Chivington manuscript, Colorado Historical Society #141, FF #65.

43. Alberts, *The Battle of Glorieta*, 141; Edrington and Taylor, *The Battle of Glorieta Pass*, 106.

44. *Daily Delta*, June 19, 1862, 2; *Cincinnati Daily Enquirer*, reprinted in the *Daily Rocky Mountain News*, June 11, 1862, 2.

45. *Weekly Rocky Mountain News*, June 7, 1862, 2; Tappan papers, Colorado Historical Society #617, FF #1.

46. Whitlock, *Distant Bugles, Distant Drums*, 222.

47. Ibid., 229; Hollister, *Boldly They Rode*, 185.

48. Edrington and Taylor, *The Battle of Glorieta Pass*, 109–10; Whitlock, *Distant Bugles, Distant* Drums, 229–30; Frazier, *Blood & Treasure*, 239–41, 276.

49. *Weekly Rocky Mountain News*, May 10, 1862, 4.

10. THE DEFENSE OF HARPERS FERRY

1. Frye, *Harpers Ferry Under Fire*, 59–60; Marvel, *Lincoln's Autocrat*, 73; *Daily Rocky Mountain News*, June 11, 1862, 2, and June 27, 1862, 3.

2. Two years later, in May 1864, Stanton described Slough as "an active and energetic man" to Ulysses S. Grant. *The War of the Rebellion*, series I, vol. 36, part II, 595, and series I, vol. 51, part 1, 641.

3. Gwynne, *Rebel Yell*, 276–77.

4. *The War of the Rebellion*, series I, vol. 12, part I, 529, 626–7, and series I, vol. 12, part III, 248.

5. Hearn, *Six Years of Hell*, 2.

6. Frye, *Harpers Ferry Under Fire*, 59–60; *The War of the Rebellion*, series I, vol. 12, part I, 639.

7. Gwynne, *Rebel Yell*, 301.

8. *The War of the Rebellion*, series I, vol. 12, part III, 262, and series I, vol. 12, part I, 639, 707; Robertson, *The Stonewall Brigade*, 100.

9. Gwynne, *Rebel Yell*, 302; Hearn, *Six Years of Hell*, 105; *The War of the Rebellion*, series I, vol. 12, part I, 640.

10. *The War of the Rebellion*, series I, vol. 12, part III, 303–4; Hearn, 104–5.

11. *The War of the Rebellion*, series I, vol. 12, part III, 285–86 and 296–97; Hearn, *Six Years of Hell*, 105.

12. Saxton's after-battle report, written on June 2, 1862, is the only record of the May 30 engagement at Camp Hill. He recorded that the fight between Slough's brigade and the Virginians lasted an hour and that the Confederates tried a second assault against the Union lines at midnight, but retreated after a brief struggle. Saxton undoubtedly embellished his account of the engagement. Assistant Secretary of War Watson reported to Stanton that Jackson's army arrived outside Harpers Ferry on May 29 and threw out skirmishers on May 30. He did not mention any engagement at Camp Hill in his final report. Winder's after-battle report and Jackson's report of the Valley Campaign made no mention of the Camp Hill engagement. Dennis Frye, chief historian at Harpers Ferry National Historical Park, writes in his history of Civil War Harpers Ferry that the Confederates rushed across Bolivar Heights under fire from Battery Stanton and Slough's brigade on Camp Hill. The rebels, however, halted three hundred yards from the federal defenses on Camp Hill. *The War of the Rebellion*, series I, vol. 12, part I, 641, 707, 738–39, and series I, vol. 12, part III, 278, 297, 303–4; Frye, *Harpers Ferry Under Fire*, 65.

13. In May 1862, Saxton received orders to become military governor of the Department of the South. While on the way to Beaufort, South Carolina, his steamer shipwrecked. He returned to New York, where he received the temporary posting to Harpers Ferry. *Alexandria Gazette*, May 28, 1862, 2; *The War of the Rebellion*, series I, vol. 12, part III, 320, 362.

14. Slough spoke at a Washington's Birthday dinner in 1863 after which a resolution was passed condemning the peace movement in the North. *Cincinnati Daily Enquirer*, June 17, 1862, 1; *Alexandria Gazette*, February 24, 1863, 2.

15. *The Sun* (New York), June 24, 1862, 1; *The Hancock Democrat* (Greenfield, IN), July 9, 1862, 1.

16. Sifakis, *Who Was Who in the Civil War*, 141; *The War of the Rebellion*, series I, vol. 12, part III, 459.

17. *The War of the Rebellion*, series, I, vol. 12, part III, 286, and series I, vol. 12, part I, 641; *Cleveland Daily Leader*, June 9, 1862, 4; *The Sun* (New York), June 24, 1862, 1; *New York Times*, June 27, 1862, 1.

18. *Weekly Rocky Mountain News*, June 7, 1862, 2; *Daily Rocky Mountain News*, July 18, 1862, 3, and August 7, 1862, 1.

19. *Daily Rocky Mountain News*, April 18, 1862, 3, and June 10, 1862, 2; Cox-Paul, "John Chivington," 131.

20. *Daily Rocky Mountain News*, June 7, 1862, 2, and June 10, 1862, 2.

21. Testimony before the Joint Committee on the Conduct of the War, National Archives, RG 128, John P. Slough testimony, February 16, 1864, U.S. Serial Set, vol. 1178, Report #54.

11. "DISORDER AND VICE HAD BEEN THE RULE"

1. The day Slough arrived in Alexandria, the *Gazette* reported, "A gentleman who visited Alexandria yesterday, represents the moral condition of the city as disgraceful, on account of the drunkenness of the soldiers in the streets. Every street and square was lined with stragglers, a large portion of whom were inebriates. A drunken dog fight occurred among the soldiers near the depot, about five o'clock in the afternoon. Several men were engaged in it, and one man was nearly beaten to death by a large stone in the hands of another, who, after pummeling his antagonist in a terrible manner, was permitted to walk off without being arrested." *Alexandria Gazette*, August 25, 1862, 2, September 16, 1862, 2, and December 10, 1862, 2; Testimony before the Joint Committee on the Conduct of the War, National Archives, RG 128 (Senate) 38th Congress, John P. Slough testimony, February 16, 1864; Berler, "A Most Unpleasant Part of Your Duties," 46.

2. Artemel, Crowell, and Parker, *The Alexandria Slave Pen*, 12, 15, 25–26; Kundahl, *Alexandria Goes to War*, 5–6; *Alexandria Gazette*, January 12, 1864, 1; Barber, *Alexandria in the Civil War*, 7–8, 13–14, 20–22; Harvey, *Occupied City*, 11; Cooling, *Symbol, Sword, & Shield*, 49, 95–96.

3. Barber, *Alexandria in the Civil War*, 27; *The Liberator*, October 17, 1862, 3; Berler, "A Most Unpleasant Part of Your Duties," 23.

4. Barber, *Alexandria in the Civil War*, 29; Berler, "A Most Unpleasant Part of Your Duties," 26; Ayoub, "Hessians in Our Midst," 3.

5. *Alexandria Gazette*, August 26, 1862, 2; Henry Whittington diary, August 26, 1862; *Philadelphia Inquirer*, August 28, 1862, 1.

6. *Alexandria Gazette*, August 26, 1862, 3, and August 28, 1862, 2.

7. *Baltimore Sun*, August 29, 1862, 4; *Philadelphia Inquirer*, August 28, 1862, 1.

8. *The Civil War Diary of Anne S. Frobel*, 101; *Alexandria Gazette*, September 1, 1862, 2, and September 16, 1862, 2; Whittington diary, September 1, 1862.

9. *The War of the Rebellion*, series I, vol. 12, part III, 791.

10. *The War of the Rebellion*, series I, vol. 19, part II, 237.

11. Ibid., 275, 309.

12. Ibid., 325–26.

13. *The War of the Rebellion*, series I, vol. 19, part II, 337; *The Civil War Diary of Anne S. Frobel*, 103.

14. William C. Stiffler, "Alexandria, Virginia," 21; Berlin et al., *Freedom*, 246; *Alexandria Gazette*, September 10, 1862, 2.

15. Stiffler, "Alexandria, Virginia," 21; *Alexandria Gazette*, September 9, 1862, 2.

16. Berlin et al., *Freedom*, 268–69; Wyman to Slough, October 21, 1862, National Archives, RG 393, Department and Defenses of Washington, Register of Letters Received; Stiffler, "Alexandria, Virginia," 22.

17. *Julia Wilbur: Part 2*, 5–6; Carol Faulkner, *Women's Radical Reconstruction*, 16.

18. Whitacre, *A Civil Life in an Uncivil Time*, 84; *Julia Wilbur: Part 2*, 23.

19. *Julia Wilbur: Part 2*, 25–26.

20. *Julia Wilbur: Part 2*, 24; Berlin et al., *Freedom*, 275.

21. *The Civil War Diary of Anne S. Frobel*, 136–37; Stiffler, "Alexandria, Virginia," 21; Tim Denneé, "African-American Civilians and Soldiers"; Wyman to Slough, November 29, 1862 (accessed on April 27, 2016), available from www.fold3-com.research.cincinnatilibrary.org/image/300447393-4; Berlin et al., *Freedom*, 276–78.

22. Denneé, "African-American Civilians and Soldiers" 6; Slough document, November 30, 1862 (accessed on April 27, 2016), available from www.fold3-com.research.cincinnatilibrary.org/image/300447395.

23. Berlin et al., *Freedom*, 276–78.

24. Quite possibly Alexandria's hospitals had an insufficient quantity of vaccine to inoculate its population. Julia Wilbur went to the Prince Street Hospital on November 28 to be inoculated but discovered that the hospital had no "virus." *Julia Wilbur: Part 2*, 31; Henry Whittington diary, December 12, 1862; *The Civil War Diary of Anne S. Frobel*, 154; Denneé, "African-American Civilians and Soldiers" 6.

25. Arabella also raised money for a dinner at Alexandria's Mansion House Hospital on Washington's birthday, 1863. *Philadelphia Inquirer*, August 28, 1862, 1; Slough to Headquarters, Department and Defenses of Washington, October 27, 1862, National Archives, RG 393, Department and Defenses of Washington, Register of Letters Received; Whitacre, *A Civil Life in an Uncivil Time*, 97–98; *Julia Wilbur: Part 2*, 50; *Alexandria Gazette*, December 18, 1862, 2, December 30, 1862, 3, January 1, 1863, 2, and February 24, 1863, 2.

26. *The War of the Rebellion*, series I, vol. 12, part II (supplement), 822; Sears, *Controversies & Commanders*, 55–56.

27. Sears, *Controversies & Commanders*, 60–61.

28. Ibid., 66.

29. Otto Eisenschiml, in his book on the Porter court-martial, repeats Fitz John Porter's claim that on his deathbed Slough expressed regret about his role in the court-martial. How Porter knew what Slough said on his deathbed is a mystery. Eisenschiml, *The Celebrated Case of Fitz John Porter*, 80–81; Anders, *Injustice on Trial*, 259; *Journal of the Executive Proceedings of the Senate of the United States* (37th Congress, 2nd session), vol. 12, 308, 418; *Journal of the Executive Proceedings of the Senate of the United States* (37th Congress, 3rd session), vol. 13, 57; Sears, *Controversies & Commanders*, 61.

30. Testimony before the Joint Committee on the Conduct of the War, Slough's testimony, February 16, 1864, National Archives, RG 128 (Senate) 38th Congress; *Alexandria Gazette*, November 22, 1862, 2, and December 2, 1862, 2.

31. *Alexandria Gazette*, December 18, 1862, 2; Wells sworn statement, February 26, 1863 (accessed on February 25, 2018), available from www.fold3.com.research. cincinnatilibrary.org/image/300519764-7; Testimony before the Joint Committee on the Conduct of the War, Wells testimony, February 22, 1864, National Archives, RG 128 (Senate) 38th Congress.

32. Petition to Edwin Stanton, February 20, 1863 (accessed on February 24, 2018), available from www.fold3-com.research.cincinnatilibrary.org/image/300519731-3.

33. Congressional request to Edwin Stanton, February 24, 1863 (accessed on February 24, 2018), available from www.fold3-com.research.cincinnatilibrary.org/ image/300519725; Slough to Stanton, February 27, 1863 (accessed on February 24, 2018), available from www.fold3-com.research.cincinnatilibrary.org/image 300519735-46.

34. See www.fold3-com.research.cincinnatilibrary.org/image/300519748-92 for the thirteen testimonial letters.

35. P. H. Watson to Slough, March 9, 1863 (accessed on February 24, 2018), available from www.fold3-com.research.cincinnatilibrary.org/image/300519727; *Journal of the Executive Proceedings of the Senate of the United States* (37th Congress, 3rd session), vol. 13, 213, 309–10.

36. *Alexandria Gazette*, March 30, 1863, 4.

37. Barber, *Alexandria in the Civil War*, 36; Gwynne to Stanton, February 27, 1863 (accessed on April 27, 2018), available from www.fold3-com.research.cincinnatilibrary. org/image/300519784-6.

38. *Alexandria Gazette*, February 2, 1863, 2.

12. ENEMIES WITHIN THE LINES

1. Ash, *When the Yankees Came*, 85; Berler, "A Most Unpleasant Part of Your Duties," 54; Barber, *Alexandria in the Civil War*, 90; *Alexandria Gazette*, May 30, 1863, 2.

2. Testimony given at the court-martial of Lt. George W. Hopkins provides a glimpse into the relationship between Alexandria's prostitutes and the soldiers stationed there. Hopkins became a regular patron of a brothel at 33 Henry Street soon after his regiment arrived in Alexandria. On July 9, 1863, after being placed in charge of a guard protecting the railroad along Henry Street, Hopkins told one of his noncommissioned officers that he could be found at the brothel if needed and left his post for almost twenty-four hours. The lieutenant visited the brothel again on July 18 and July 21. On July 26, he welcomed two prostitutes to his tent and then walked with them the length of the dress parade, "in presence of all the wives and families of the officers and men." Later that same day, while drunk, he escorted the prostitutes through Alexandria's streets, and that evening he took one of them to a "respectable public house." When the proprietor asked that the prostitute leave the premises, an inebriated Hopkins shook his fist in the proprietor's face and said, "I can whip any damned and God-damned son of a bitch who says my woman is a prostitute." Hopkins was arrested the next day and was charged with conduct prejudicial to good order and military discipline, conduct unbecoming an officer and a gentleman, and breach of arrest. Stiffler, "Alexandria, Virginia," 23; Pennsylvania Reserves (accessed on June 19, 2016), available from www.pareserves.com/?q=node/2539; Slough to Stanton, February 27, 1863 (accessed on February 25, 2018), available from www.fold3.com. research.cincinnatilibrary.org/image/300519735–46.

3. *Julia Wilbur: Part 2*, 32n58, 61; Testimony before the Joint Committee on the Conduct of the War, Wells testimony, February 22, 1864, National Archives, RG 128 (Senate) 38th Congress.

4. Berlin et al., *Freedom*, 251; Testimony before the Joint Committee on the Conduct of the War, Slough testimony, February 16, 1864, National Archives, RG 128 (Senate) 38th Congress.

5. Whitacre, *A Civil Life in an Uncivil Time*, 119–20; *Julia Wilbur: Part 2*, 12, 25n29, 59.

6. Berlin et al., *Freedom*, 281–83.

7. Ibid., 283, 286.

8. Ibid., 284–86.

9. Faulkner, *Women's Radical Reconstruction*, 19–21; Whitacre, *A Civil Life in an Uncivil Time*, 96.

10. Berlin et al., *Freedom*, 286.

11. Whitacre, *A Civil Life in an Uncivil Time*, 122; Barber, *Alexandria in the Civil War*, 94; *Julia Wilbur: Part 2*, 88, 102n151; Berlin et al., *Freedom*, 250.

12. *Cleveland Daily Leader*, May 22, 1863, 1; Slough to Headquarters, Department and Defenses of Washington, May 9, 1863, and May 14, 1863, National Archives, RG 393, Letters Received and Registry of Letters Received.

13. *Julia Wilbur: Part 2*, 86; *The War of the Rebellion*, series I, vol. 25, part II, 514–16.

14. Wert, *Mosby's Rangers*, 64; Ramage, *Gray Ghost*, 85–86; Harvey, *Occupied City*, 22; Thomas, Nash, and Shepard, "Places of Exchange," 366.

15. *The Civil War Diary of Anne S. Frobel*, 187; *Julia Wilbur: Part 2*, 86–88; Henry Whittington diary, May 31, June 1, and June 3, 1863; *The War of the Rebellion*, series I, vol. 25, part II, 181, and series I, vol. 27, part III, 440; Slough to Headquarters, May 31, 1863, National Archives, RG 393, Department and Defenses of Washington, Letters Received and Registry of Letters Received.

16. Berler, "A Most Unpleasant Part of Your Duties," 52, 55; *The Civil War Diary of Anne S. Frobel*, 187; Slough to Headquarters, May 31, 1863, National Archives, RG 393, Department and Defenses of Washington, Registry of Letters Received.

17. Alexandria's first military governor, Gen. William R. Montgomery, adhered strictly to the conciliatory policy. He chose not to fly the American flag over his headquarters to avoid offending Southern sensibilities, treated the city's ladies with extreme courtesy, and attempted to deal even-handedly with all its residents, loyal or secessionist. Berler, "A Most Unpleasant Part of Your Duties," 28; Barber, *Alexandria in the Civil War*, 27; Ash, *When the Yankees Came*, 26–30; Grimsley, *The Hard Hand of War*, 8–9.

18. Ash, *When the Yankees Came*, 51; Riker, "This Long Agony," 4.

19. *The Civil War Diary of Anne S. Frobel*, 183, 185.

20. Slough to Heintzelman, June 18, 1863, National Archives, RG 393, Department and Defenses of Washington, Registry of Letters Received; *The War of the Rebellion*, series I, vol. 27, part III, 260; Riker, "This Long Agony," 2.

21. Guelzo, *Gettysburg*, 48, 74; *Julia Wilbur: Part 2*, 91, 93.

22. *Julia Wilbur: Part 2*, 94; Riker, "This Long Agony," 3.

23. Anne Frobel estimated that Slough's list numbered one hundred families, although Diane Riker, in her article about Slough's efforts to deport disloyal residents, counted 243 names of individuals and families on a roll found in the United Daughters of the Confederacy museum in Alexandria. *The Civil War Diary of Anne S. Frobel*, 203; Riker, "This Long Agony," 4.

24. Henry Whittington diary, July 6, 1863; *The Civil War Diary of Anne S. Frobel*, 204.

25. Henry Whittington diary, July 7 and July 9, 1863; Riker, "This Long Agony," 8–9.

26. *National Republican*, October 14, 1863, 3, and November 19, 1863, 3.

27. Union officers and politicians intent on holding Chivington accountable for the Sand Creek massacre turned to Slough for support. Lt. Joseph Cramer sent an account of the massacre to Maj. Edward Wynkoop on December 19, 1864. In a postscript to the letter, Cramer told Wynkoop that he intended to send a report to Slough "in hopes that he will have the thing [the massacre] investigated." Hiram P. Bennet, Colorado's

delegate to the United States Congress, learned from Wynkoop about Cramer's report and wrote Slough on January 20, 1865, to ask for a copy. By sharing Cramer's report with the House of Representatives, Bennet intended to lay blame for the massacre on Chivington, showing the country the colonel's "true colors." At the end of the letter, Bennet asked Slough for "such suggestions as you may think proper." It is unknown if Slough received Cramer's report or followed through with his promise to Stanton to help push Chivington out of the service. Slough to Stanton, September 13, 1863 (accessed on April 23, 2016), available from www.fold3.com.research.cincinnatilibrary. org/image/304609295; Lt. Joseph A. Cramer to Maj. Edward Wynkoop, December 19, 1864 (accessed on March 10, 2018), available from www.nps.gov/sand/learn/ historyculture/joseph-cramer-biography.htm; Hiram Pitt Bennet to John Slough, January 20, 1865, Western Americana Collection, Beinecke Rare Book and Manuscript Library, Yale University.

28. "Testimony taken before the Judiciary Committee of the House of Representatives in the investigation of charges against Andrew Johnson," *US Serial Set*, vol. no. 1314, 667; Marvel, *Lincoln's Autocrat*, 525n25.

29. Blustein, *Preserve Your Love for Science*, 86; Marvel, *Lincoln's Autocrat*, 313; Zeidenfelt, "The Embattled Surgeon," 26–27, 29.

30. Blustein, *Preserve Your Love for Science*, 26–28, 73–75; Marvel, *Lincoln's Autocrat*, 314.

31. Zeidenfelt, "The Embattled Surgeon," 30; Marvel, *Lincoln's Autocrat*, 314.

32. Zeidenfelt, "The Embattled Surgeon," 31; Blustein, *Preserve Your Love for Science*, 91; Marvel, *Lincoln's Autocrat*, 316.

33. After the Union army's fiasco at the battle of Ball's Bluff, the committee imprisoned Brig. Gen. Charles Stone for six months because it doubted his loyalty to the federal government. *Reports of the Committees of the Senate of the United States for the First Session of the Thirty-Eight Congress* (Washington, DC: Government Printing Office, 1864); Tap, *Over Lincoln's Shoulder*, 75.

34. Testimony before the Joint Committee on the Conduct of the War, Slough's testimony, February 16, 1864, National Archives, RG 128 (Senate), 38th Congress; *New York Times*, February 16, 1864, 1; *Cincinnati Daily Enquirer*, February 18, 1864, 3.

35. Wilbur knew such prominent abolitionists as Amy Post, Lucy Coleman, Frederick Douglass, and Susan B. Anthony. Whitacre, *A Civil Life in an Uncivil Time*, 58, 68, 80; *Julia Wilbur: Part 2*, 104; Yellin, *Harriet Jacobs*, 169.

36. Berlin et al., *Freedom*, 299–301.

37. Ibid., 302; *Julia Wilbur: Part 2*, 105n153.

38. *Julia Wilbur: Part 2*, 129, 137.

39. The Joint Committee did not require a quorum to conduct its meetings. Sen.

Zachariah Chandler, Congressman Moses Odell, and an unnamed third person—possibility the committee's counsel—examined the witnesses during the committee's investigation of Alexandria's military government. Testimony before the Joint Committee on the Conduct of the War, Wyman testimony, February 12, 1864, National Archives, RG 128 (Senate), 38th Congress.

40. *Julia Wilbur: Part 2*, 144; *New York Times*, February 16, 1864, 1; Testimony before the Joint Committee on the Conduct of the War, Slough testimony, February 16, 1864, National Archives, RG 128 (Senate), 38th Congress.

41. Wells had served as provost marshal of the Defenses of Washington south of the Potomac since June 2, 1863, while Gwynne had served as Alexandria's provost marshal since November 7, 1863. Testimony before the Joint Committee on the Conduct of the War, Travis testimony, February 18–19, and Gwynne testimony, February 19, 1864, National Archives, RG 128 (Senate), 38th Congress.

42. Testimony before the Joint Committee on the Conduct of the War, Wells testimony, February 22, 1863, National Archives, RG 128 (Senate), 38th Congress.

43. The Alexandria liquor sellers also lobbied the loyal government of Virginia to act against Slough. On February 8, 1864, the Virginia general assembly appointed a committee to "aid and advise" the Joint Committee in its investigation. Although the Joint Committee agreed to cooperate with the Virginia committee, the Virginians failed to move forward with their own inquiry. *Reports of the Committees of the Senate of the United States for the First Session of the Thirty-Eight Congress.*

13. "WHY THEN AM I KEPT HERE SO LONG?"

1. *Evening Star*, April 22, 1864, 3.

2. Capt. John Wyman responded to Slough's toast by commenting that America "had been taught what liberty truly was by the great act which liberated millions of Russians from slavery and serfdom" and then raised his glass saying, "Russia and the United States—bound together by the interests of a common humanity—indissoluble now and forever." *Alexandria Gazette*, December 7, 1863, 4, and January 20, 1864, 2; *Evening Star*, March 18, 1864, 3; *Lincoln Praises Sanitary Commission for Work with Troops* (accessed on February 6, 2017), available from www.history.com/this-day-in-history/lincoln-praises-sanitary-commission-for-work-with-troops.

3. Email from Carolyn Laceky, January 22, 2014; *Academy Journal*, December 9, 1873, 1.

4. *The War of the Rebellion*, series I, vol. 33, 438; *Julia Wilbur: Part 2*, 152; *National Republican*, February 1, 1864, 2; *Evening Star*, January 11, 1864, 1; Denneé, "African-American Civilians and Soldiers," 7; Denneé, "A House Divided Still Stands," 12

(accessed on April 21, 2016), available from http://www.freedmenscemetery.org /resources/documents/contrabandhospital.pdf.

5. *Julia Wilbur: Part 2*, 154; Denneé, "African-American Civilians and Soldiers," 10.

6. *Julia Wilbur: Part 2*, 157, 177–79.

7. *Alexandria Gazette*, March 3, 1864, 3, March 29, 1864, 3, June 14, 1864, 3, and June 24, 1864, 3; *Virginia State Journal*, June 30, 1864, 3.

8. *Julia Wilbur: Part 2*, 175.

9. Slough to Stanton, July 8, 1864 (accessed on April 24, 2016), available from www. fold3.com.research.cincinnatilibrary.org/image/300986919.

10. McPherson, *Battle Cry of Freedom*, 756.

11. Henry Whittington diary, July 10, 1864; *Alexandria Gazette*, July 13, 1864, 2.

12. Stanton considered sending Slough to serve as military governor of Freder−icksburg, Virginia, in early May 1864. On May 10, worried that "matters are not well organized in Fredericksburg," Stanton ordered Slough to "take command of the forces in that city, guard the hospitals, and perform the duties of the military governor there." Before Slough could leave for his new assignment, Stanton suspended the order. *The War of the Rebellion*, series I, vol. 36, part II, 595 and 616; Slough to Townsend, July 30, 1864 (accessed on April 24, 2016), available from www.fold3.com.research.cincinnatili−brary.org/image/300986921.

13. *The War of the Rebellion*, series I, vol. 27, part III, 442, and series I, vol. 27, part I, 56–57.

14. Slough to Potter, October 28, 1863, and Slough to Augur, November 1, 1863, National Archives, RG 393, Department and Defenses of Washington, Letters Received.

15. Slough to Augur, June 25, 1864, National Archives, RG 393, Department and Defenses of Washington, Register of Letters Received.

16. By July 1864, Provost Marshal Henry Wells had assumed oversight of stragglers and deserters apprehended in Alexandria. *Alexandria Gazette*, July 19, 1864, 1.

17. *The War of the Rebellion*, series I, vol. 29, part II, 253, and series I, vol. 43, part II, 197–98.

18. *The War of the Rebellion*, series 1, vol. 43, part II, 274, 290, 298–99, 301, 355, 366–67.

19. *The War of the Rebellion*, series 1, vol. 43, part II, 388–89; Ramage, *Gray Ghost*, 204; *The Civil War Diary of Anne S. Frobel*, 207; Henry Whittington diary, October 28, 1864.

20. *The War of the Rebellion*, series I, vol. 43, part II, 554; *Evening Star*, November 7, 1864, 1; Wert, *Mosby's Rangers*, 237, 274; *Cincinnati Daily Enquirer*, November 15, 1864, 3.

21. *The War of the Rebellion*, series I, vol. 43, part II, 620; *Julia Wilbur: Part 2*, 196–97; Denneé, "A House Divided Still Stands," 23–24.

22. Miller, "Volunteers for Freedom," 10.

23. Ibid., 10; Paula Tarnapol Whitacre, "Written in Stone but Petitioned on Paper," 6 (accessed on June 19, 2016), available from https://static1.squarespace.com/static/51cdecffe4b04906f65fdecb/t/56b270a81d07c09746111a76/1454534826668/LOuvertureForWeb.pdf.

24. *Julia Wilbur: Part 2*, 199, 210; Miller, "Volunteers for Freedom," 10–11; Whitacre, "Written in Stone but Petitioned on Paper," 7; Whitacre, *A Civil Life in an Uncivil Time*, 186.

25. Slough to Stanton, January 5, 1865 (accessed on April 22, 2016), available from www.fold3.com.research.cincinnatilibrary.org/image/3050722292-4.

26. *Alexandria Gazette*, April 4, 1865, 2; *Evening Star*, April 4, 1865, 2.

27. *Evening Star*, April 11, 1865, 2, and April 13, 1865, 4; *Julia Wilbur: Part 2*, 230.

28. *Alexandria Gazette*, April 12, 1865, 2, and May 1, 1865, 3.

29. As late as mid-June 1865, Slough dispatched a squad of cavalry to Aldie and Upperville, Virginia, to search for "marauders and guerrillas" suspected of murdering Unionists. Slough to Headquarters, June 13, 1865, National Archives, RG 393, Department and Defenses of Washington, Telegrams Received.

30. Swanson, *Manhunt*, 113, 123–24; Telegrams to Slough, April 14–16, National Archives, RG 393, Department and Defenses of Washington, Telegrams Received; Slough to Lt. Col. J. H. Taylor, April 17, 1865 (accessed on June 18, 2016), available from http://rememberinglincoln.fords.org/node/635.

31. Swanson, *Manhunt*, 253.

32. *Julia Wilbur: Part 2*, 230–31.

33. *Evening Star*, April 21, 1865, 2; *Weekly Republican*, April 27, 1865, 2.

34. *Virginia State Journal*, May 4, 1865, 3; Berlin et al., *Freedom*, 358–60.

35. Manning, *Troubled Refuge*, 205–6, 230.

36. William Silvey, an assistant special Treasury agent assigned to Alexandria, noted that the freed people's efforts to build homes, schools, and churches had the effect of "disarming almost the prejudice of everyone." Thomas, Nash, and Shepard, "Places of Exchange," 390.

37. *Alexandria Gazette*, May 2, 1865, 3; Slough to Stanton, June 8, 1865, National Archives, RG 94, Generals' Papers (Various).

38. *Alexandria Gazette*, July 7, 1865, 2.

14. CHIEF JUSTICE

1. *New York Times*, June 13, 1865, 5.

2. Evans to Slough, June 14, 1865, Chicago Historical Society.

3. John Evans (accessed on March 25, 2018), available from https://www.colorado
.gov/pacific/archives/john-evans; Bergeron, ed. *The Papers of Andrew Johnson*, 8:543.

4. Bergeron, *The Papers of Andrew Johnson*, 8:543.

5. Historian Gary Roberts writes that Slough withdrew his name from consideration as territorial governor because his outspoken criticism of Evans had disqualified
him. He draws this conclusion from the single letter that Slough wrote Johnson on
August 7 about Evans's incompetence as an administrator. Given that mid-nineteenth-century politicians frequently savaged their opponents' reputations, it seems
unlikely that Slough would have stood down because he had criticized Evans to Johnson. Roberts, *Death Comes to the Chief Justice*, 25; *Madison County Courier*, October 21,
1865, 1; *Times Picayune*, October 28, 1865, 1.

6. Slough apparently wrote Governor Charles Anderson of Ohio to lobby him for
the chief justice's position, but Anderson declined to help him. The governor wrote
Slough that "as a rule," he refused to recommend appointees to the Johnson administration. *National Republican*, October 27, 1865, 2; Charles Anderson to Slough, December 18, 1865, Cincinnati History Library and Archives; Roberts, *Death Comes to the
Chief Justice*, 26 and 166 n43; *New York Times*, January 27, 1866, 1.

7. *Junction City Weekly Union*, February 14, 1866, 3; *Santa Fe Weekly Gazette*, March
3, 1866, 2.

8. Poldervaart, *Black-Robed Justice*, 1; *Santa Fe Weekly Gazette*, March 17, 1866, 2,
April 14, 1866, 2, April 21, 1866, 2, and June 30, 1866, 2.

9. New Mexico's new superintendent of Indian affairs, A. B. Norton, also traveled
with the party. *Santa Fe New Mexican*, April 27, 1866, 2; Roberts, *Death Comes to the
Chief Justice*, 167 n47.

10. Horn, *New Mexico's Troubled Years*, 116–17; Sifakis, *Who Was Who in the Civil War*,
452.

11. *Santa Fe Weekly Gazette*, June 6, 1866, 2, and June 30, 1866, 2; *Santa Fe New
Mexican*, July 7, 1866, 2; Anderson, *History of New Mexico*, 143; Santa Fe, New Mexico
(accessed on May 1, 2017), available from https://en.wikipedia.org/wiki/Santa_Fe
_New_Mexico; Horgan, *The Centuries of Santa Fe*, 223, 249.

12. *Santa Fe Weekly Gazette*, July 28, 1866, 2; John Clark diary, June 23, 1867, and
June 30, 1867.

13. Hispano describes Spanish-speaking people who populated New Mexico during
the colonial period. Nuevomexicano is used interchangeably with Hispano. Hispanos
in New Mexico (accessed on January 6, 2020), available from https://en.wikipedia.org
/wiki/Hispanos_of_New_Mexico; John Clark diary, January 27, 1867, and April 6, 1867;
Hall, *Social Change in the Southwest*, 211.

14. *Santa Fe Weekly Gazette*, July 28, 1866, 2; Poldevaart, *Black-Robed Justice*, 3–4;

Roberts, *Death Comes to the Chief Justice*, 43; Masich, *Civil War in the Southwest Borderlands*, 36, 251.

15. Hollister, *Boldly They Rode*, 56–57; Richard H. Jackson to President Andrew Johnson, November 1, 1866, Bergeron, *The Papers of Andrew Johnson*, 11:413.

16. *Santa Fe Weekly Gazette*, August 25, 1866, 2; Masich, *Civil War in the Southwest Borderlands*, 158, 207, 289; Slough to Stanton, August 17, 1866 (accessed on April 22, 2016), available from www.fold3-com.research.cincinnatilibrary.org/image/3050722297–8.

17. Slough had firsthand knowledge of efforts in the eastern states to erect memorials to the Union dead. In June 1865, he had joined an excursion to the Bull Run battlefield for the purpose of dedicating two monuments there. *Evening Star*, June 12, 1865, 2; *Santa Fe Weekly Gazette*, December 15, 1866, 2.

18. *Santa Fe Weekly Gazette*, February 9, 1867, 2.

19. *Santa Fe New Mexican*, December 8, 1866, 2, and January 12, 1867, 2; *Julia Wilbur: Part 2*, 28.

20. Poldevaart, *Black-Robed Justice*, 7–8; *Santa Fe New Mexican*, January 26, 1867, 2.

21. Hunt, *Kirby Benedict*, 107–9; Masich, *Civil War in the Southwest Borderlands*, 279.

22. Murphy, "Reconstruction in New Mexico," 103; *Santa Fe Weekly Gazette*, February 2, 1867, 2.

23. The United States Congress passed the Peonage Abolition Act in March 1867, which was followed by Governor Mitchell's April 14 proclamation freeing New Mexicans held in peonage. Despite the Territorial Supreme Court's ruling, the Peonage Abolition Act, and Mitchell's proclamation, Nuevomexicanos continued to practice peonage until the movement for statehood in the late nineteenth century. Murphy, "Reconstruction in New Mexico," 109–10.

24. Gonzales, *Política*, 532–33.

25. Ibid., 514, 518, 521; Santa Fe County District Court Record Book, 1863–67.

26. John Clark diary, February 25, 1867, February 28, 1867, March 6, 1867, and August 1, 1867.

27. Roberts, *Death Comes to the Chief Justice*, 43.

28. *Santa Fe Weekly Gazette*, March 2, 1867, 2, April 20, 1867, 2, April 27, 1867, 2, and May 11, 1867, 2.

29. *The American Almanac and Repository of Useful Knowledge*, 377; Slough to Santiago Hubbell, June 30, 1867, Hubbell Family papers; John Clark diary, June 19, 1867.

30. John Clark diary, June 25, 1867; *Santa Fe Weekly Gazette*, June 29, 1867, 2, and July 6, 1867, 2.

31. *Santa Fe Weekly Gazette*, August 10, 1867, 2; *Santa Fe New Mexican*, August 10, 1867, 2; Santa Fe County District Court Record Book, 1867–1870.

32. Gomez, *Manifest Destinies*, 94–97; *Annual Report of the Commission of Indian Affairs, for the Year 1867*, 217–21.

33. Masich, *Civil War in the Southwest Borderlands*, 229, 270, 280.

34. *Santa Fe Weekly Gazette*, August 3, 1867, 2; John Clark diary, July 26, 1867.

15. DISINTEGRATION

1. Gonzales, *Política*, 531; *The Daily Commonwealth*, April 1, 1875, 2.

2. "Be careful what you write: Agonies of a double-talking Democrat" (accessed on July 27, 2017), available from www.confederatesfromiowa.com/category/iowa-democrats/; Roberts, *Death Comes to the Chief Justice*, 30–32.

3. Roberts, *Death Comes to the Chief Justice*, 32; Berwanger, *The West and Reconstruction*, 93–99.

4. Roberts, *Death Comes to the Chief Justice*, 32–33.

5. *Santa Fe New Mexican*, June 1, 1867, 2; *Santa Fe Weekly Gazette*, August 10, 1867, 2; Roberts, *Death Comes to the Chief Justice*, 49.

6. Samuel Duncan to John Slough, October 14, 1867, Grand Jury Reports, mixed materials, 1865–1880, New Mexico State Records Center and Archives; Bernalillo County District Court, Report Book "F," 1865–1872, New Mexico State Records Center and Archives.

7. Bernalillo County District Court, Report Book "F," 1865–1872, New Mexico State Records Center and Archives.

8. John Clark diary, October 17, October 19, and October 31, 1867.

9. *Santa Fe Weekly Gazette*, August 17, 1867, 2.

10. Ibid., October 19, 1867, 2.

11. Ibid., October 26, 1867, 2.

12. A third plaque read, "To the heroes who have fallen in various battles with savage Indians in the Territory of New Mexico." In 1974, an unidentified man posing as a city worker obliterated the word "savage" from the inscription. *Santa Fe Weekly Gazette*, October 26, 1867, 2; John Clark diary, November 2, 1867.

13. *Santa Fe Weekly Gazette*, May 18, 1867, 2.

14. *Santa Fe Weekly Gazette*, September 28, 1867, 2.

15. *Santa Fe Weekly Gazette*, May 11, 1867, 1–2, and June 1, 1867, 2; Hall, *Social Change in the Southwest*, 207, table IX.I.

16. *Santa Fe Weekly Gazette*, November 22, 1867, 2, and November 29, 1867, 2.

17. *Santa Fe Weekly Gazette*, November 29, 1867, 2.

18. Roberts, *Death Comes to the Chief Justice*, 93.

19. Ibid., 40–41, 52; *Santa Fe New Mexican*, August 10, 1867, 2; John Clark diary, August 1, 1867.

20. Roberts, *Death Comes to the Chief Justice*, 52–53; *Santa Fe New Mexican*, December 3, 1867, 2.

21. Ironically, Heath did not have the authority to administer the oath. Refusing to resort to Slough, the legislature turned to Santa Fe County probate judge Antonio Ortiz to administer the oath the following day. John Clark diary, December 2, 1867; *Santa Fe Weekly Gazette*, December 7, 1867, 2; Gonzales, *Política*, 618.

22. Murphy, *Frontier Crusader*, 85, 91; *Cincinnati Daily Enquirer*, February 20, 1861, 1.

23. Murphy, *Frontier Crusader*, 120–21, 123–25; Roberts, *Death Comes to the Chief Justice*, 36.

24. Roberts, *Death Comes to the Chief Justice*, 54.

25. Ibid., 60; John Clark diary, December 4, 1867.

26. John Clark diary, December 4, 1867; *Santa Fe New Mexican*, December 3, 1867, 2, and December 10, 1867, 2.

27. *Santa Fe Weekly Gazette*, December 7, 1867, 2.

28. John Clark diary, September 24, 1867, and December 2, 1867; Gonzales, *Política*, 606–7.

29. Roberts, *Death Comes to the Chief Justice*, 45–48.

30. *Santa Fe Weekly Gazette*, December 14, 1867, 2.

31. *Santa Fe Weekly Gazette*, December 14, 1867, 2; *Santa Fe New Mexican*, December 10, 1867, 2.

32. *Santa Fe Weekly Gazette*, May 2, 1868, 2; Roberts, *Death Comes to the Chief Justice*, 62.

33. Miller, "William Logan Rynerson in New Mexico," 101–3; Roberts, *Death Comes to the Chief Justice*, 57–58, Gonzales, *Política*, 614.

34. Roberts, *Death Comes to the Chief Justice*, 63–65.

35. Ibid., 65.

36. Secord, *Santa Fe's Historic Hotels*, 11, 16–17; Historical Society of New Mexico, *The California Column*, 29.

37. Slough's charge that Rynerson stole while in the army recalled the accusation of misconduct when Rynerson served with the 1st California. His claim that Rynerson stole his legislative seat referred to the recently disputed Doña Ana County election. Roberts, *Death Comes to the Chief Justice*, 57; *Santa Fe Weekly Gazette*, January 11, 1868.

38. *Santa Fe Weekly Gazette*, January 11, 1868, 2.

39. *Santa Fe New Mexican*, January 14, 1868, 2.

40. *Santa Fe Weekly New Mexican*, January 14, 1868, 2; *Daily Ohio State Journal*, January 7, 1870, 2.

EPILOGUE

1. *Santa Fe Weekly Gazette*, December 21, 1867, 2, and January 11, 1868, 2.

2. John Clark diary, October 3, 1867, October 5, 1867, and December 15, 1867.

3. Santa Fe County Probate of Wills and Testaments, Record Book "C," 1859–1870, 355–56; John Clark diary, December 16, 1867, and December 17, 1867.

4. On May 4, 1868, Slough's remains were exhumed so that they could be returned to Cincinnati. His family had sent a walnut coffin lined with zinc to carry his body back, first by "government wagon" and then by rail. He was interred in the family plot at Spring Grove Cemetery at 5:00 p.m. on June 20, 1868. *Santa Fe Weekly Gazette*, December 21, 1867, 2, and May 9, 1868, 2; *Santa Fe New Mexican*, December 17, 1867, 2, and December 24, 1867, 2; John Clark diary, December 17, 1867; *Cincinnati Daily Enquirer*, June 20, 1868, 2.

5. *Santa Fe New Mexican*, January 14, 1868, 2.

6. *Santa Fe Weekly Gazette*, December 21, 1867, 2, and February 15, 1868, 2.

7. *Ohio Daily Statesman*, May 1, 1868, 1; *Council Bluffs Nonpareil*, February 1, 1868, 2; *Dubuque Herald* reprinted in the *Santa Fe Weekly Gazette*, January 26, 1868, 2.

8. *Highland Weekly News*, January 16, 1868, 1; *Daily Kansas Tribune*, December 27, 1867, 2.

9. Slough's death gained widespread coverage among American newspapers and was even reported in the *Guardian* of London. *Brooklyn Daily Eagle*, December 28, 1867, 2; *Detroit Post* reprinted in the *Tennessean*, January 3, 1868, 1; *Montana Post*, January 18, 1868, 7; *Guardian* (London), January 9, 1868, 5.

10. Roberts, *Death Comes to the Chief Justice*, 70; *Santa Fe Weekly Gazette*, January 11, 1868, 2.

11. Roberts, *Death Comes to the Chief Justice*, 90, 93–98.

12. Ibid., 100–101.

13. Ibid., 102.

14. Ibid., 107–9.

15. John Clark diary, January 6, 1868; *Daily Kansas Tribune*, January 19, 1868, 2.

16. Slough left his eldest son Willie the presentation sword that admiring citizens and officers gave him in Alexandria. The citizens of Alexandria also presented him with a watch, chain, and key, which he left to his second son, John. To his youngest son, Martin, was left a silver pitcher, two goblets, two meerschaum pipes, and some "photographs of army views." In Slough's world, daughters apparently did not merit

much inheritance; he left his daughter Sallie the "large picture frame of myself and staff officers." Santa Fe County Probate Record of Wills and Testaments, Record Book "C," 1859–1870, 355–56.

17. *Daily Ohio State Journal*, January 7, 1870, 2.

18. United States Census 1880; *Pensions and Increases of Pensions for Certain Soldiers and Sailors of the Civil War*, Serial Set, vol. 5223, 78.

19. Johnson, "Placer Gold Deposits of New Mexico," 4; "Virginia City, Colfax County, New Mexico (accessed on May 31, 2017), available from https://www.family search.org/wiki/en/Virginia_City,_Colfax_County,_New_Mexico_Geneology.

Bibliography

PRIMARY SOURCES

CINCINNATI CITY DIRECTORIES

The Cincinnati Directory for the Year 1829

The Cincinnati Directory for the Year 1834

The Cincinnati Directory Advertiser for the Years 1836–37

Shaffer's Advertising Directory for 1839–40

The Cincinnati Directory for the Year 1842

The Cincinnati Directory for the Year 1843

Williams' Cincinnati Directory and Business Advertiser for 1851–52

Williams' Cincinnati Directory, City Guide, and Business Mirror, 1853

MANUSCRIPTS

Bernalillo County District Court, Report Book "F," 1865–1872

Charles Gordon Matchette Journal, 1855–1856, Cincinnati History Library and Archives

Charles Anderson to Slough, December 18, 1865, Cincinnati History Library and Archives

Daniel Mulford Valentine diary, Kansas State Historical Society

Declaration for Widow's Pension, Washington, DC, January 1908, Civil War Pension File Certificate, No. 639,330

Department and Defenses of Washington, Registry of Letters, Telegrams Received, and Letters Received, 1862–1865, National Archives Record Group 393 Generals' Papers (Various), National Archives Record Group 94

Henry Whittington diary, Local History Special Collections, Alexandria Public Library

Hiram Pitt Bennet to John Slough, January 20, 1865, Western Americana Collection, Beinecke Rare Book and Manuscript Library, Yale University

Hubbell Family papers, New Mexico State Records Center and Archives

Jacob Downing scrapbook, Stephen H. Hart Library and Research Center

John Clark diary, Fray Angélico Chávez Historical Library

John Evans to John Slough, June 14, 1865, Chicago Historical Society

John James Ingalls collection, Kansas State Historical Society

John M. Chivington, "The First Colorado Regiment," 1884, Stephen H. Hart Library and Research Center

John Chivington, "The New Mexico Campaign," 1890, Stephen H. Hart Library and Research Center

Miscellaneous Cincinnati Water Works manuscripts, 1853–1854, Cincinnati History Library and Archives

Miscellaneous newspaper clippings about the 1st Colorado Volunteer Infantry, Stephen H. Hart Library and Research Center.

Morning Reports, 1st Cavalry, Military Affairs, Colorado State Archives

Nelson Van Vorhes collection, Mahn Center for Archives and Special Collections, Ohio University Libraries

"Report of the Committee Established to Examine the Feasibility of Using the Cincinnati College Building for a Female Academy," n.d., Cincinnati History Library and Archives

Samuel Duncan to John Slough, October 14, 1867, Grand Jury Reports, mixed materials, 1865–1880, New Mexico State Records Center and Archives

Samuel F. Tappan manuscripts, Stephen H. Hart Library and Research Center

Santa Fe County District Court Record Books, 1863–1867 and 1867–1870, New Mexico State Records Center and Archives

Santa Fe County Probate Record of Wills and Testaments, Record Book "C," 1859–1870, New Mexico State Records Center and Archives

Testimony before the Joint Committee on the Conduct of the War, February 12–22, 1864, National Archives, Record Group 128

Thomas Ewing Jr. collection, Kansas State Historical Society

United States Census, 1850, 1860, 1870, and 1880

William Gilpin collection, Chicago Historical Society

NEWSPAPERS

Alexandria Gazette

Anti-Slavery Bugle (Lisbon, Ohio)

Ashland (Ohio) Union

Baltimore Sun

Brooklyn Daily Eagle

Cincinnati Daily Gazette

Cincinnati Enquirer

Colorado Republican and Rocky Mountain Herald (Denver, Colorado)

Commercial Gazette (Kansas City, Kansas)

Council Bluffs (Iowa) Nonpareil
Daily Commonwealth (Topeka, Kansas)
Daily Kansas Tribune (Lawrence, Kansas)
Daily Leader (Cleveland, Ohio)
Daily Ohio State Journal (Columbus, Ohio)
Daily Ohio Statesman (Columbus, Ohio)
Evening Star (Washington, DC)
Findlay (Ohio) Jeffersonian
The Guardian (London)
Highland Weekly News (Hillsboro, Ohio)
Junction City (Kansas) Weekly Union
Kansas Chief (White Cloud, Kansas)
Kansas Herald of Freedom (Wakarusa, Kansas)
Leavenworth Daily Times
Leavenworth Weekly Herald
The Liberator
Madison County Courier (Edwardsville, Indiana)
The M'Arthur (Ohio) Democrat
Meigs County (Ohio) Telegraph
Montana Post (Virginia City, Montana)
National Republican (Washington, DC)
New York Times
Perrysburg (Ohio) Journal
The Philadelphia Inquirer
Preble County (Ohio) Democrat
Republican (Holmes County, Ohio)
Rocky Mountain News (Denver, Colorado) (daily and weekly)
Santa Fe New Mexican
Santa Fe Weekly Gazette
Spirit of Democracy (Woodsfield, Ohio)
Squatter Sovereign (Atchison, Kansas)
Times Picayune (New Orleans, Louisiana)
Topeka Tribune
Virginia State Journal (Alexandria, Virginia)
Weekly Champion and Press (Atchison, Kansas)
Weekly Portage Sentinel (Ravenna, Ohio)
Weekly Republican (Plymouth, Indiana)
Western Reserve Chronicle (Warren, Ohio)

PRINTED MATERIAL

Academy Journal (St. John's Academy, Alexandria Virginia), vol. 4, #10 (December 1873).

"*An Address, delivered by John A. Martin, at the Re-Union of the Members and Officers of the Wyandotte Constitutional Convention, Held in Wyandotte, Kansas, July 29, 1882.*" Atchison, Kansas: Haskell & Sons, Printers, 1882.

The Alumna: An Annual Published by the Alumnae of the Wesleyan Female College, Cincinnati. Cincinnati: Robert Clarke & Co. Printers, 1877.

The American Almanac and Repository of Useful Knowledge for the Year 1861, vol. xxxii. Boston: Crosby, Nichols, Lee and Company, 1861.

Annual Report of the Commission of Indian Affairs, for the Year 1867. Washington, DC, Government Printing Office, 1867.

Bergeron, Paul H., ed. *The Papers of Andrew Johnson*, vol. 8 (May–August 1865). Knoxville: University of Tennessee Press, 1989.

Catalogue and Circular of the Law Department of the Cincinnati College, 1846–1847.

Catalogue of the Officers and Students of the Cincinnati College, 1841. Cincinnati History Library and Archives.

Celebration of the Forty-Seventh Anniversary of the First Settlement of the State of Ohio by Native Citizens. Cincinnati: Lodge, L'Hommedieu & Co. 1835.

Cist, Charles. *Cincinnati in 1841: Its Early Annals and Future Prospects.* Cincinnati: Charles Cist, 1841.

———. *Sketches and Statistics of Cincinnati in 1851.* Cincinnati: W. H. Moore & Co. 1851.

The Civil War Diary of Anne S. Frobel of Wilton Hall, Virginia. McLean, VA: EPM Publications, 1992.

Eighteenth Annual Report of the Trustees and Visitors of Common Schools to the City Council of Cincinnati. Cincinnati: Daily Times, 1847.

Gallatin, E. L. *What Life Has Taught Me.* Denver: Jno. Frederic, Printer, 1900.

Gardiner, Charles, letter, May 3, 1862, reprinted in "The 'Pet Lambs' at Glorieta Pass." *Civil War Times Illustrated* XV, no. 7 (November 1976) 30–37.

Hollister, Ovando James. *Boldly They Rode: A History of the First Colorado Regiment of Volunteers.* Reprint Lakewood, CO: Golden Press, Publishers, 1949.

Journal of the Executive Proceedings of the Senate of the United States.

Journal of the House of Representatives of the State of Ohio: Being the First Session of the Fifty-Second General Assembly Commencing on Monday, January 7, 1856, vol. LII. Columbus, OH: Statesman Steam Press, 1856.

Journal of the House of Representatives of the State of Ohio, being the Second Session of the Fifty-Second General Assembly, vol. LIII. Columbus, OH: Statesman Steam Press, 1857.

Journal of the Senate of Ohio at the First Session of the Thirty-Ninth General Assembly. Columbus, OH: Samuel Medary, 1840.

Kansas Constitutional Convention: A Reprint of the Proceedings and Debates of the Convention Which Framed the Constitution of Kansas at Wyandotte in July 1859. Topeka: Kansas State Printing Plant, 1920.

Lieber, Francis. *The Character of the Gentleman*. Philadelphia: J. B. Lippincott & Co., 1864.

A List of Graduates of the Cincinnati Law School, Law Department of the University of Cincinnati from the Time of its Establishment, 1833–1904.

Memorial of the Citizens of Cincinnati to the Congress of the United States Relative to the Navigation of the Ohio and Mississippi Rivers. Cincinnati: Daily Atlas Office, 1844.

Nelson, William, ed. *Documents Relating to the Colonial History of the State of New Jersey*, vol. xix. Paterson, NJ: Press Printing and Publishing Co., 1897.

Niven, John, ed. *The Salmon P. Chase Papers*, vol. 1. Kent, OH: Kent State University Press, 1993.

Notices of the House of Representatives of the State of Ohio in the Fifty Second General Assembly. Columbus, OH, 1857.

Official Proceedings of the Democratic National Convention Held in 1860 at Charleston and Baltimore. Proceedings at Charleston, April 22—May 3. Cleveland: Nevins' Print, Plain Dealer Job, 1860.

Official Proceedings of the National Democratic Convention Held in Cincinnati, June 2–6, 1856. Cincinnati: Enquirer Company Steam Printing Establishment, 1856.

Pensions and Increases of Pensions for Certain Soldiers and Sailors of the Civil War, Serial Set, vol. 5223.

Reports of the Committees of the Senate of the United States for the First Session of the Thirty-Eight Congress. Washington, DC: Government Printing Office, 1864.

Richardson, Albert D. *Beyond the Mississippi*. Hartford, CT: American Publishing Company, 1867.

Simpson, Benjamin F. "The Wyandotte Convention." *Kansas Historical Collections* 3 (1883–1885) 385–89.

U. S. Congressional Serial Set.

The War of the Rebellion: A Compilation of the Official Records of the Union and Confederate Armies. 128 vols. Washington, DC: Government Printing Office, 1881–1901.

Wharton, J. E. *History of the City of Denver from Its Earliest Settlement to the Present Time*. Denver: Byers and Dailey, Printers, News Office, 1866.

Julia Wilbur: Part 2: The Civil War Years in Alexandria and Washington, D.C. (October 1862–1865). Diaries transcribed and annotated by Paula T. Whitacre, Magill Library Special Collections Division, Haverford College.

Wilder, Daniel W. *The Annals of Kansas*. Topeka: George W. Martin, Kansas Publishing House, 1875.

Williams, William G. *Laws and General Ordinances of the City of Cincinnati.* Cincinnati: The Cincinnati Gazette Company, 1853.

SECONDARY SOURCES

Alberts, Don E. *The Battle of Glorieta: Union Victory in the West.* College Station: Texas A&M University Press, 1998.

Anders, Curt. *Injustice on Trial: Second Bull Run, General Fitz John Porter's Court-Martial, and the Schofield Board Investigation that Restored His Good Name.* Zionsville, IN: Guild Press Emmis Publishing LP, 2002.

Anderson, George. *History of New Mexico: Its Resources and Its People.* 2 vols. Los Angeles: Pacific States Publishing Co., 1907.

Ash, Stephen V. *When the Yankees Came: Conflict & Chaos in the Occupied South, 1861–1865.* Chapel Hill: University of North Carolina Press, 1995.

Artemel, Janice G., Elizabeth A. Crowell, and Jeff Parker. *The Alexandria Slave Pen: The Archeology of Urban Captivity.* Washington, DC: Engineering Science, Inc., 1987.

Ayoub, Michael. "Hessians in Our Midst: Provost Duty in Alexandria 1861–62: The 88th Pennsylvania Volunteers." *Alexandria Chronicle* (Fall 2008): 1–15.

Baker, Jean H. *Affairs of Party: The Political Culture of Northern Democrats in the Mid-Nineteenth Century.* New York: Fordham University Press, 1998.

Bancroft, Hubert Howe. *History of the Life of William Gilpin: A Character Study.* San Francisco: History Company, Publishers, 1889.

Barber, James G. *Alexandria in the Civil War.* Lynchburg, VA: H. E. Howard, Inc., 1988.

Berler, Anne Karen. "A Most Unpleasant Part of Your Duties: Military Occupation in Four Southern Cities, 1861–1865." PhD dissertation, University of North Carolina at Chapel Hill, 2013.

Berlin, Ira, Steven F. Miller, Joseph P. Reidy, Leslie S. Rowland, eds. *Freedom: A Documentary History of Emancipation, 1861–1867.* Series 1, vol. II (*The Wartime Genesis of Free Labor: The Upper South*). Cambridge, England: Cambridge University Press, 1993.

Berwanger, Eugene H. *The West and Reconstruction.* Urbana: University of Illinois Press, 1981.

Billington, Ray Allen. *America's Frontier Heritage.* Albuquerque: University of New Mexico Press, 1974.

Billington, Ray Allen, and Martin Ridge. *Western Expansion: A History of the American Frontier,* 5th ed. New York: Macmillan Publishing Co. Inc. 1982.

Biographical Annals of Lancaster County, Pennsylvania. J. H. Beers & Company, 1903.

Biographical Directory of the American Congress, 1774–1949.

Blum, Carol Jean. "'A Devotion in the West': The Settlement of Cincinnati, 1788–1810," *Queen City Heritage* 48, no. 1 (Spring 1990): 2–19.

Blustein, Bonnie Ellen. *Preserve Your Love for Science: Life of William A. Hammond, American Neurologist.* Cambridge, England: Cambridge University Press, 1991.

Brinkerhoff, Fred W. "The Kansas Tour of Lincoln the Candidate." *Kansas Historical Quarterly* 13 (February 1945): 294–307.

Bromwell, Henrietta E. *Fiftyniners' Directory: Colorado Argonauts of 1858–1859,* vol. I. Denver, CO: 1926.

Brown, Richard Maxwell. *No Duty to Retreat: Violence and Values in American History and Society.* New York: Oxford University Press, 1991.

Cawelti, John G. *Apostles of the Self-Made Man: Changing Concepts of Success in America.* Chicago: University of Chicago Press, 1965.

Cheatham, Gary L. "Slavery All the Time or Not at All: The Wyandotte Constitution Debate, 1859–1861." *Kansas History: A Journal of the Central Plains* 21 (Autumn 1998): 168–87.

Cincinnati Pioneer. Cincinnati: John D. Caldwell, 1873.

Clampitt, Bradley R. *Occupied Vicksburg.* Baton Rouge: Louisiana State University Press, 2016.

Clayton, Andrew Robert Lee. *Ohio: History of a People.* Columbus: Ohio State University Press, 2002.

Cooling, B. Franklin. *Symbol, Sword, & Shield: Defending Washington during the Civil War.* Hamden, CT: Archon Books, 1975.

Colton, Ray C. *The Civil War in the Western Territories: Arizona, Colorado, New Mexico, and Utah.* Norman: University of Oklahoma Press, 1959.

Cox-Paul, Lori. "John Chivington, 'The Reverend Colonel,' 'Marry Your Daughter,' 'Sand Creek Massacre,'" *Nebraska History* 88 (2007) 126–37, 142–47.

Cozzens, Peter. *Shenandoah 1862: Stonewall Jackson's Valley Campaign.* Chapel Hill: University of North Carolina Press, 2008.

Denneé, Tim. "African-American Civilians and Soldiers Treated at Claremont Smallpox Hospital, Fairfax County, Virginia, 1862–1865." www.freedmencemetery.org/resouces/documents/claremont.pdf. Accessed on November 12, 2016.

———. "A House Divided Still Stands: The Contraband Hospital and Alexandria Freedmen's Aid Workers." www.freedmencemetery.org/resources/documents/contraband_hospital.pdf. Accessed on April 21, 2016.

Dexter, Julius. "Historical Sketch of Cincinnati College," circa 1880. Cincinnati History Library and Archives mss.

Donald, David Herbert. *Lincoln.* New York: Touchstone, 1995.

Donald, David Herbert, Jean Harvey Baker, and Michael F. Holt. *The Civil War and Reconstruction*. New York: W. W. Norton & Company, 2001.

Dorsett, Lyle W. *The Queen City: A History of Denver*. Boulder, CO: Pruett Publishing Company, 1977.

Downs, Gregory. *After Appomattox: Military Occupation and the Ends of War*. Cambridge, MA: Harvard University Press, 2015.

Early Ohio Settlers: Purchasers of Land in Southwestern Ohio, 1800–1840. Baltimore: Genealogical Publishing Company, Inc. 1986.

Edrington, Thomas S., and John Taylor. *The Battle of Glorieta Pass: A Gettysburg in the West, March 26–28, 1862*. Albuquerque: University of New Mexico Press, 1998.

Eisenschiml, Otto. *The Celebrated Case of Fitz John Porter: An American Dreyfus Affair*. Indianapolis: Bobbs-Merrill Company, Inc. 1950.

Enoch, James C. "A Clash of Ambitions: The Tappan-Chivington Feud." *Montana: The Magazine of Western History* 15, no. 3 (July 1965): 58–67.

Etcheson, Nicole. *Bleeding Kansas: Contested Liberty in the Civil War Era*. Lawrence: University Press of Kansas, 2004.

Faulkner, Carol. *Women's Radical Reconstruction: The Freedmen's Aid Movement*. Philadelphia: University of Pennsylvania Press, 2004.

Foner, Eric. *Free Soil, Free Labor, Free Men: The Ideology of the Republican Party Before the Civil War*. Oxford: Oxford University Press, 1970.

———. *Reconstruction: America's Unfinished Revolution, 1863–1877*. New York: Harper & Row, 1988.

Foote, John P. *The Schools of Cincinnati and its Vicinity*. Cincinnati: C. F. Bradley & Co.'s Powell Press, 1855.

Foote, Lorien. *The Gentlemen and the Roughs: Violence, Honor and Manhood in the Union Army*. New York: New York University Press, 2010.

Ford, Henry A., and Mrs. Kate B. Ford. *History of Cincinnati, Ohio, with Illustrations and Biographical Sketches*. Cleveland: L. A. Williams & Co., n.d.

Frazier, Donald S. *Blood & Treasure: Confederate Empire in the Southwest*. College Station: Texas A&M University Press, 1995.

Frye, Dennis E. *Harpers Ferry Under Fire: A Border Town in the American Civil War*. Virginia Beach, VA: Donning Company Publishers, 2012.

Gaeddert, G. Raymond. *The Birth of Kansas*. Lawrence: University Press of Kansas, 1940.

Gambone, Joseph G. "Starving Kansas: The Great Drought and Famine of 1859–1860." *The American West* VIII, no. 4 (July 1971): 30–35.

Garrison, Webb. *Mutiny in the Civil War*. Shippensburg, PA: White Mane Books, 2001.

Gienapp, William E. *The Origins of the Republican Party, 1852–1856*. Oxford: Oxford University Press, 1987.

Goldfield, David. *America Aflame: How the Civil War Created a Nation*. New York: Bloomsbury Press, 2011.

Gomez, Laura E. *Manifest Destinies: The Making of the Mexican American Race*. New York: New York University Press, 2007.

Gonzales, Phillip B. *Política: Nuevomexicanos and American Political Incorporation*. Lincoln: University of Nebraska Press, 2016.

Goodrich, Thomas. *War to the Knife: Bleeding Kansas, 1854–1861*. Mechanicsburg, PA: Stackpole Books, 1998.

Gordon, Lesley J. *A Broken Regiment: the 16th Connecticut's Civil War*. Baton Rouge: Louisiana State University Press, 2014.

Goss, Charles Frederick. *Cincinnati: The Queen City, 1788–1912*. Chicago: S. J. Clarke Publishing Company, 1912.

Gower, Calvin W. "Kansas Territory and Its Boundary Question: 'Big Kansas or Little Kansas,'" *The Kansas Historical Quarterly* 33, no. 1 (Spring 1967): 1–12.

Greve, Charles Theodore. *Centennial History of Cincinnati*, vol. 1. Chicago: Biographical Publishing Company, 1904.

Grimsley, Mark. *The Hard Hand of War: Union Military Policy toward Southern Civilians, 1861–1865*. Cambridge, England: Cambridge University Press, 1995.

Guelzo, Allen C. *Gettysburg: The Last Invasion*. New York: Alfred A. Knopf, 2013.

Gwynne, S. C. *Rebel Yell: The Violence, Passion and Redemption of Stonewall Jackson*. New York: Scribner, 2014.

Hagedorn, Ann. *Beyond the River: The Untold Story of the Heroes of the Underground Railroad*. New York: Simon & Schuster, 2004.

Halaas, David Fridtjof. *Boom Town Newspapers: Journalism on the Rocky Mountain Frontier: 1859–1881*. Albuquerque: University of New Mexico Press, 1981.

Hall, Jesse A., and Leroy T. Hand. *History of Leavenworth County, Kansas*. Topeka, KS: Historical Publishing Company, 1921.

Hall, Thomas D. *Social Change in the Southwest, 1350–1880*. Lawrence: University Press of Kansas, 1989.

Harvey, Jeremy J. *Occupied City: Portrait of Civil War Alexandria, Virginia*. Alexandria, VA: Alexandria Convention & Visitors Association, 2003.

History of Cincinnati and Hamilton County, Ohio: Their Past and Present. Cincinnati: S. B. Nelson & Co. Publishers, 1894.

Hearn, Chester G. *Six Years of Hell: Harpers Ferry During the Civil War*. Baton Rouge: Louisiana State University Press, 1996.

Historical Society of New Mexico. *The California Column: Its Campaigns and Services in New Mexico, Arizona, and Texas during the Civil War, with Sketches of Brigadier General James H. Carleton, It's Commander, and Other Officers and Soldiers.* Santa Fe: New Mexican Printing Company, 1908.

Hoffer, William James Hull. *The Caning of Charles Sumner: Honor, Idealism, and the Origins of the Civil War.* Baltimore: Johns Hopkins University Press, 2010.

Holt, Michael F. *The Political Crisis of the 1850s.* New York: John Wiley & Sons, 1978.

———. *Political Parties and American Political Development from the Age of Jackson to the Age of Lincoln.* Baton Rouge: Louisiana State University Press, 1992.

Horgan, Paul. *The Centuries of Santa Fe.* New York: E. P. Dutton & Company, Inc., 1956.

Horn, Calvin. *New Mexico's Troubled Years: The Story of the Early Territorial Governors.* Albuquerque: Horn & Wallace, Publishers, 1963.

Hunt, Aurora. *Kirby Benedict: Frontier Federal Judge.* Glendale, CA: Arthur H. Clark Company, 1961.

James, Marquis. *The Life of Andrew Jackson.* Garden City, NY: Garden City Publishing Co. Inc., 1938.

Joblin, M. *Cincinnati Past and Present: Or Its Industrial History as Exhibited in the Life Labors of Its Leading Men.* Cincinnati: Elm Street Printing Company, 1872.

Johnson, Maureen G. "Placer Gold Deposits of New Mexico." In *Geological Survey Bulletin 1348.* Washington, DC: United States Government Printing Office, 1972.

Karnes, Thomas L. *William Gilpin: Western Nationalist.* Austin: University of Texas Press, 1970.

Keleher, William A. *Turmoil in New Mexico, 1848–1868.* Santa Fe: Rydal Press, 1952.

Kundahl, George G. *Alexandria Goes to War: Beyond Robert E. Lee.* Knoxville: University of Tennessee Press, 2004.

Laceky, Carolyn. "John Potts Slough: Frontier Lawyer: Hero, Villain, Victim." Unpublished article.

———. "Triumph and Treachery: John P. Slough in New Mexico." Unpublished article.

Leonard, Stephen J., and Thomas J. Noel. *Denver: Mining Camp to Metropolis.* Niwot: University Press of Colorado, 1990.

Linderman, Gerald F. *Embattled Courage: The Experience of Combat in the American Civil War.* New York: The Free Press, 1987.

Logan, James K., ed. *The Federal Courts of the Tenth District: A History.* Denver: US Court of Appeals for the Tenth Circuit, 1992.

McGrath, Maria Davies. *The Real Pioneers of Colorado*, vol. 1. Denver: Denver Museum, 1934.

Maizlish, Stephen E. *The Triumph of Sectionalism: The Transformation of Ohio Politics, 1844–1856*. Kent, OH: Kent State University Press, 1983.

Manning, Chandra. *Troubled Refuge: Struggling for Freedom in the Civil War*. New York: Alfred A. Knopf, 2016.

Marvel, William. *Lincoln's Autocrat: The Life of Edwin Stanton*. Chapel Hill: University of North Carolina Press, 2015.

Masich, Andrew E. *Civil War in the Southwest Borderlands, 1861–1867*. Norman: University of Oklahoma Press, 2017.

McPherson, James M. *Battle Cry of Freedom: The Civil War Era*. New York: Oxford University Press, 1988.

Miller, Darlis A. "William Logan Rynerson in New Mexico, 1862–1893." *New Mexico Historical Review* 48, no. 2 (April 1973): 101–31.

Miller, Edwin A. Jr. "Volunteers for Freedom: Black Civil War Soldiers in Alexandria National Cemetery, Part I." *Historic Alexandria Quarterly* (Fall 1998): 1–14.

Miller, T. Michael. "Prison Life in Civil War Alexandria." *Northern Virginia Heritage* 9, no. 3 (October 1987): 9–13.

Minor, Craig. *Kansas: The History of the Sunflower State, 1854–2000*. Lawrence: University Press of Kansas, 2002.

Morgan, Perl W. *History of Wyandotte County Kansas and Its People*. Chicago: Lewis Publishing Company, 1911.

Moore, H. Miles. *Early History of Leavenworth City and County*. Leavenworth, KS: Sam'l Dodsworth Book Co., 1906.

Murphy, Lawrence R. *Frontier Crusader—William F. M. Arny*. Tucson: University of Arizona Press, 1972.

———. "Reconstruction in New Mexico." *New Mexico Historical Review* 43, no. 2 (April 1968): 99–115.

Nevins, Allan. *The Emergence of Lincoln: Douglas, Buchanan, and Party Chaos, 1857–1859*, vol. 1. New York: Charles Scribner's Sons, 1950.

———. *Ordeal of the Union: A House Dividing, 1852–1857*. New York: Charles Scribner's Sons, 1947.

Niven, John. *Salmon P. Chase: A Biography*. Oxford: Oxford University Press, 1995.

Oertel, Kristen Tegtmeier. *Bleeding Borders: Race, Gender, and Violence in Pre-Civil War Kansas*. Baton Rouge: Louisiana State University Press, 2009.

Poldervaart, Arie W. *Black-Robed Justice*. 1948. Reprint, Holmes Beach, FL: Gaunt, Inc., 1999.

Portrait and Biographical Record of Denver and Vicinity, Colorado. Chicago: Chapman Publishing Company, 1898.

Powell, Thomas E., ed. *The Democratic Party of the State of Ohio*. 2 vols. Ohio Publishing Company, 1913.

Price, David H. "Sectionalism in Nebraska: When Kansas Considered Annexing Southern Nebraska, 1856–1860," *Nebraska History* 53 (Winter 1972): 447–62.

Ramage, James A. *Gray Ghost: The Life of Col. John Singleton Mosby*. Lexington: University Press of Kentucky, 1999.

Rawley, James A. *Race and Politics: Bleeding Kansas and the Coming of the Civil War*. Lincoln: University of Nebraska Press, 1979.

"The Reception of Colorado's First Governor." *The Colorado Magazine* vii, no. 5 (September 1930): 233–35.

Reeves, William F. "A Brief History of the First 150 Years of the Cincinnati Water Works." Cincinnati History Library and Archives manuscript.

Reid, Whitelaw. *Ohio in the War: History of Ohio During the War and the Lives of Her Generals*, vol. 1. Cincinnati: Moore, Wilstach & Baldwin, 1868.

Riker, Diane. "'This Long Agony:' A Test of Civilian Loyalties in an Occupied City." *Alexandria Chronicle* (Spring 2011): 1–10.

Roberts, Gary L. *Death Comes to the Chief Justice: The Slough-Rynerson Quarrel and Political Violence in New Mexico*. Niwot: University Press of Colorado, 1990.

Robertson, James I. *The Stonewall Brigade*. Baton Rouge: Louisiana State University Press, 1963.

Ross, Steven J. *Workers on the Edge: Work, Leisure, and Politics in Industrializing Cincinnati, 1788–1890*. New York: Columbia University Press, 1985.

Samito, Christian G. "The Intersection between Military Justice and Equal Rights: Mutinies, Courts-Martial, and Black Civil War Soldiers." *Civil War History* 53, no. 2 (July 2007): 170–202.

Sandage, Scott A. *Born Losers: A History of Failure in America*. Cambridge, MA: Harvard University Press, 2005.

Sanford, Albert B. "Camp Weld, Colorado." *Colorado Magazine* xi, no. 2 (March 1935): 46–50.

———, ed. "Life at Camp Weld and Fort Lyon in 1861–62: An Extract from the Diary of Mrs. Byron N. Sanford." *Colorado Magazine* vii, no. 4 (July 1930): 132–39.

Scheetz, Jim. "When Kansas Became A State." *Kansas Historical Quarterly* 27, no. 1 (Spring 1961): 1–21.

Sears, Stephen W. *Controversies & Commanders: Dispatches from the Army of the Potomac*. New York: Houghton Mifflin Company, 1999.

Secord, Paul R. *Santa Fe's Historic Hotels*. Charleston, SC: Arcadia Publishing, 2013.

SenGupta, Gunja. *For God & Mammon: Evangelicals and Entrepreneurs, Masters and Slaves in Territorial Kansas, 1854–1860*. Athens: University of Georgia Press, 1996.

Shotwell, John B. *A History of the Schools of Cincinnati*. Cincinnati: School Life Company, 1902.

Sides, Hampton. *Blood and Thunder: The Epic Story of Kit Carson and the Conquest of the American West*. New York: Anchor Books, 2006.

Silbey, Joel H. *The Partisan Imperative: The Dynamics of American Politics Before the Civil War*. New York: Oxford University Press, 1985.

———. *A Respectable Minority: The Democratic Party in the Civil War Era, 1860–1868*. New York: W. W. Norton & Company, 1977.

Sifakis, Stewart. *Who Was Who in the Civil War*. New York: Facts on File Publications, 1988.

Smiley, Jerome C. *History of Denver, With Outlines of the Early History of the Rocky Mountain Country*. Denver: Times-Sun Publishing Company, 1901.

Smith, Mertis. "An Exercise in Deception: John M. Chivington at the Battle of Glorieta Pass." *Undergraduate Research Journal at UCCS* 2, no. 1 (Spring 2009): 20–43.

Stanton, F. J. "History of the First Regiment of Colorado Volunteers, 1861." *The Trail: A Magazine for Colorado* I, no. 12 (May 1909): 5–15.

Stiffler, William C. "Alexandria, Virginia: A Time of Turbulence, January 1, 1861—July 1, 1863." Unpublished manuscript in the Local History Collection, Alexandria Public Library.

Swanson, James L. *Manhunt: The 12-Day Chase for Lincoln's Killer*. New York: HarperCollins Publishers, 2006.

Tap, Bruce. *Over Lincoln's Shoulder: The Committee on the Conduct of the War*. Lawrence: University Press of Kansas, 1998.

Taylor, John. *Bloody Valverde: A Civil War Battle on the Rio Grande, February 21, 1862*. Albuquerque: University of New Mexico Press, 1995.

Thomas, William G. III, Kaci Nash, and Robert Shepard. "Places of Exchange: An Analysis of Human and Materiél Flows in Civil War Alexandria, Virginia." *Civil War History* 62, no. 4 (December 2016): 359–98.

Thompson, Jerry, ed. *Civil War in the Southwest*. College Station: Texas A & M University Press, 2001.

Ubbelohde, Carl, Maxine Benson, and Duane Smith. *A Colorado History*, 7th ed. Boulder, CO: Pruett Publishing Company, 1995.

Volo, James M., and Dorothy Denneen Volo. *Family Life in 19th-Century America*. Westport, CT: Greenwood Press, 2007.

Weisenburger, Francis P. *The Life of John McLean: A Politician on the United States Supreme Court*. Columbus: Ohio State University Press, 1937.

Wert, Jeffrey D. *Mosby's Rangers: The True Adventures of the Most Famous Command of the Civil War*. New York: Simon & Schuster, 1990.

West, Elliott. *Contested Plains: Indians, Goldseekers, and the Rush to Colorado*. Lawrence: University of Kansas Press, 1998.

Whitacre, Paula Tarnapol. *A Civil Life in an Uncivil Time: Julia Wilbur's Struggle for Purpose*. Sterling, VA: Potomac Books, 2017.

Whites, LeeAnn, and Alecia P. Long, eds. *Occupied Women: Gender, Military Occupation, and the American Civil War*. Baton Rouge: Louisiana State University Press, 2009.

Whitford, William Clarke. *Colorado Volunteers in the Civil War: The New Mexico Campaign in 1862*. Denver: State Historical and Natural History Society, 1906.

Whitlock, Flint. *Distant Bugles, Distant Drums: The Union Response to the Confederate Invasion of New Mexico*. Boulder: University Press of Colorado, 2006.

Woodworth, Steven E. *Beneath a Northern Sky: A Short History of the Gettysburg Campaign*, 2nd edition. Lanham, MD: Rowman & Littlefield Publishers, Inc., 2008.

The WPA Guide to Cincinnati. Cincinnati: Cincinnati Historical Society, 1987.

Wright, Arthur A. "Colonel John P. Slough and the New Mexico Campaign, 1862." *Colorado Magazine* 29, vol. 2 (1962): 89–105.

Wright, Richard. *"It's Your Misfortune and None of My Own:" A New History of the American West*. Norman: University of Oklahoma Press, 1991.

Yellin, Jean Fagan. *Harriet Jacobs: A Life*. New York: Basic Civitas Books, 2004.

Yanuck, Julius. "The Garner Fugitive Slave Case." *Mississippi Valley Historical Review* XL, no. 1 (June 1953): 47–66.

Zeidenfelt, Alex. "The Embattled Surgeon, General William A. Hammond." *Civil War Times Illustrated* XVII, no. 6 (October 1978): 24–32.

Index

—as major of 1st Colorado Volunteer
Infantry, 93, 97, 113, 117; admired by
soldiers of 1st Colorado, 99, 137; at
battle of Apache Canyon, 118; captures
Confederate wagon train at Johnson's Ranch, 122–23; conspires against
Slough, 106, 125, 138, 165; undermines
Slough's authority, 95, 98, 102, 103, 106,
111, 122–23

Cincinnati, OH, 3, 9, 10, 228n10; coffee
houses and taverns in, 6–7; growth
of, 4–5, 27; life in early, 4; politics in
antebellum, 13–14, 15, 16; racial violence
in, 27; steamboat construction in,
5, 6. *See also* Democratic national
convention

Cincinnati College, 8

Cincinnati Law School, 8, 10, 229n17

Civil War, Union approach to southern
sympathizers, 161–62. *See also* Chivington, John: as major of 1st Colorado
Volunteer Infantry; 1st Colorado
Volunteer Infantry; Harpers Ferry: defense of; New Mexico Territory: Civil
War in; Slough, John: in Civil War,
as colonel of 1st Colorado Volunteer
Infantry

—army of: Northern Virginia, 134, 141–42,
143, 159–60, 162, 164, 182; the Potomac,
130, 134, 143, 159, 162, 164, 175, 177, 182;
the Rappahannock, 130, 134; the Valley,
132; of Virginia, 135, 141–42, 148

—battles and campaigns of: Antietam, 143; Chancellorsville, 159, 160;
1st Manassas, 101, 160; Fort Sumter,
89; Gettysburg, 164; Monocacy, 176;
Overland, 175, 176; Petersburg, 182; Red
River, 172; 2nd Manassas, 141–42, 148;

Sevens Days, 134, 148; Valley (1862),
130, 134; Valley (1864) 178, 180

Clark, John, 197, 201, 213, 214, 220;
criticizes Slough's performance as
chief justice, 199, 202, 207

Clever, Charles, 198, 216; contested
election with José Francisco Chávez,
202, 214–15; fight over appointment as
attorney general, 199, 203

Colorado Territory: gold rush in, 81,
85, 92; recruitment of volunteers
during the Civil War, 91, 92; reliance
on credit to supply 1st Colorado
Volunteer Infantry, 97, 243n30; threat
of insurrection in, 88, 90

Confederate Army of New Mexico, 102,
112–13, 116, 126

Confederate Territory of Arizona, 101

Connelly, Henry, 103

Cooper, James, 131, 133, 134, 135–36

Corry, William, 38–39, 43–44, 45

Davis, Jefferson, 101, 182, 204

Delgado, Felipe, 207, 208, 209

Democratic national convention, 32, 78–79

Denver, Colorado Territory, 82, 102, 106;
early life in, 86–88; founding of, 85,
242n12

Douglas, Stephen A., 14, 31, 33, 53, 78–79

Downing, Jacob, 104, 106, 126, 245n16,
245n17; arrested by John Slough,
105, 108–9; writes under pseudonym
"Union," 103, 136, 248n39; conspires
with John Chivington, 106

Duncan, Samuel, 206, 218

Early, Jubal, 164, 176, 180

Elkins, Stephen B., 197, 201, 202, 223; fight

with John Slough, 211–12, 216;
background of, 193: as New Mexico
territorial governor, 198–99, 208, 209,
210, 213
Monroe, James (Ohio legislator), 24, 25
Mosby, John S., 160, 179, 180

Native American peoples: Apache, 196;
Arapaho, 82, 90, 165, 196, 242n13;
Cheyenne, 82, 165, 196, 200; Pueblo,
194, 201–2, 211
New Mexico Territory: erection of
memorial to Union dead, 197, 207–8;
judicial system of, 193, 197; mining
districts in, 201, 210, 224; political
turmoil in, 198–99, 202, 214–15. *See also*
Native American peoples: Pueblo;
Slough, John: in Civil War in New
Mexico Territory
—Civil War in: battle of Apache Canyon,
117, 118–19, 208; battle of Pigeon's
Ranch, 119–22, 208, 247n27; battle of
Valverde, 113, 118, 121, 208; invasion by
Confederate forces, 101, 102

Ohio House of Representatives, 52nd
General Assembly, 17–18, 19, 33; debate
over expansion of slavery to Kansas
Territory, 22, 27–28; debate over habeas
corpus law and fugitive slaves, 24,
25–26; expulsion of John Slough from,
38, 39; investigates Slough-Cadwell
altercation, 35, 36–37; passes resolution
for repeal of Fugitive Slave law, 28;
Republicans seek to expel John Slough
from, 36, 37–42
Orange and Alexandria Railroad, 160, 173,
178–80

Paul, Gabriel, 112–13, 115, 116, 246n13
peonage, 197–98, 203, 261n23
Perkins, George W., 59, 81, 85, 238n21
personal liberty laws, 24
Pierce, Franklin, 20, 53
Pigeon's Ranch, 117, 118, 119. *See also* New
Mexico Territory: Civil War in: battle
of Pigeon's Ranch
Pope, John, 135, 141, 148, 195
popular sovereignty, 14, 18, 21, 31, 57, 59, 64,
78–79
Porter, Fitz John, 141; court-martial of,
148–49
Pyron, Charles, 117–19

Reeder, Andrew, 20, 166
Ritchie, John, 67, 68
Robinson, Charles, 20, 22
Rochester Ladies Anti-Slavery Society,
144, 157, 167
Rynerson, William, 215; altercation
with John Slough, 217–19; blamed
for Slough's death, 221–22; introduces
resolutions censuring Slough, 216;
tried for Slough's murder, 222–23

sack of Lawrence, 30–31, 41
Sand Creek massacre, 165, 191, 255n27
Santa Fe, New Mexico Territory, 113,
122, 201, 209, 214, 215; burial of John
Slough, 220; description of, 194–95
Santa Fe trail, 113, 116–17, 118, 119
Saxton, Rufus, 129, 130–34, 136, 250n12,
250n13
Scurry, William, 117, 119–22
Seward, William, 106, 183–84
Shannon, Wilson, 20, 21
Sheridan, Philip, 178, 180

Sibley, Henry Hopkins, 101–2, 114, 116, 126

Sibley's Brigade. *See* Confederate Army of New Mexico

Sigel, Franz, 134–35

Slave Pen (Alexandria, VA), 145, 157, 170, 171

Slave Power, 15, 19, 21, 22, 26, 32

Slough, Arabella McLean, 11–12, 13, 230n24; in Alexandria, 147–48, 173, 252n25; family in Ohio politics, 11; lobbies for husband's promotion, 129; marriage to John Slough, 11, 28, 56, 82; in Santa Fe, 193–94, 195, 197, 201, 220; as widow, 223–24

Slough, John P., 3, 56, 78, 134–36, 196, 255n27; assaults against life, 56, 125, 153, 165, 218–19; attitudes about Blacks, 26–27, 64, 66, 135–36, 155, 159, 186–87; attitudes about Hispanos, 195, 199–200; birth and early years of, 5; death and funeral of, 220, 224, 264n4; Democratic Party affiliation of, 16, 17, 41; education of, 8, 10; family of, 13, 28, 55, 56, 82, 147, 173, 193, 210–11, 218, 231n30, 237n14, 264n16; marriage to Arabella McLean, 11, 12, 16; personality of, 12, 29, 40, 41–42, 43, 55, 171, 200, 226; physical description of, 12; political apprenticeship of, 10–11, 13, 15, 33; position on the franchise for Native Americans and women, 66, 71, 202; religion of, 8, 197, 229n16; siblings of, 5, 12, 229n16, 230n29

—in Civil War: attitude toward secession, 135, 175; participates as official in Lincoln's funeral, 185; promoted to brigadier general, 129, 149, 152; at defense of Harpers Ferry, 129, 131, 133, 134; serves as court-martial judge, 148, 149, 164, 165, 166, 172

—in Civil War in Alexandria, VA: 173, 178–79, 180, 181–82, 187–88; acts to suppress southern sympathizers in, 161, 162, 163, 179; addresses problem of refugees in, 144, 155, 157–58, 168, 169, 174, 187; addresses problem of smallpox in, 146, 174; addresses public nuisances in, 154, 175; clashes with other officers, 177–78; honored by subordinates, 152–53; investigated by the Joint Committee on the Conduct of the War, 166–67, 169–70, 171; involved in Booth manhunt, 184; requests transfer from, 175–76, 177, 178; responds to threats of Confederate attack, 160–61, 173; restores order to, 140–41, 142–43, 151; returns power to civil authorities, 183, 187; struggles with liquor dealers, 149–52, 187

—in Civil War in New Mexico Territory: at battle of Pigeon's Ranch, 119–24; leads campaign, 113, 115–16, 246n13, 249n41

—as colonel of 1st Colorado Volunteer Infantry, 91, 94–95, 242n16; criticized for cowardice, 103–5, 108, 136–37; disciplinary problems, 95, 96, 97–98, 100, 102, 108, 110–11; disliked by men, 99, 100, 111–12, 113; resigns command, 124–25

—in Colorado Territory, 85–86, 126; emigrates to, 82, 86; lobbies for appointment as territorial governor, 191–92; rises to prominence, 90, 91–92

—in Kansas Territory: emigrates to, 45, 51, 53; opposes Lecompton constitution, 58–59; raises drought relief funds, 80–

81; rises in territorial Democratic party,
61–62; runs for office, 73–75, 77, 79–80.
See also Lecompton constitution
—as lawyer: in Cincinnati, 10, 13;
in Denver, 86, 92, 243n17; in
Leavenworth, 45, 54, 55–56, 61, 82; in
Washington, DC, 192
—as New Mexico territorial chief justice,
197, 198, 199, 200; appointment, 192;
censured by territorial council, 216, 217;
key rulings, 198, 201–2, 203; presides
over First Judicial District, 193, 195–96,
200, 211; presides over Second Judicial
District, 200, 206; Republicans criticize
Slough's performance, 199, 203, 207
—in New Mexico Territory: advocates
for railroad development, 209;
altercation with Charles McClure,
210–11; altercation with John Mitchell,
211–12, 216; altercation with William
Arny, 212–13, 214, 216; altercation
with William Rynerson, 217–19;
involvement in territorial politics,
198, 202; leads effort for memorial to
Union dead, 197, 207–8, 212, 261n17;
seeks improvement of Union cemetery
at Pigeon's Ranch, 196–97, 207;
speculates in mining ventures, 201, 210
—in Ohio House of Representatives,
17–19, 27–29, 33–34, 231n8, 232n10; altercation with Darius Cadwell, 34–36, 37,
40, 233n7; election to, 15, 16; expulsion
from, 38–39; seeks re-election to, 42–
44, 236n34; speeches, 18, 24, 26, 36, 37
—at Wyandotte constitutional
convention, 60, 62, 67, 68–69, 70;
fights to seat delegates, 63, 64; leads
Democratic contingent, 61, 62–63,

71–72; opposes signing constitution,
70–72; position on rights of Blacks, 65,
66. *See also* Wyandotte constitution;
Wyandotte constitutional convention
Slough, Martin: Democratic affiliation
of, 7, 16, 229n14; early years of, 3–4,
230n28; occupations of, 5, 6; rises in
prominence in Cincinnati, 7–8, 12;
wealth of, 12, 241n14
Slough, Mary Potts, 5, 9, 12, 228n3, 228n10,
230n29
Slough, Matthias, 4, 228n9
Stanton, Edwin: appoints Slough
military governor of Alexandria, VA,
138; relationship with John Slough, 136,
149, 175–76, 177, 178, 196; as Secretary of
War, 129, 130, 160, 184
—addresses problems in Alexandria,
VA: of refugees, 144, 168; of smallpox,
146–47; of liquor dealers, 150–51, 152; of
southern sympathizers, 162, 164
—involvement in courts-martial: of
Fitz John Porter, 148–49; of William
Hammond, 165–66
Stimson, Samuel A., 62, 65, 68, 69, 69–70
Stonewall Brigade, 132
Stuart, James Ewell Brown (JEB), 160
Sumner, Charles, 31–32, 41

Tappan, Samuel F., 91, 93–95, 112–13, 125,
137, 245n8, 245n17
Thacher, Solon, 64, 67, 69–70, 72
Topeka constitution, 20, 23, 60, 61

"Union" (Jacob Downing): attacks
Slough and Weld for inactivity, 103,
107, 137–38; criticizes Slough's actions
at the battle of Pigeon's Ranch, 123, 136

Union Pacific Railroad, 208–9
United States Colored Troops, 159, 187;
    protest against burial in Contrabands'
    Cemetery, 180–81
United States Military Railroads, 160, 184
United States Sanitary Commission,
    165, 173

Valentine, Daniel Mulford, 54–55
Van Vorhes, Nelson, 17, 22, 35, 44
Virginia City Town Company, 210, 224

Wade, Benjamin, 22, 167
Wakarusa War, 20–21, 50
Washington, DC, 130, 132, 143, 144;
    defenses of, 140, 159, 160, 177;
    threatened by Jubal Early's army,
    176–77
Weld, Lewis Lanyard, 93, 97, 103, 107,
    108, 138
Wells, Henry H., 150, 151, 152, 154, 157;
    questioned by the Joint Committee
    on the Conduct of the War, 170–71;
    responds to Julia Wilbur's complaints,
    155, 157; suppresses southern

sympathizers in Alexandria, VA, 161,
    162, 163, 164
Western Anti-Slavery Society, 23–24
Whittington, Henry, 147, 164, 176
Wilbur, Julia, 147, 160, 162, 164, 181, 184–85,
    256n35; criticizes treatment of Black
    refugees, 154–58, 171, 174; observes living
    conditions of refugees in Alexandria,
    VA, 144–46, 174; opposes Albert
    Gladwin, 155–56, 157, 167–68, 180, 181
Winchell, James, 62, 68, 69–70, 72
Wyandotte constitution, 60, 212;
    Democrats refuse to sign, 71, 72,
    239n34; ratification of, 72, 73
Wyandotte constitutional convention, 60,
    61, 73; achievements of, 68, 71, 72
—debate over: allegations of bribery, 68–
    70; annexation of southern Nebraska
    Territory, 67–68; rights of Black
    Kansans, 65–67; seating of delegates,
    63–64
Wyandotte, Kansas Territory, 60
Wyman, John G., 144, 146, 154–55, 169
Wynkoop, Edward (Ned), 98, 102, 126,
    245n17, 255n27